continued . . .

"*Transition Game* holds up as an **insightful** crash course in Indiana basketball at every level, and **should be required reading** for high school and college players to make them understand what a bigger whole they are part of." —*Northwest Indiana Times*

"This book is **funny, sweet, and beautifully bizarre**. Jon Wertheim writes with the fluidity of a waterfall, but *Transition Game*, more than any book I can think of in recent memory, cements just how much sports has changed in this country."

—Buzz Bissinger, **author of** *Friday Night Lights*

"*Transition Game* takes us deep inside the sport—as well as the culture that surrounds it. It's the type of great book that is worthy of a place on the national bestseller list." —InsideHoops.com

"Jon Wertheim has done **a masterful job** of weaving the golden threads of Indiana basketball into a garment that reveals not only a great deal about Indiana today, but also about the whole sports world around us."

—Frank Deford

ALSO BY L. JON WERTHEIM

Venus Envy

TRANSITION GAME

HOW HOOSIERS WENT HIP-HOP

L. JON WERTHEIM

RIVERHEAD FREESTYLE

New York

THE BERKLEY PUBLISHING GROUP
Published by the Penguin Group
Penguin Group (USA) Inc.
375 Hudson Street, New York, New York 10014, USA
Penguin Group (Canada), 90 Eglinton Avenue East, Suite 700, Toronto, Ontario M4P 2Y3, Canada
(a division of Pearson Penguin Canada Inc.)
Penguin Books Ltd., 80 Strand, London WC2R 0RL, England
Penguin Group Ireland, 25 St. Stephen's Green, Dublin 2, Ireland (a division of Penguin Books Ltd.)
Penguin Group (Australia), 250 Camberwell Road, Camberwell, Victoria 3124, Australia
(a division of Pearson Australia Group Pty. Ltd.)
Penguin Books India Pvt. Ltd., 11 Community Centre, Panchsheel Park, New Delhi–110 017, India
Penguin Group (NZ), cnr Airborne and Rosedale Roads, Albany, Auckland 1310, New Zealand
(a division of Pearson New Zealand Ltd.)
Penguin Books (South Africa) (Pty.) Ltd., 24 Sturdee Avenue, Rosebank, Johannesburg 2196,
South Africa

Penguin Books Ltd., Registered Offices: 80 Strand, London WC2R 0RL, England

First G. P. Putnam's Sons hardcover editions: March 2005
First Riverhead Freestyle trade paperback edition: March 2006
Riverhead Freestyle trade paperback ISBN: 1-59448-187-3

The Library of Congress has catalogued the G. P. Putnam's Sons hardcover edition as follows:

Wertheim, L. Jon.
Transition game: how Hoosiers went hip-hop / L. Jon Wertheim.
    p. cm.
ISBN 0-399-15250-4
1. Basketball—Indiana—Bloomington.   2. School sports—Indiana—Bloomington.
3. Coaches (Athletics)—Indiana—Bloomington—Biography.   I. Title.
GV885.73.B56W47   2005   2004057344
796.323'.09772—dc22

PRINTED IN THE UNITED STATES OF AMERICA

10 9 8 7 6 5 4 3 2 1

Basketball may have been born in Massachusetts,

but it grew up in Indiana.

JAMES NAISMITH

CONTENTS

TRANSITION GAME

PROLOGUE

AS MY FATHER FOUGHT THE GOOD FIGHT AGAINST CANCER—
a battle that he would eventually lose—I was making regular trips
from my home in Manhattan to the mother country in south-central
Indiana. On a particularly bitter night a few years ago, eager to escape
the grim sterility of the hospital, uninspired by the options at the mul-
tiplex, I decided to venture to the Bloomington High School North
gym and catch a basketball game for the first time since I graduated in
1989.

I often write about basketball for my day job at *Sports Illustrated*
and have spent more nights than I care to count courtside at NBA
games. But I had stopped following the Bloomington North Cougars.
I had heard that the basketball program had made vast improvements
from the late '80s, when I sat on uncomfortable bleachers and watched

my classmates play the standard "Indiana-style" basketball that was predicated on the vaunted fundamentals and featured floor-bound types, passing and scrapping and unfurling jump shots. I was vaguely aware that the team had managed to summit the pinnacle of high school hoops, winning the state title in 1997, a year destined to be remembered as the season before "class basketball" poisoned the Indiana basketball culture. I occasionally scanned the Bloomington North report on the website of the local newspaper, the Bloomington *Herald-Times,* though not closely enough to notice that many players had decidedly "un-Hoosier" surnames.

My father, an academic who militantly refused to be baptized at the church of hoops, once joked that the state motto ought to be "Dribble ergo sum." And he was right. It's hard to exaggerate just how deeply basketball is embedded in Indiana's fabric, just how loudly the thump of a leather ball on a wooden floor echoes through the culture. Basketball is a statewide touchstone, the filament that threads together towns from Auburn to Zionsville. It's no coincidence that nine of the ten biggest high school basketball gyms in the country are in Indiana. Jacques Barzun is credited with the bromide "Whoever wants to know the heart and mind of America had better learn baseball . . . the rules and realities of the game and do it by watching first some high school or small-town teams." If you want to know the heart and mind of latter-day Indiana, you'd better do the same with basketball. It is the state's esperanto. The marquee outside a church not far from Bloomington North's sprawling campus once read BASKETBALL FLOOR IS FINISHED. LEAGUE PLAY IS UNDERWAY. Underneath, in smaller letters, was another message: COME WORSHIP WITH US EVERY SUNDAY. From double-wide trailers to faux Tudor mansions, nearly every Indiana home is adorned with goals—never "baskets" or "hoops"—where kids can practice their free throws and jump shots until dark, Indiana's version of solitaire.

As I was growing up, the importance of basketball was reinforced in high school. The student body of Bloomington North was, as it is today, exceptionally varied, a mix of National Merit Scholars and kids who excelled in the auto body courses taught in the school's vocational wing. There was a Latin Club and an ace Academic Decathlon team filled with future Ivy Leaguers. But so was there an active Future Farmers of America chapter and an on-site babysitting center so girls who'd gotten pregnant could stay in school. Naturally, the usual high school constituencies—stoners, geeks, punks, preps, freaks—were all represented.

Yet the basketball team, unremarkable though it was, formed a ripple of concentric circles that determined one's popularity at school. Those who had reached the apotheosis of playing for the varsity team made up the innermost ring and were conferred the prestige of royalty. Swaddled in faux leather letterman's jackets—shrouds of Turin in the halls of Indiana high schools—they congregated each morning outside the main entrance, there to be admired but not addressed. It was an unwritten rule that the prime spaces in the student parking lot were reserved for the basketball dignitaries. Even before the season started, a brigade of unfailingly cute, apple-cheeked cheerleaders and eternally tanned pom-pom squad members—the distinction between the two eludes me now as it did then—decorated the players' locker room with bunting, candy and personalized signs.

Then came those of us who lacked the talent, height or both to play on the team, but did something—anything—else to feel as though we had some small connection to the Cougars. Some joined the pep band, which numbered more than fifty. Some served as "team trainers," essentially glorified towel boys, ascertaining that the players' uniforms were washed, their water bottles filled. My means of insinuating myself, however peripherally, into the culture was by covering the team for the school newspaper, the *North Star*. I spent untold nights in the ad hoc press box, logging every basket, rebound and assist.

It wasn't that the team was particularly good. Physically, the players looked as if they had walked off the set of the movie *Hoosiers*. They were stout, almost uniformly white, sporting buzz-cut hairstyles. They fashioned their games after Larry Bird, that archetype of southern Indiana, who could shoot the lights out but played on the X and not the Y axis. The Cougars had a winning record only once in my four years, my senior year, 1988–89, when a new, no-nonsense coach named Tom McKinney was starting to put his imprint on the program. That season, the team went 15–9 and won the local sectional, an achievement that warranted much more than the standard pep rally. Team members met the mayor, served as guest DJs on the local radio station and didn't pay for another lunch the rest of the school year.

Now, a decade after my graduation, as I drove up the winding route to the school and entered the gym, it brought back a tide of memories. The familiar signposts were everywhere: the sweet smell of basketball leather, the sound of the angry buzzer, the school fight song, the sight of Coach McKinney—clad in his trademark maroon sweater–white socks–dress shoes ensemble—unobtrusively stalking the sidelines. Same violently ugly, tapioca-colored walls. Same uniforms. Same chiropractors' dream bleachers.

But the closer I looked, the more difference I saw. The floor surface, no longer uneven slats of hardwood, was expensive, glistening parquet. The goals were adorned with breakaway rims, an innovation meant to accentuate the aesthetics of dunks and save the goals from wear and tear. Jay-Z and Christina Aguilera, not Mellencamp, Springsteen or Bon Jovi, blared during the warm-ups. Most conspicuously, a mammoth sign commemorating the State Championship, the ne plus ultra of Indiana sports, was slathered on one of the walls. I later learned that over the past five years, Bloomington North had won more games than any other team in the state. A high school team in a college town—located roughly two miles up the road from one of the most gilded programs in college basketball—the Cougars, no matter how good they were, were consigned to playing second fiddle to the Indiana University Hoosiers in Bloomington. But on this night the gym crackled with an electricity never in evidence during my four years.

It wasn't just the *place* that looked different. The players did too. The height of the frontline forwards and center made them leviathans for a high school program. At least the programs that I could recall from a decade ago. What was once a fairly paradigmatic Indiana high school team was now variegated, filled with players of all shapes and sizes. Though there were players with the familiar buzz cuts, the others had dreads and braids. As if someone had been tinkering with the tint knob on an old television set, the players came in a variety of shades. Jared Jeffries, a senior swingman with a café au lait complexion, a smooth touch and lanky licorice ropes for legs, was already pegged as a player with NBA-caliber talent. College coaches and scouts had been regular fixtures in the stands throughout Jeffries's career, but eventually he decided to stay in Bloomington and committed to play for Indiana University. A few weeks later, he would win Indiana's coveted Mr. Basketball Award. Perhaps the stronger NBA prospect was sophomore Sean May, already an ox of a power forward, whose father, Scott, was the hero of Indiana's 1976 undefeated NCAA title team and had played for the Chicago Bulls. The team's slashing reserve guard was Mike Davis, Jr., whose father was months away from becoming Indiana University's head basketball coach.

Then it was game time. In the first few minutes it was apparent that the deliberate, plodding style—filled with screens, picks and cuts—that the Cougars had deployed in my day was a cultural relic. Crossover dribbles almost subliminal in their quickness were the order of the day. A jamboree of fast breaks enabled Bloomington North to score more points by halftime than they usually had managed during an entire game a decade earlier. A horizontal game was now being played vertically. Within the first few minutes, Bloomington North had dunked three times—en route to winning in a blowout. Like a caterpillar that had metamorphosed into a butterfly, the program not only looked unrecognizably different but it was now airborne. "What are these guys ranked, anyway?" I asked my seatmate. He responded with an are-you-kidding? look. "They're Number One in the state."

At halftime, I walked past the team's trophy display on the main concourse. The recent team pictures suggested a mini UN. I noticed that for all the Matts and Davids there were also pan-ethnic names like Kueth and Djibril and Mario. I struck up a conversation with a former chemistry teacher whom I recognized as he worked the concession stands. Immediately, he sensed my awe. At the facilities. At the multi-hued team. At the caliber of basketball being played. At the former players in the stands who were headed to big-time college programs, if not the NBA. "Like the *Twilight Zone*, isn't it?" he said with a proud smile. "Everything is different from when you were here."

And the Bloomington North team was hardly the only basketball program buffeted by the winds of change. At Indiana University, epochal coach Bob Knight, an iconic figure for twenty-nine years who cleaved public opinion, inspiring both fierce loathing and unconditional affection, was about to be fired. His replacement, Mike Davis, is a deeply pious African-American—the first black coach in school history, in fact—who would be as accommodating with his players as Knight was exacting, as candid and personable as Knight was antisocial and choleric. As a neighbor of my parents put it, "If Notre Dame can have a black football coach [Ty Willingham], I guess we can't be surprised IU has a black basketball coach."

An hour up State Road 37 in Indianapolis, the NBA's Indiana Pacers had recently moved out of dowdy Market Square Arena. Their new home was a state-of-the-art, basketball-themed palace named Conseco Fieldhouse, replete with luxury suites, a gleaming practice facility, miles of fiber-optic wiring, a matzoh ball soup concessionaire and a scoreboard probably worth more than the value of the entire franchise twenty years ago. Once a sad-sack team, the Pacers now were an elite franchise, although their personnel was a motley crew of veterans, journeymen, a Slovenian project and three players who hadn't spent so much as a day in a college classroom, having graduated directly from high school to the NBA.

Another hour up Interstate 65 in West Lafayette, women's basketball—at best an afterthought between men's games not all that long ago—was all the rage. The Lady Boilermakers at Purdue routinely packed Mackey Arena, winning a recent NCAA title with players who would go on to play in the WNBA, the women's professional league. (Not only that, but their head coach hired her *husband* to be her assistant.) Farther north in South Bend, the Notre Dame women's team was also a powerhouse that won the 2001 NCAA title, beating . . . Purdue in the final.

The high school all-class state tournament, an institution since 1911, was replaced by an ill-conceived, soul-sucking, underdog-euthanizing format dividing the schools into four classes, a move that was nothing less than a crime against the culture. (What's next, no CART cars at the Indy 500?) And if Indiana remained a fertile crescent for basketball, a state that mints a disproportionate number of NBA players, the template had changed. Instead of churning out pros in the image of Scott Skiles and Kyle Macy and Steve Alford—who were long on heart, modestly endowed with native talent and could stroke the J like nobody's business—Hoosiers now came on the order of Shawn Kemp and Bonzi Wells and Zach Randolph. That is, players who could soar above the rim *Matrix*-like or create their own shot against any defender or unspool velveteen finger rolls, but couldn't be counted on to hit an open fifteen-footer.

So too was the game changing recreationally. The best young

players were burnishing their skills not on hoops affixed to russet-colored barns but, more often than not, on scraggly asphalt courts. They didn't emulate that peach-fuzzed sharpshooter from the local high team or even a state legend like Larry Bird. To a person, they fashioned their games after a midair acrobat who—though he played just a few miles from the Indiana state line—was a global icon: Michael Jordan.

Larry Bird shared a story with me about how he and four starting teammates in French Lick had spent their summers playing against the rival starting five from West Baden High. No referees, no scoreboards, no fans. "Just ten guys going at it." Now, any half-decent player is immersed in the Amateur Athletic Union (AAU), a controversial summer circuit that offers kids a chance to raise their stock with recruiters, traversing the country, playing dozens of organized games. Another sign of the times: As I drove around town I noticed fewer and fewer goals came with nets attached to the rims. Hoosier hotshots once took pleasure in hearing the zip of an immaculate jumper passing through the net and watching the nylon sway like a flag in a breeze. Now the euphoria came from a different source. They dunked and they blocked shots, and if they detached a bit of twine in the process, all the better: It was a tangible totem of their athleticism.

It became clear that the same forces that were transforming the fabric of Indiana more generally—globalization, multiculturalism, technology, commercialization, a centrifugal demographic pull driving folks from rural communities to cities, a world that is, at once, growing smaller and more complex—were affecting basketball in much the same way. Slick Leonard, the inimitable Pacers announcer, former coach, star of IU's 1953 championship team, and quintessential lifelong Hoosier, puts it thusly: "You can argue that basketball is better. You can argue it's worse. But you can't argue that it's changed. Buddy, the game ain't like it used to be."

My boyhood barber and current Indiana basketball sounding

board in Bloomington had a tidy explanation for the paradigm shift: "Indiana basketball," he explained matter-of-factly, "is going hip-hop." Or, as another veteran observer condensed it for me, "Homeboys have replaced the farmboys." In my mind, this was clearly code that black was supplanting white, urban was trumping rural. But the more I thought about it, the more I realized that—unintentionally perhaps—it was a darn good analogy. Yes, just as African-Americans are disproportionately represented in the world of hip-hop, so too do they comprise the majority of basketball players, at least at the highest levels. But both cultures are less about race than about ethos. In hip-hop, as in present-day basketball, formal training is less important than improvisational skills. The parameters of acceptability have broadened. There is no single path to the promised land. Substance matters, but so does style. For all the tough talk and testosterone, the field is open to women. If Eminem has the requisite skills and appeal, he can be a major player in the rap world, never mind that he is a gawky white kid from industrial Detroit. Same in the NBA, where Steve Nash, a scrawny, shaggy-haired guard from British Columbia, is an All-Star.

Some folks don't "get" these new frontiers, despairing that *their* game is fading away. Locked in a time warp, they cling stubbornly to the way it was. Others are tenuous converts accepting some of the changes more readily than others. Still others are devoted admirers who don't remember any preceding genres and have no interest in preserving the past. Whatever. For better or worse, "Indiana basketball" connotes something altogether different than it used to.

One of my beloved home state's many quirks and distinctions, Indiana refuses to change its clocks twice a year. Putatively, this accommodates Hoosier agrarians seeking to max out their daylight hours, but the running joke is that "Indiana is hopelessly behind the times." I'd submit an alternative metaphor. In Indiana, time is elastic. Sometimes Hoosiers are in synch with the methodical, soporific Midwest. Other times they're in lockstep with the up-tempo, chaotic East Coast. In some cases, Indiana clings obstinately to the past. In others, it is on the cultural vanguard.

Consider: Indiana is, unequivocally, a red state. So much so that neither political party's presidential candidate spends much time campaigning in the state. Yet the mayors from the biggest cities are consistently Democrats. Indiana is known as an unregenerate agricultural state, but in truth it is also a heavily industrial state—birthplace of au courant products ranging from silicone breast implants to Humvees, the gas-guzzling sport utility vehicles favored by pro athletes—that often leads the country in manufacturing. It is also a hotbed for biotech and life science firms. Indiana is a heavily Christian, deeply traditional state; the *Indianapolis Star*, the state's newspaper of record, features Scripture from Corinthians at the top of the front page and there are no high school sporting events scheduled on Sundays. On the other hand, the headquarters for Hebrew National are located in the state, as are dozens of mosques and Baha'i temples. Culturally, too, there is a push-pull between the past and the present. From Cole Porter (born in Peru, 1891) to Michael Jackson (Gary, 1958) to Axl Rose (born William Bruce Rose, Lafayette, 1962) to Babyface (born Kenneth Edmonds, Indianapolis, 1959), some of the most innovative musical acts of their time have come from Indiana. But the state's most popular station, Q-95, traffics in classic rock, its morning shock jocks fixtures for twenty years. Plus, if you scan your radio while driving the state's highways, you'd be forgiven for wondering whether a state ordinance mandates that John Cougar Mellencamp's quintessentially Indiana rock tune "Jack and Diane" (now more than twenty years old) be played at least twice every hour.

I figured Indiana, with its ambivalent, on-again, off-again relationship with change as a backdrop, was as good a place as any to try to get a handle on basketball's transition, trace the arc of this transformative wave. How are these shifting tectonics being received by the millions of parishioners who worship at various basketball cathedrals? How do the trends and fault lines in basketball mirror the ones in society? Where, finally, is the sport headed? So I spent a good chunk of the winter of 2003–04 in the great Hoosier State, traveling the interstates and back roads that thread the Indiana countryside, trying to locate the soul of basketball circa A.D. 2004. I went back to my old stomping ground, Bloomington North, and spent a season with a typically contemporary, topflight high school team seeing what would refract through that narrow prism. Without leaving the state, I also looked at how the college game, the pros, even basketball venues are in a state of flux.

After dozens of games and innumerable colorful conversations, I reached a conclusion about the state of basketball in the state of basketball: The rhythms may have changed convulsively, but basketball's heart is still beating just fine.

1

OPENING NIGHT

THE SCHOOL BUS TRANSPORTING THE BLOOMINGTON NORTH basketball team rolled down State Road 37, rumbling like an empty stomach as a marmalade sun ducked beneath the horizon. The bus trip is one of the touchstones of high school sports in the Midwest. It is on obscure state roads in the soupy black of night that bonds cohere, nicknames get coined, bawdy stories get swapped. But it was almost hauntingly quiet this evening during the half-hour trip from Bloomington to Bedford. The passenger manifest included five coaches in the front of the bus; the juniors and seniors from the varsity team in the back; the freshmen and sophomores from the jayvee team in the steerage of the middle.

In stereo and surround sound, there was a murmur of "Nasty" when the bus passed a particularly large slab of roadkill, an unfortunate deer that had likely gotten the business end of a pickup. Otherwise, in keeping with a team rule, the players sat in silence as the countryside of southern Indiana—baby-blue water towers, flotillas of tractors, roadside churches, corn-stubbled fields, the late-fall foliage, trains bound to Louisville and St. Louis—whipped by. Their ears wrapped in headphones, the players lost in the music from their Discmen and MP3 players and iPods, islands unto themselves. "Man, your boys are quiet," the driver told Bloomington North coach Tom McKinney as the bus stopped and the team disembarked. "No," responded McKinney, stingy, as usual, with his words. "They just know they have a job to do."

It was opening night for the Bloomington North Cougars. And if such an occasion is usually fraught with nervous energy, it was particularly pronounced as this 2003–04 season began. The maiden game is the first chapter of the unique narrative that wends through every season. But for the first time in recent memory, no one had even a rough sense of how Bloomington North's story would unfold. Practices and scrimmages were generally encouraging and had revealed some promise. But those sessions have limited value. You can try and trick yourself into thinking that a simulated game really counts, but, in the end, there's no substitute for the real thing. The Cougars were ranked No. 8 in the state preseason poll, but that seemed to come as much out of deference to the program's recent history as anything else.

There was still the lingering, deeply unpleasant aftertaste of the previous season. In 2002–03, the Cougars had been ranked as high as No. 2 in Indiana and had had a realistic chance of winning the state title—as they had done in 1997 and had come within a game of achieving in 2000. Run through a quick checklist of the prerequisites for a successful team—depth, athleticism, senior leadership, height, shooting, commitment to defense—and it was hard to find an insuperable weakness. The 2002–03 team cruised through the regular season, losing just two games, one of them to Indianapolis's Pike High

School, the best team in the entire country, according to many polls. How good was Bloomington North? Errek Suhr, a proletarian guard, was *fourth* on the team in scoring, yet he was able to walk onto the Indiana University team in the fall of 2003.

But the season ended in bitter disappointment. After rolling over crosstown rival Bloomington South in the regular season by 25 points, North stumbled against the same team a few weeks later in the sectional final of the state tournament. One sloppy, atrociously officiated 32-minute game and so much promise ended with a deadening thud. Now, if the Cougars weren't starting from scratch, they had a good many cracks in need of spackling. "It's not easy to graduate three senior starters and stay at the same level," said McKinney, his voice a rolling bass that originates somewhere deep in his gut. "We got a lot of questions we need answered."

Among them: Could Anthony Lindsey make the switch from shooting guard to point guard? Would Josh Macy, the star of the school's baseball team, forget about hitting fastballs long enough to knock down jump shots as Bloomington North's starting two-guard? Would Josh Norris, a versatile, athletic senior who never quite seemed to pull it all together in games, figure out a way to elevate his performance? Would Kyle Thomas, a 6'4", 240-pound block of solid granite, play his hardest and risk injury now that he had committed to playing football at Indiana University the following fall? Would Reed Ludlow remember how to catch a basketball? At 6'8" Ludlow was the tallest player on the team, but he had forsaken basketball and instead played hockey since seventh grade. After doctors discovered a benign tumor on his brain, he quit pucks and, as a senior, was playing organized basketball for the first time. Could bench players such as Michael Philippsen, an unfailingly upbeat and well-liked senior, fill the vacuum left by the graduating class before him?

But the biggest "if" encircled swingman Bil Duany who potentially, anyway, was the team's best player and the linchpin for whatever success the team would or would not have. The last in a lineage of five Duany siblings to play for Bloomington North, Bil stood 6'7" and was the type of versatile player who would jump for the opening tap and then bring the ball upcourt. His oldest brother graduated from Bloomington North in 1996 and played for the University of Wisconsin. Another older brother was class of 1998 and played for Syracuse, starting alongside Carmelo Anthony on the 2003 team that won the NCAA title. Two older sisters had gone to college on basketball scholarships as well.

As Bil was beginning to fill out his frame and plane the rough edges in his game, he suffered back-to-back knee injuries—one to the left, one to the right—both requiring extensive surgery and rehab. In part because he was missing so much class time and in part because he wanted to preserve his eligibility, he had taken a year off from school. Because he had been out of commission for much of the past eighteen months, college recruiters had stopped calling his house. Over the summer, a few smaller schools had offered him a full ride, but Duany demurred, thinking he could do better. He had played a good amount of basketball, including seventy AAU games in June and July, and he told the North coaches that his explosive leaping ability was returning. But would his knee trouble—even at some subconscious level—manifest itself when the games began?

Adding to the aura of flux was the rumor that McKinney, North's coach for the past seventeen years, would retire after the season. McKinney had taken a dormant Bloomington North program—lucky to finish a season with a winning record during my day—and, mostly through hard work, transformed it into a powerhouse. Over the past decade, McKinney had a higher winning percentage than any other coach in Indiana. He minted players who routinely made all-state teams, graduated to big-time college programs and even landed in the

NBA. Solemn and soft-spoken, McKinney was not what one would call a "players' coach." He was fifty-six and didn't think of his role as being a playmate for teenage kids. He was there to teach them, there to make them better basketball players and, trite as it sounds, better people. The players didn't necessarily connect with him personally, but he commanded their respect—sometimes of the grudging variety— and his authority was unquestioned. No one wanted to see McKinney's career end on a sour note.

Basketball arrived in Indiana more than a century ago, imported in 1893 by Nicolas McKay, a Presbyterian minister from Crawfordsville, a somewhat typical Indiana town northwest of Indianapolis. McKay was a disciple of Dr. James Naismith and had worked alongside the sport's founder in Springfield, Massachusetts. When he returned to Indiana, McKay ventured to the Crawsfordsville YMCA and taught the locals how to play this game that entailed hurling a ball into a ten-foot-high net hanging from a round rim that had been fashioned by a local blacksmith.

For a variety of reasons that sports sociologists will always debate, basketball was a perfect match for the state's ethic. Its emphasis on both teamwork and the individual struck a resonant chord in Indiana, a state where a sense of community and a sense of self-sufficiency are valued in equal measure. The sport is played indoors, no small consideration given Indiana's dreary, subfreezing winters. Small communities that didn't have the requisite number of kids for a football team could field a starting five for basketball.

But the sport also served a social function. In Bedford, where Bloomington was playing on this night, as in hundreds of other small towns in Indiana, basketball was once the single biggest representation of the community. The players were *their* boys, defending the town's honor; and they were to be supported no matter what. As the fields lay fallow and the weather dipped below freezing, basketball was the source of entertainment on winter weekend nights. The symbiosis between the town and the team quickly ossified.

Today, basketball doesn't have the same hold. Beset by the fragmentation of community, and by other choices of divertissement—high-speed Internet access, satellite television, a casino on the Ohio River, to name three—residents of hundreds of small towns like Bedford don't ritually converge on the high school gym. Especially when the local teams are unremarkable.

During my four years at Bloomington North, Bedford beat the Cougars five times in six games, and ranked among the hegemonic programs in the state. The next Nobel Prize winner could be a BNL alum and the school would still be best known as the alma mater of Damon Bailey. An Indiana hoops deity, Bailey piloted the team to the Indiana state title in 1990. During those years you could arrive at games two hours before tip-off and end up parking on a knoll because fans had already filled the school's parking lot.

But lately Bedford North Lawrence had fallen from the ranks of the elite. The team had gone seventeen seasons without a losing record, but this was partly because they'd been able to lard their schedule with games against smaller schools. The crowd support is still ample—this is, after all, southern Indiana. Giddy cheerleaders still sell programs for fifty cents outside the main entrance, looking into their compact mirrors between sales to make some last-minute pregame adjustments. The team's broadcasters from WBIW radio still call the games from a nook above the court. Members of a local men's club still give away "suckers," the rural locution for lollipops. But even as the junior varsity game—something of a warm-up act in the world of high school basketball—drew to a close, the stands were only half-filled and

Class in session: Even in his final season as a high school basketball coach, Tom McKinney (*center*) was an intense taskmaster. (*Jeremy Hogan/Bloomington* Herald-Times)

any anticipatory buzz was muted. No doubt because the game came during Thanksgiving break, there wasn't even a pep band: as the home team took the court, a tinny rendition of the team's Sousa-esque fight song crackled over the p.a. system.

McKinney spent much of the time before the game watching the North jayvee team play Bedford North Lawrence's. As ten kids with nascent facial hair and physiques that were more boy than man engaged in scrums, silly fouls and the occasional made basket for four six-minute periods, McKinney removed the ever-present pen from behind his left ear to take a few notes. Midway through the third period, he met the varsity team in the locker room and addressed them for the last time in the preseason in his usual deep, rolling cadences that suggest he deliberates long and hard about every word that comes out of his mouth. "We've been waiting a long time for tonight, for the season to start," he said. "At least I know I have. The crowd's going to be into the game, it's their first game, too. We know what we have to do. Let's just get after it." *Win one for the Gipper* it was not. But the players responded, putting their hands together and yelling "Defense." That Duany was the first player to charge out of the locker room was lost on no one.

As the varsity teams warmed up, it was clear that the half-court hashes could have doubled as dividing lines between basketball past and present. On Bedford's side of the court, the Stars ran through variations of the three-man weave with almost paramilitary precision. This was a monochromatic team of buzz-cut Hoosiers whose very names—Riley and Kory and Scotty and Trent and the euphonious Dax Duncan—were straight out of a Booth Tarkington novel. In short, it was vintage, throwback Indiana basketball, the stuff of grainy black-and-white videotape.

At the other end of the floor, the North team emerged from the locker room sporting the look du jour—that is, silky black warm-ups, the obligatory billowy shorts that extended below the knee, the latest black Nikes, price tag: $200. As the players ran cursorily through a layup line, their shots grew increasingly ornate. Twisting, rococo reverses. Velveteen finger rolls. Double-clutch up-and-under moves. The Cougars complied with perhaps the most arcane rule in Indiana high school basketball and refrained from dunking ("stuff shots" during warm-ups result in a technical foul). But more than a few forearms and elbows brushed the rim of the Cougars' basket.

McKinney would insist throughout the season that this was as unathletic and as slow a team as he had coached in years. No player on this aggregation would have started on the 1997 or 2000 team, he maintained. This lament was testament to how dramatically the standards had shifted. Bloomington's final team drill before the tip-off entailed players on both sides of the goal passing the ball off the backboard while airborne—an exercise, it occurred to me, that the team fifteen years before was insufficiently athletic to pull off. As the Cougars kept the ball in play, Bedford's assistant, Alan Bush, the point guard on the Bailey-era teams, turned with raised eyebrows to another assistant. "Man, those guys'r bigger'n I thought."

By my notes, it took precisely twelve seconds for Bloomington North to impose its will on Bedford. Duncan, Bedford's tallest starter at 6'5", caught the ball on the right side of the paint and tried to deke Thomas with a series of fakes. Thomas wasn't buying. When Duncan finally went up for a shot, Thomas joined him midair and didn't block the shot so much as he smote it. The ball hit the floor violently with a high-pitched *zingggg*, Lindsey retrieved it and Bloomington was suddenly in fast-break mode. After a few dribbles downcourt, Lindsey fed the ball to Duany in stride. As a defender approached from the left, Duany elevated.

Jim Carroll, who wrote *The Basketball Diaries*, observed that the best basketball players can correct their mistakes immediately and beautifully in midair. Duany did just that. Before the defender could swipe at the ball, Duany tucked it near his body and changed his angle of attack. As he twisted, he transferred the ball to his right hand and laid it in the basket as delicately as a parent placing a blanket over a sleeping child. For emphasis he slapped the backboard on his descent. *I'm back.*

And so it went. It wasn't that Bedford was a bad team. It was just that the Stars were competing against a completely different phylum of athlete. Time and again they would reach for a rebound only to have either a lengthier or thicker arm of a Bloomington player—usually the ones belonging to Thomas and Duany—eclipse their grasp. Watching the undersized Bedford players grapple for position with the North frontline players was like watching a regular Joe wrestle the gargantuan man at the county fair. On offense Bedford's team had trouble orchestrating anything effective against Bloomington's harassing man-to-man defense. On several possessions the Stars were unable to infiltrate the *perimeter*, much less the paint. Were it not for their ability to shoot the three-pointer—the shot Indiana native John Wooden rightfully once called "the great equalizer"—Bedford would have been hard-pressed to score. As it was, Bloomington led 31–20 at halftime. Duany and Thomas each had accumulated more rebounds than the entire Bedford team combined.

It wasn't a flawless opening-night performance. Not by any stretch. But there were surprisingly few flubbed lines. Players from both teams cut at the right times, switched defensively and generally avoided bumping into one another. For a game that was only marginally competitive, there was actually a fair amount of rhythm. On a few occasions, a North player looked querulously at McKinney, as if to say, *What do you want me to do, Coach?* He shot back a look that conveyed a clear message: *You're the one on the floor, buddy. You figure it out.*

Though it was just the first game, it would in many ways serve as a blueprint for the season. The roles and personalities that would define players were already starting to form. Flush with seniors and lacking anything resembling an *enfant terrible*, this was a smart team that played with either an abundance of aplomb or a deficit of feral intensity. The players were motivated by joy and not by hunger: sometimes this served them well, sometimes it worked to their detriment. To their way of thinking, a basketball game was just that. A game. That it never represented anything more was a source of constant dismay to McKinney.

Anthony Lindsey, who was a few weeks removed from his last game as the star quarterback of the North football team, would play the same role on the basketball court. A natural-born leader whose mother was a member of the Bloomington North faculty, he guided the offense with poise, precision and practicality—if not panache. In many ways he was cut from the same cloth as Coach McKinney, a speak-softly-and-hit-your-late-game-free-throws type. Lindsey was being recruited to play football at West Point. When I once asked him if the prospect of possibly going to war had any chilling effect on his desire to go to the Academy, he shook his head and gave the kind of disbelieving look you would shoot at someone who burned a winning lottery ticket. "I wouldn't think twice about serving my country," he said solemnly.

Lindsey cut a confident figure, free of that awkward teenage shoulder-slumping. His thick eyebrows crest to form an "M" over his pupils and he is handsome enough to pass for a young James Van Der Beek. But for all the pretty-boy earmarks on the surface, there was a good deal of grit to his game. He spent much of the night swabbing the floor with his body, sacrificing nonvital organs for the good of the team. Plus he played heartfelt defense on Bedford's best player, Andy Root.

Sometimes for better, sometimes for worse, Kyle Thomas, too, exhibited many of the same characteristics that served him so well on the football field. An unmovable object, clogging the lane with his immense frame, much as he did the line of scrimmage in football, Thomas blocked, challenged and discouraged countless shots. Time and again, he used his strength and surprisingly agile footwork to get superior positioning. But just as Thomas, the star defensive tackle, was a nonentity on offense in football, he was out of his element when the Cougars had the ball. He simply lacked anything resembling touch. But to his credit, he knew it, shooting only when he was within a few feet of the basket—and even then doing so with palpable reluctance.

Then there was Bil Duany, the team's wild card. His gifts were not a matter of debate, but he had a tendency to play on cruise control, a characteristic maddening to many, including his older brother Duany Duany, who sat in the stands and shook his head at the silly fouls and careless box-outs. "You have to want to rip out the other guy's heart," said Duany, spending the holidays in Bloomington before heading back to Europe to play for a club team. "Bil's not like that."

In the fourth quarter, Bil gathered the ball at midcourt and had a clear path to the goal for a basket that would have sealed the game. From the stands, one could all but see the gears in his head underneath all those cornrows spinning furiously as he contemplated which variety of dunk he would throw down. As he took one last dribble near the free throw line and began to soar, his reverie was interrupted when the ball trickled off his bony fingers and out of bounds. Like a human jack-in-the-box, McKinney popped off the Cougars' bench. "Bil," he bellowed, "just lay the ball in next time." Duany smiled broadly and nodded in agreement, not upset in the least.

Otherwise, McKinney watched the action on the court as if he were staring at a calm sea. As his counterpart, Bedford's coach Mark Ryan, paced the sidelines and was often so animated that his red tie was perpendicular to his chest, McKinney sat on the bench pensively. Absentmindedly fingering the neckline of his sweater, he mumbled a few observations to assistants and gave some pointers to players. A few risibly bad calls from the officials, one of them directly in front of the North bench, went unremarked upon. It was the 559th game of McKinney's career and he was pacing himself for the season, rationing his energy.

The only real spasm of drama came midway through the fourth quarter. As Bloomington North began to bring the ball downcourt after a Bedford miss, one of the referees interrupted play to whistle Josh Norris for a technical foul. Norris's face registered a look of utter confusion. McKinney shot up from his seat. "What did he say?" McKinney asked the referee in a measured voice.

" 'He's holding me, ref!' " responded the official.

"That's it?" McKinney asked, wondering if the ref had decided to censor a choice word or two in the retelling.

"That's it."

McKinney has a long-standing policy that any player who draws a technical foul won't play again for the rest of the game. Two seasons ago, Sean May, the best player on a team that many picked to win the state title, was whistled for a technical foul during a state tournament game. Without a second thought, McKinney benched May, who, to that point, had never been less than a model citizen in his four years on the team. Bloomington North lost, ending its season.

But this time, McKinney made an exception and let Norris stay on the court. "When a senior captain informs the ref that he's being held," said McKinney afterward, "you sure don't expect to get a 'T' for that."

In the NBA, technical fouls—generally occasioned by fighting, flagrant fouls and supremely profane tirades—result in a single free throw for the opposition. Big deal. But in high school games, the virtues of sportsmanship and fair play are emphasized. A technical foul affords the opposition not only two free throws but possession of the ball. It's makings for a huge swing in momentum. Bedford, sure enough, subsequently scored eight straight points to close the deficit to seven. It was as close as they would get. Like so many Bloomington North opponents that would follow, the Bedford team was resilient and competed honestly, but was, finally, nonthreatening.

There are some distinguishing features about the waning moments of Indiana high school basketball games. Fans remain until the bitter end, no matter how sadistically lopsided the score. Some of these folks are the parents and neighbors and girlfriends of the players and can't afford to have their faith questioned. But the majority simply find it somehow *disrespectful*—to the team, to the school, to the sport of basketball—to leave before the final horn. (It's probably worth adding that by the time of the pregame national anthem, you could get an accurate attendance count. Hoosiers aren't hip to the concept of arriving late, a bad habit that Los Angeles Lakers fans have turned into an art form.)

Perhaps taking their cue from the display of loyalty in the stands, players would sooner join the cheerleading squad than concede defeat. Teams trailing late in the game by the most insurmountable margin will still deploy the time-honored strategy: intentionally foul the opposition and then jack three-pointers when you get the ball back. Down by 11 points with 35 seconds to play, Bedford continued to foul the Cougars, unwilling to accept the inevitable. This tactic ended up padding the Cougars' final margin of victory, 62–48. It made for an agonizingly long last few minutes. It always does. "What are they going to do, set up for an eleven-point field goal?" the press row cynic next to me asked. Still, you had to appreciate this show of pride and optimism.

When the flatulent horn sounded for the last time, putting an end to the evening, the players lined up in front of their benches for a postgame "handshake line," another noble, if quaint, feature of Indiana games. Standing directly underneath a Bedford banner reading SPORTSMANSHIP IS OUR MOTTO; VICTORY OUR GOAL, the players passed each other and brushed palms, repeating "Good game" and "Nice game," not unlike flight attendants bidding passengers adieu at the gate.

The Bedford locker room was a study in bleakness. It wasn't that Bedford had lost. It was that they had been demoralized. You play hard for the entire 32 minutes of the game, you make your free throws, you hit your three-point shots and you expect, if not to win, at least to be competitive. But Bedford was barely in the game. "They pounded us in every way possible," lamented Ryan, Bedford's exasperated coach. "Physically, they just manhandled us, and I don't know what we could have done, if anything. Maybe just try to block out better, but all I saw was maroon jerseys above us." It hadn't been a fair fight. The echoes from Bedford's glory years were growing ever more faint.

Tom McKinney was in only marginally happier spirits as he sat on the bench of the visitors' locker room, a subterranean space perfumed by teenage sweat and institutional cleaner. As he combed over the stat sheet—dutifully delivered by North's retired chemistry teacher James Van Osdol, the team scorer—like a detective seeking clues to a mystery, McKinney winced at the capacious room for improvement. Bil Duany had 18 points and 15 rebounds, which, in a vacuum, was a hell of a game. However, were it not for the missed dunk, some errant free throws and a stretch when he did a convincing impression of a somnambulist, he could have put up 25 and 20, easily. Anthony Lindsey had played a terrific floor game, but neither he nor backcourt mate Josh Macy shot well. The team, in fact, missed all 11 of their three-point attempts. "We're not quick and we don't shoot well," McKinney said in succinct summation. "That means our defense is going to have to win us some games."

There were other gripes and other sources of stress. McKinney would stay up the rest of the night, as he always did, playing and replaying the game in his head. Still, it was basketball season again. And as he stepped out of the gym into the dark Indiana night and breathed the chilly air, he was warmed, at least slightly, knowing that his team was 1–0.

2

THE CAN'T-MISS KID

HALF AN HOUR SOUTH OF BLOOMINGTON ON STATE ROAD 37, Bedford, Indiana, is the seat of Lawrence County, which prides itself on being the world's limestone capital. Shrouded in a curtain of residual dust, the quarries that dot the landscape have provided the rock for the Empire State Building, the Alamo, the Taj Mahal and Rockefeller Center. Until recently, the first son of Lawrence County was Virgil "Gus" Ivan Grissom, an astronaut who served as command pilot for the first three-man Apollo flight. In the middle of Grissom's hometown of Mitchell lies an obelisk—appropriately enough made of limestone; appropriately enough adjacent to a basketball court—memorializing his space travel.

Lawrence County is also home to Heltonville, Indiana, a blink-and-miss-it hamlet of 1,300. There, at the junction of State Roads 58 and 744, lies another limestone monument paying homage to a local boy made good. Except this memorial is more elaborate than Grissom's and has been photographed by countless more tourists who have made a detour on a winding, undulating state road. The sign reads DAMON BAILEY, FROM YOUR HOMETOWN FANS IN RECOGNITION OF ALL YOU HAVE ACHIEVED—WITH GREAT PRIDE AND MUCH LOVE. So there, set in stone, are dueling monuments to Indiana's priorities. Venturing to outer space is all well and good. But it is ultimately dwarfed by the status of being a Hoosier basketball star.

There was a time when references to Bailey, at least in Indiana, did not require a surname. For a decade, from the mid-'80s until the mid-'90s, the mere mention of "Damon" would have resonated with every Hoosier. At the height of Damon-mania circa 1990, most Hoosiers would not merely have recognized the name but been able to rattle off Bailey's line score from the previous game. Indiana has had a raft of schoolboy stars whose aptitude for shooting a leather ball through a metal rim has afforded them the apotheosis of full-bore celebrity around the time they received their driver's licenses. But Bailey surpassed them all. He was Oscar Robertson, Larry Bird and Rick Mount all rolled into one—with Jimmy Chitwood's flair for the dramatic.

Had Angelo Pizzo, the Bloomington native who wrote the scripts for *Hoosiers* and *Rudy*, submitted a treatment of Bailey's boyhood in Bedford, it likely would have been laughed out of Hollywood for being excessively hokey. Even the protagonist's surname appeared to be lifted from Capra. The plotline: A homegrown, small-town Indiana kid with folksy twang takes to basketball. When not discharging his chores, or helping rescue the neighbor's kitten out of the oak tree, he's polishing his skills on the hardwood. Silhouetted by darkness, he works on his jump shots, free throws and dribbling until his mother calls him in for dinner. He's big for his age, and by the time he's in sixth grade, he can touch the rim. Still, he tells everyone that "a dunk isn't worth more points than a jumper and you're a lot more likely to get an open jumper than an open dunk." He dates the prettiest cheerleader (whom he will later marry) and never turns down an autograph request. When he is a senior playing in the championship game in front of half the friggin' state, it seems, his team is trailing in the waning moments. (Cue piano tinkling.) He single-handedly wins the game, appropriately on the free throws he grew up practicing before the dawn had broken and after the sun had set. In addition to leading his team to the state title in his valedictory game, he claims the Mr. Basketball Award, Indiana's equivalent of the Heisman Trophy. Dissolve to final scene: He leaves his beloved small town to play for the famed crusty coach up the road at State U.

Bailey lived in a different county and was a year behind us in school, but my friends and I were keenly aware of the embryonic Cult of Damon long before it became a statewide phenomenon. As a seventh-grader, Bailey was the star of the eighth-grade squad at Shawswick, a school often derided among the middle school sophisticates in Bloomington because its team was called the Farmers. The youngest kid on the court, Bailey was also the best, a virtuoso who could dunk with two hands, throw preposterous passes, post up a center on one possession and dribble past an opposing guard on the next. Quite apart from his physical gifts, he also had a basketball cortex more advanced than anyone else's. He knew every angle on the court and anticipated moves before the opponent even considered making them. I still recall vividly that after Shawswick beat my middle school, Tri-North, my classmate Pat (Son of Bob) Knight reported to anyone who would listen that Bailey was the "best player I've ever seen." As if it were necessary, he added the codicil, "And that includes black guys."

As an eighth-grader with a low threshold for awe, I once recognized Bailey at the College Mall and trailed him in the manner of a pimple-faced paparazzo. *How was Damon at Donkey Kong? What flavor Slurpee did he like?* Even in civvies, he walked with the confidence of someone who had just hit the game-winning shot. Bailey was something of a celebrity in southern Indiana, akin to the local band that you knew would one day hit it big and you could brag you liked them before they went commercial. But his status as a local—at best a regional—treasure was short-lived. Bob Knight had heard plenty about Bailey from his vast network of amateur scouts and toadies, to say nothing of his son, Pat. In early 1986, when Bailey was an eighth-grader, Knight the Elder took in a Shawswick game. Not one given to hyperbole, Knight came away a believer in a precocious fourteen-year-old kid. "Damon Bailey is better than any guard we have right now," he famously told his assistants. "I don't mean potentially better, I mean better today."

On its face, it was uncharacteristic gushing. But it was vintage Knight. Ever the puppeteer, his remarks were surely intended to motivate Indiana's incumbent guard, Steve Alford, a terrific player who had been a member of the gold medal 1984 U.S. Olympic team but was in the throes of a slump at the time. Regardless, Knight's sentiments were picked up, not only by the local cognoscenti but also by John Feinstein, in the process of writing a national bestseller. By the time Bailey was a freshman in high school and Feinstein's *Season on the Brink* was in its gazillionth printing, the small-town basketball savant with the perfect, feathered hair had pierced the national consciousness.

It's almost impossible to exaggerate the proportions of Bailey's popularity. You were more likely to land floor seats for a concert by southern Indiana's other boy wonder, John Cougar Mellencamp, than tickets to one of Bailey's Bedford North Lawrence High School games, which introduced the subspecies of ticket scalper to the southern

Indiana prep hoops scene. Bedford's 6,300-seat gymnasium was sold out weeks in advance. When Bedford played road games, a convoy from Lawrence County inevitably barreled through the Indiana countryside to pack the visiting gym. On account of Bailey, the Bedford North Lawrence Stars routinely outdrew the Pacers, Indiana's entrant in the NBA.

Bailey stopped going out in public because he could scarcely suck on a chili dog outside the Tastee-Freez without being mobbed. "Then they found out where I lived," Bailey recalls. "I open my window one morning and two guys are taking clumps of grass." Clumps of grass? "I guess they wanted a souvenir." (And this was pre-eBay.) Then there was the Indianapolis businessman who made the papers when he named his son Damon and daughter Bailey. Bedford's coach during Bailey's reign, Danny Bush, likes to tell a story from Bailey's freshman season. The team played against Floyd Central, a large school on the Indiana–Kentucky border. Bailey performed at his typically peerless level; Bush took him out with several minutes remaining. Bailey slurped down some water and placed the cup near the bench. As Bush directed his team, he felt something at his arm. The coach was so caught up in the game that he paid no attention until the tapping became tugging. He turned to see that an elderly lady had sidled up to him and was pointing to Bailey's discarded paper cup. "Can I have that?" she asked.

When Bedford North Lawrence played against Bloomington North, some of my classmates loitered near the visitors' entrance armed with notepads, Sharpie pens and cameras. As Damon walked sheepishly off the team bus, he dutifully signed autographs for kids no older than he was. His expression never changed. Clearly, this was standard operating procedure at every road game. I can also recall going to a formal-wear shop to pick up a rented tuxedo for the junior prom. The store's counter was festooned with a framed copy of Bailey's prom photo. Naturally, it was autographed. "Damon got his tux here," the proprietress volunteered with pride. The kid was fifteen at the time and already, if unbeknownst to him, a commercial pitchman.

Handsome and terminally clean-cut, Bailey left the girls screaming. But shrouded in a cloak of unattainable coolness in that Fab Four, Steve McQueen kind of way, he engendered respect—genuine respect, not the reluctant kind—among his male peers. We all played basketball, so we had an instant appreciation for his manifold gifts. But his aura also made it hard for us to begrudge him his status. At once assured and humble, he played with supreme confidence. And while he never talked trash, he subtly let everyone know he was the proverbial Man. At the same time, the frequency with which he passed, the encouragement he gave teammates, the slaps on the butt he conferred on opposing players—it all suggested that he was an authentically cool guy, a suspicion that anyone who knew Bailey was happy to confirm.

Demographically, Bailey probably scored his highest approval ratings among southern Indiana's adult population. At a time when the working definition of "Indiana basketball" was first starting to change, Bailey was not merely a star athlete but, to many, a sort of cultural affirmation. He was a throwback, a player who stood for discipline, self-reliance and decorum at a time when many felt those virtues were losing their importance. He was not just from Indiana, he was *of* Indiana. If he was a basketball god, many fans liked to think that he was created in their own image.

We had heard fables and, quite literally, urban myths from the heathen lands of northern Indiana where a man-child star named Shawn Kemp strutted into gyms with a battery pack in his back pocket attached to Christmas lights that flickered in his "ramp"-style Afro. He drove a tricked-up car of dubious provenance, wore fur coats and passed his classes despite being illiterate. (Most of it was pure fiction, of course.) Kemp could, to use the code, "jump out of the gym" and he possessed a palette of dunks that recalled Michael Jordan. But, the Damon apostles wondered, could Kemp hit an open jump shot, recognize a 1-3-1 defense or step to the line and make his free throws with the game hanging in the balance? That Kemp went on to sign with the enemy, Kentucky—where he allegedly stole a teammate's jewelry and was caught trying to pawn it—and turned pro at age nineteen, confirmed in the eyes of many his status as the devil incarnate.

Bailey was the polar opposite. His game was predicated on that racially charged alliteration "heart and hustle." His jump shot was a guided missile that, more often than not, flitted through the net. One heard (ad nauseam) that "he played the right way," integrating his teammates, sublimating the personal for the collective. He spoke in the authentic, flinty Indiana patois that turns school into "skill," Louisville into "Laville" and Hoosier into "Hissure." Early in his high school career, he committed to play for Indiana University, further confirmation of Hoosier bona fides. "He became so much more than a basketball player," says Bush, his coach. "He was an icon. I don't know how else to put it."

Throughout Bailey's high school career, his story continued to break like one of those formulaic sports movies. For four years he justified his steadily ballooning hype. He improved every year, scored from all coordinates on the floor and balanced his utilitarian game with a few "highlight reel" flourishes—a bloodless no-look pass, a snazzy reverse layup, a fierce dunk. (When, as a senior, he broke the state's all-time scoring record, he did so not with a downy-soft jumper or a calibrated bank shot but on an alley-oop pass, soaring over two defenders to retrieve the ball before softly dropping it in the basket.) Above all, Bailey was *consistent*, a virtue that Hoosiers hold in the highest regard. He was not just excellent, he was ritually excellent. Though he could have coasted through most games and still given a good accounting of himself, he didn't take possessions—much less games—off. "Even now, I'm really proud of that," he says. "I can honestly say that I never gave any game less than a hundred percent."

During Bailey's senior year, when Damon-mania reached its apex, he led Bedford to the state final, the Elysian fields of high school basketball. In front of 41,046 fans, more than double the next-largest crowd ever to watch a high school game anywhere in the world—the finals, many suspected, were moved from Market Square Arena to the cavernous Hoosier Dome to accommodate the Cult of Damon—Bailey cemented his place in the Indiana basketball temple. In the waning moments of the championship game, Elkhart's Concord High led Bedford by six points when Bailey rallied the team and demanded the ball. Bailey scored 11 points in the final 2:30, most, fittingly enough, on free throws. Final score: Bedford North Lawrence 63, Concord 60. Bedford's record during the Bailey Era: 99–11. As the capstone on his career—as if there had been another candidate—he was named Mr. Basketball. Concord's coach, Jim Hahn, suggested after the game, "This is the final chapter in the Damon Bailey story."

Hahn knew more than he knew.

If Bailey were ever the feature of the basketball version of a VH1 *Behind the Music* segment, this is the point at which the lugubrious horn strains would kick in and the inevitable "dark period" would commence. When Bailey ventured to Bloomington, the All-American parable that had been his life story to that point veered from fairy tale to drama. It's not that his fortunes came crashing down; rather, they wafted to earth like leaves from an oak tree in an Indiana autumn. He came to Indiana University weighted with greater expectations than any other freshman basketball player in school history. On the eve of

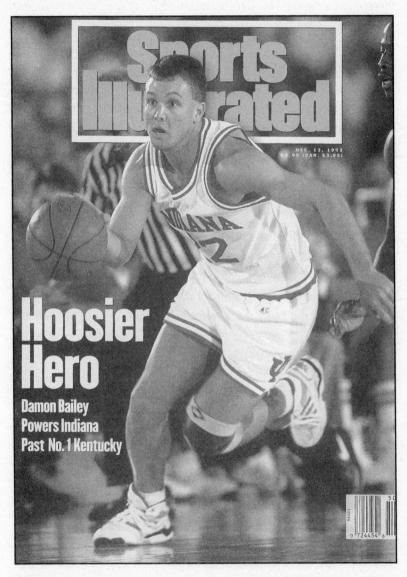

Sports Illustrated

DEC. 13, 1993
$2.95 (CAN. $3.95)

Hoosier Hero

Damon Bailey Powers Indiana Past No. 1 Kentucky

Hoosier hero: Damon Bailey never made it to the NBA but is still the exemplar for Indiana basketball. (*John W. McDonough*/ Sports Illustrated)

his first game for the Hoosiers in the fall of 1990, the *Indianapolis Star* proclaimed on the front page of the newspaper, "Bailey Era Finally Set to Tip Off."

Donnie Walsh, the Indiana Pacers' revered team president, asserts that the only player to leave high school with more hype has been LeBron James. And James was the first pick in the 2003 NBA draft. Bailey made a fairly seamless transition to college ball. He cracked the regular rotation on a team stacked with talented upperclassmen, averaged a respectable 11.4 points and was named to various national All-Freshman teams.

And yet there were flaws in his college game that had never before surfaced. Bailey developed a troubling tendency to disappear during games, scoring prolifically in a short stretch and then, unaccountably, going six or eight or ten minutes without so much as attempting a shot. What his supporters claimed was a conscious effort to integrate his teammates into the game was perceived by others as passivity. What's more, the versatility that served him so well in high school worked, at times, to his detriment in the college ranks. At 6'3", Bailey was too small to be a frontline player. At the same time, at 200 pounds, he lacked the lateral foot speed to defend many guards. He was neither fish nor fowl—in Indiana terms, he was an El Camino, neither a bona fide truck nor a full-fledged car—and he never found a niche on the court. Compounding matters, apart from the usual autograph requests and media circus, there was a horrible off-court distraction: in Damon's freshman year his sister Courtney was diagnosed with leukemia.

Then there was the strain of playing for Knight. Like all players who committed to serve as foot soldiers in the General's boot camp, Bailey knew the terms of the deal before he enlisted. Even forewarned, he was taken aback by Knight's stentorian tirades, the verbal shrapnel, the pains the coach took to humiliate players, the absence of mirth that enshrouded the program. "It was so gloomy there were times when you would say, 'Why am I putting myself through this?'" Bailey once said. The emotional peaks and valleys (or, more accurately, plateaus and valleys) of playing for Knight exacted such a psychic price that on more than one occasion, Bailey thought seriously of transferring. A former Indiana assistant says that at one point Bailey and his father, Wendell, sat in Damon's off-campus apartment and were close to fashioning an exit strategy and decamping to Florida State. They were eventually talked out of it by Knight's "good cop" assistants. Bailey made it through four years, trying his best to suppress any disdain for Knight. He was a good soldier during his time at Indiana, but eventually he stood up to the bully. In 2003, he cowrote the book *Damon: Beyond the Glory* and surprised even some of those closest to him with a savage account of Knight. "The coach is a complex contradiction who demands respect but gives little in return," he writes. "He is controlling of others but resents the authority of his superiors. He is rude but expects others to be polite. He wants others to work to correct their imperfections, but makes little effort to amend his faults."

He goes on to characterize Knight as "a very egotistical person" who bleached the fun out of basketball. He observes that Knight's lapses in decorum were a constant distraction and maintains that while Knight's coaching ability is estimable, "he is not a person to emulate." He even offers a thorough compendium of Knight's various misdeeds through the years.

But in truth it was not Knight's tyranny that stunted Bailey's growth as a player. It was nagging injuries that neutered his athleticism. His speed and jumping ability reduced dramatically from his high school days, Bailey struggled creating his shot against defenders. He had trouble penetrating against fleet-footed guards. On defense, he was average at best, his instincts no match for other players' ability to soar higher or blow past him with a crossover dribble. The hand-eye coordination, his sixth sense for the game, his iron will hardly compensated for the physical deficiencies. "I think he might have been one of those guys who just peaked early," says Walsh. "Other players who are athletic but not skilled in high school put it together during college."

Had it been any other player, Bailey's career at Indiana would be deemed an unqualified success. His four teams were consistent winners, including the 1992 consortium that reached the Final Four. At a school with perhaps the richest basketball tradition in the country, he finished among the top ten players of all time in both scoring and assists. To boot, he graduated with a degree in general studies. But there was an unmistakable sense in Hoosier Nation that Bailey's college years were tinged with disappointment. Fans expected perfection. Or, at the very least, general excellence. They discovered that the Mona Lisa had pockmarks. And as Bailey's aura diminished, so did his prospects of playing in the NBA.

*T*he 1994 NBA draft was held in Indianapolis. In one of those Walter Mitty episodes, I represented the Portland Trail Blazers and sat at their designated table. My highly complex mission entailed jotting down the name of the draft pick emanating from Portland's war room on the other end of the phone line and handing the paper to NBA commissioner David Stern. After warmly shaking my hand, Stern read out the player's name. Aaron McKie. While any monkey could have performed the job with equal skill, I was privy to internal reports on a hundred or so prospects, prepared by the team's fine general manager at the time, Brad Greenberg. Next to Bailey's name was a dismissive, two-word summation: *Not athletic.*

With the first pick in the draft, the Bucks selected Glenn Robinson, a player well known to the local crowd. Before deciding to turn pro after his junior year, Robinson, a silky forward with a soft jump shot, an ability to use either hand and an utter indifference to defense, had been a star at Purdue. Before that, he had led Gary Roosevelt High School to the 1991 Indiana high school title. Still, in the pantheon of Indiana basketball stars, Robinson wasn't even in the same wing as Bailey. Yet here he was three years later as the top pick in the NBA draft. By the end of the summer his agent was demanding a $100 million contract, causing the Bucks' owner, Senator Herb Kohl, to utter the classic one-liner "I'll tell you what: I'll take your contract and you can have my franchise." (Robinson settled for $68 million over ten years.) A decade later he is still starting in the NBA, a solid, if defensively apathetic player.

Jason Kidd. Tony Dumas. Shawnelle Scott. As draft night continued and the names grew increasingly obscure, the restless natives began lobbying vocally for Bailey. Finally, with their second-round pick (and the forty-fourth selection overall) the hometown Pacers selected Bailey. The few remaining fans cheered, but it was a sympathetic cheer, much like the one that forms when the twelfth man is finally allowed to play out the final minutes of a blowout. Pacers executives would later admit that the decision to select Bailey was a public relations move in Indiana as much as anything else. The Pacers signed Bailey to a contract with the proviso that he undergo knee surgery at the team's expense. He spent an exasperating year—albeit one for which he was handsomely remunerated—in rehab, sitting on the end of the Pacers' bench in street clothes. After two seasons on the inactive list, he was released in training camp in 1996, beaten out by Fred Hoiberg for the final roster spot. "Athletically, he just couldn't make the jump," says Walsh. "Everything else was there but . . ." Walsh's voice trails off, leaving the thought to hang in the air like a long jumper. "If this had been twenty years ago, it would have been a different story." Larry Bird, who had followed Bailey's career as intently as any other Hoosier, was more direct: "The bottom line is that Damon just wasn't good enough for the NBA."

Bailey's failure to make it to basketball's highest level wasn't just an unsatisfying ending to a basketball fable that began with so much promise. It was a vivid illustration of a paradigm shift. For decades, dozens of Hoosiers who grasped the game, competed feverishly and possessed a reliable jump shot made their mark on the NBA, regardless of athletic limitations. Don Buse and Kyle Macy and Jerry Sichting and Scott Skiles all had lengthy pro careers. Even Steve Alford played in 169 games with the Dallas Mavericks and the Golden State Warriors. In a prior era, Bailey, bum knees and all, would have been a serviceable player if not a star. But this was the mid- and late '90s. His level of athleticism didn't meet the NBA's minimum standards, and his style of play resembled a dance craze from a bygone era, now hopelessly out of vogue. It was hard to consider his fate and not conclude that he and his ilk were dinosaurs of sorts, picking and rolling their way into the basketball tar pits.

By 1996, Bailey, like so many NBA aspirants, was choosing between the lesser of two basketball evils: staying in America and playing in the no-frills Continental Basketball Association (CBA) or playing for some deep-pocketed team in Uruguay or Portugal or the Philippines, where you don't speak the language, don't know the culture and can't be sure you'll get paid. With debatable accuracy, the CBA refers to itself as the "second-best basketball league in the world." But reminders abound that the players are more than a long jump shot from the big time. Cash-strapped teams from backwater markets such as Yakima, Washington, and Rapid City, South Dakota, often travel to games by bus and stay at fleabag motels. When the teams are home, the players often lodge at the local hotel and fritter away the bulk of their mornings and afternoons watching bad television. As one CBA refugee once joked to me, "The league should have a sponsorship deal with Prozac."

The biggest differences between the CBA and the NBA are financial. The *minimum* NBA salary comes close to covering the season payroll for a CBA team, on which the best player is likely to earn $1,000 a week for the five-month season. Stories abound of players getting summoned to the NBA and suddenly receiving more in meal money—thanks to the NBA Players' Association it is now $110 per day, which goes a long way at Taco Bell—than they were making in salary in the CBA.

The CBA's Fort Wayne Fury held Bailey's rights, so he hardly had to worry about adjusting to a foreign culture. And fortunately for Bailey, he could handle the CBA's wage scale. He had received two seasons' worth of salary, in excess of $500,000, from the Pacers and had his various side ventures and Indiana-based endorsements. Plus, unlike the vast majority of NBA players who cannot avoid the temptation to purchase an armada of cars or subsidize the business venture of every distant cousin, Bailey was fiscally responsible.

A tougher adjustment was adapting to the CBA's style of play. Rare is the minor leaguer in any sport who does not carry a monstrous chip on his shoulder, cursing "the system," bemoaning "politics," lamenting "the numbers game," able to rattle off a list of big-league players with skills and abilities inferior to his own. The way out of this purgatory is to put up numbers that catch the eye of the parent teams. It works fine in baseball: The disgruntled minor leaguer who can hit .350 or strike out ten batters a game can rest assured that he'll be upwardly mobile. Basketball is trickier. When there are five players on the court who each want to score 25 points a game, the results can be disastrous. While the CBA rosters are chock-full of players with NBA-worthy talent, the games can feature less passing and defense than a lunchtime YMCA action. To say that the CBA's style of basketball ran counter to Bailey's basketball instincts would be an understatement. "Damon would make the extra pass or help his man on defense—it's the only way he knew how to play the game," says Rich Coffey, who was the Fury's general manager during Bailey's tenure and now runs the Fort Wayne Arena Football League franchise. "Then the next trip down he would be wide open and wouldn't see the ball because one of his teammates would want to put up twenty points and impress the scouts. He put on a good face, but no question it wore on him. I think it also hurt when he didn't get much of a chance in the NBA and other teammates—guys he knew in his heart he was better than—got a chance."

One such player was Moochie Norris, a typical basketball Bedouin inasmuch as he had attended three colleges and played for six teams in four years when he landed in Fort Wayne. Norris was one of those characters straight out of a movie like *Slap Shot* or *Bull Durham* that romanticize the quirks of the bush leagues. Named after the Cab Calloway song "Minnie the Moocher," Norris was a six-foot dervish who thrilled the fans in Fort Wayne with his dunking and hair that alternated between braids and a prodigious Afro. He also had insomnia and rarely slept more than two hours a night. In the infomercial hours, he would don glasses that flashed lights and emitted a thumping sound when he closed his eyes. But Norris could play a little, and Bailey was instrumental in bolstering the kid's confidence, feeding him the ball and moving to off-guard when an NBA scout was in town so Morris could demonstrate his ballhandling skills. Before long Norris had gone from a wacky cult figure to a solid CBA player. By season's end he was called up, made the most of the opportunity and now plays for the New York Knicks, where he is midway through a guaranteed $22 million contract. Naturally, at the time, Bailey expressed nothing but happiness for his former teammate. Still, consider their fates—the wacky, well-traveled insomniac is in the NBA and the paragon of basketball virtue isn't—and you can't help but marvel that the basketball gods work in strange ways.

By 2000, Bailey's frustrations were mounting. And, after he married his school sweetheart, his family had burgeoned to three kids. It was no fun calling his daughter on her birthday from a motel in Yakima or Rapid City. Burned out on a sport that had consumed him for twenty years, Bailey walked away with the most cursory, fanfare-free of retirement announcements. And that's how it ended for Damon Bailey. The "can't-miss kid" retired from basketball, never having played a solitary minute in the NBA. The limestone memorial to Bailey in Heltonville is engraved with various accomplishments. The last entry: 1994, First Team, All–Big Ten. Not a word about the pros.

If Hoosiers ever needed convincing that a mastery of the vaunted fundamentals, an XXXL heart and an unassailable attitude were no longer sufficient credentials for reaching basketball's highest ranks, this was it. His basketball odometer had rolled over. Before he had turned thirty, Damon Bailey was no longer a basketball icon. He was a cultural relic.

In the spring of 2003, I had a pleasant phone conversation with Bailey. We made tentative plans to meet in person for this project and for a "Where Are They Now?" article for *Sports Illustrated.* He was traveling a lot for business, so just to be sure we could connect, he gave me his cell phone number.

Then Bailey disappeared. A series of calls and messages and voice mails went unreturned. A letter sent Federal Express to Bailey's office went ignored. Intermediaries tried to help out, but nothing materialized. Had Bailey still been playing, I would have persisted a bit more. But given that he was out of basketball, a "civilian" whose life was in repose, I couldn't very well blame him for seeking some privacy. He had been under media surveillance since middle school. By this point, he was well within his rights to decline being badgered.

Having left his twenties behind, currently encroaching on middle age, Bailey has settled easily into the next phase of his life. While he was never accorded the millions bestowed on even the NBA's lesser lights, he is financially secure. When his playing days ended, there was a slight temptation to relocate elsewhere—Phoenix, for instance, which would have done wonders for his golf game. But, finally, he was hopeless to resist the tug, the undertow really, of southern Indiana. To borrow from another icon who lives in the region, Bailey could be himself in this small town.

Damon, his wife, Stacey, the former Bedford cheerleader he began dating in middle school, and their three kids live in a spacious house on twenty-three acres east of Bedford on Route 58. Bailey's parents, his in-laws, his grandparents, his church, his old high school gym—they're all a few minutes away. He spends his days at the Hawkins-Bailey Warehouse (note which name comes first), a business that, according to its brochure, "distributes filtration and lubrication materials to coal mines and construction companies." Physically, Bailey is still handsome and athletic-looking. His shoulders and torso still look as though they could be cut from the Indiana limestone behind his home. But the Glory Days have, without question, passed him by. The steady stream of requests for interviews and autographs has slowed to a trickle. In his 2003 book, *Beyond the Glory*, Bailey casually included his business card as one of the graphics. That he would—whether by accident or design—commit his contact information to print speaks volumes to how much life has changed since Bailey would take a circuitous route home from games, just to be sure no one was following him.

Sure, in his weaker moments he might reflect on the arc of his basketball career and ask himself the unanswerable "what ifs." What if he hadn't gone to Indiana University, where the autocratic coach made it damn near impossible to have any fun on the court? What if his knees hadn't betrayed him? What if his emotional makeup had enabled him to coast through games, and what if he hadn't ravaged his body with his unstinting effort? What if he had gone to the training camp of an NBA team that had different roster needs? What if he'd been born a decade or two earlier, when the demands of the basketball labor force were much different and horizontal skills were as prized as vertical ones? But, ultimately, the thoughts are fleeting. He doesn't yearn for a life that he isn't living.

Life being heavy into irony, I saw Bailey at a Bedford game during my winter in Indiana. Given how clear he had made it that he had no interest in being interviewed, I decided not to introduce myself. Bailey, I was told, makes it to a handful of games, more because his wife is the school's varsity cheerleading coach than to watch basketball or to troll for any residual glory. He was uniformly recognized as he sat in the stands. But he was not mobbed. Just another thirty-something fan watching kids half his age play basketball, assessing the team now tasked with representing the Bedford community.

After the game, I spoke with a coach in the visitors' locker room. As I walked back toward the court, there were a dozen or so kids of various shapes and sizes milling about, shooting on the goals as parents chatted and custodians swept up the empty popcorn boxes and paper cups. Stacey Bailey, exuding warmth and grace even from a distance, stood on the side of the court chatting up, one assumed, the parents of a cheerleader. Damon waited patiently off to the side, when a loose ball trickled over to him. Unsure about the origins, he shrugged and hoisted a twenty-five-footer. Damn if the shot, like countless others—millions perhaps—he'd attempted on the same goal didn't find a home in the hoop. You couldn't help thinking it would have made for a hell of a final scene in the Damon Bailey movie. The credits roll and the audience leaves smiling, knowing that the "can't-miss kid" who missed the NBA is making it just fine after all.

3

EMPIRE BUILDER

TOM MCKINNEY'S OFFICE IS A WINDOWLESS BOX NOT MUCH larger than an airplane lavatory. Vestigial fumes from the adjacent locker room seep under the door. The desk is entirely too small to accommodate McKinney's sturdy 6'2" frame. There is little on the walls to suggest it is the workspace of one of the state's most accomplished and successful basketball coaches, a man who has won 88 percent of his games over the past decade. In fact, the only basketball relics are the pair of shoes his father wore when he played in 1938 and the shoes his son, David, wore when he played for Bloomington North in 1997. And still, for nearly twenty years, its inhabitant has relished few things more than opening the door to this lair after the last school bell had tolled, changing from his sweater and slacks into his polyester shorts and gray T-shirt and reviewing the meticulous practice schedule he would deploy later that afternoon.

It's an article of faith that basketball players of all levels tend to regard practice as a necessary evil, the broccoli before the steak and ice cream that are the games. It's all toil and trouble, sweat without adulation. In truth, a good many coaches feel the same way. They would rather be performing under klieg lights, with the pep band playing, the cheerleaders cheering and the scoreboard defining and quantifying their success.

But even after thirty-four years of retreating to the gym every day after school, McKinney greets practice with a sort of exhilaration. It's when basketball is stripped of its window dressing, distilled to its purest form. Free of distractions, he can decode his players, figuring out what makes them tick both as individuals and as a collective. He can play alchemist, mixing and matching until the disparate parts form something resembling a whole. Most of all, he can teach. Not just the niceties of the drop step and half-court trap—though there was plenty of that. A bulwark against eroding values, McKinney teaches discipline and respect and accountability and honor. "Character building" has become the hoariest of sports clichés, but that's what McKinney does.

During practices, as McKinney barks orders and watches the action, his eyes unfailing surveillance cameras, there is a constancy to him. His tone, his facial expression, even his posture are unchanged the entire time. His carping and caviling is nonstop, never especially vulgar or especially personal but unceasing nonetheless, delivered in a glacially slow cadence so every word is dragged out for emphasis. Much like Vince Lombardi, McKinney doesn't congest his players' heads with dozens of plays. But those he has, he expects them to know. "Do a few things, but do them well" is a favorite McKinney expression.

Likewise, there is only one team rule, but it is an all-encompassing one: "Don't embarrass the program."

As both his Hoosier accent and his disdain for self-promotion immediately suggest, McKinney is as Indiana as Indiana gets. To start with, it is, pointedly, Tom McKinney. Never Thomas. He was born and raised in Columbus, Indiana, forty miles southeast of Bloomington, graduated from Indiana University in 1970 and has never lived outside the state. Basketball is the filament that has run through his life. He has hardly gone a day without hearing the squeak of canvas soles against a maplewood floor. By the time he had finished playing forward for Columbus High School, a deadeye shooter (but, surprisingly, a lousy defender not just by his own reckoning) on one of the best teams in Indiana, he knew he wanted to become a high school coach. McKinney comes from a family of educators; his father was a principal in Columbus and his uncle Lawrence was a longtime principal in the South Bend system who taught alongside John Wooden. McKinney entered the field as well, graduating from IU with a degree in education and becoming a versatile teacher in a variety of humanities subjects. But his real classroom was always 84 feet long with ten-foot goals on each end. On one of his first dates with Judy Earnshaw, the woman he would later marry, he confided that his dream was to coach a high school team to a state title one day. She didn't flinch.

Fresh out of college, McKinney started his ascent up the high school coaching ladder. Like everything he does, it was slow, methodical and steady. He had served as an assistant for nearly a decade, spending untold hours traversing those two-lane state roads that curl intestine-like through the countryside, to scout opponents. After the school day, he would decamp to the gym to organize practices, diagram plays, stay late to work with kids on whatever parts of their game needed fine-tuning. Then, on game nights, he would recede into the background.

He was in his early thirties when he finally landed a head coaching job at Franklin High School. He was there eight years when the call came, in 1987. Would he like to coach Bloomington High School North? It was an opportunity to move to a bigger, more vibrant school, but the job came with a few caveats. A high school team in a college town, Bloomington North was hardly the community epicenter and, unlike in so many other Indiana towns, life doesn't stop when the high school basketball team plays. Anything McKinney did was guaranteed to be obscured by the Indiana Hoosiers. Plus, for reasons no one could quite pin down, the school's basketball program routinely under-achieved; winning seasons were rare. Worse still, the team's starting forward was Pat Knight. Not only was he the son of the most accomplished and influential basketball coach in the country, but there were murmurs that Bob Knight and his ex-wife, Nancy, displeased with how Pat was being used, had pushed out the previous coach.

It was the perfect fit for McKinney. Reflexively, almost pathologically, modest, McKinney recoils from attention as if it were a hot flame. He liked nothing more than coaching on a Saturday night and then going grocery shopping or taking his son and daughter out for breakfast the next morning. In a basketball-mad state, where anyone who coaches a church league team of third-graders thinks he's the second coming of Wooden, McKinney had known too many small-town coaches who couldn't fill up their car at the Amoco without having to justify their substitution patterns to overzealous fans. The specter of Knight would be a blessing.

Bloomington North's history of futility wasn't a turnoff either. Ever the pragmatist, McKinney figured it just meant the expectations would be manageable. As for coaching Bob Knight's son, McKinney's concerns were abated when Knight *père* called a meeting and, with characteristic finesse, said, "I only ask one thing of you. Don't let my son be a limp dick." After that, save offering the Bloomington North team the use of Indiana University facilities, Knight never meddled. Any concern that the new coach would be Bob Knight's patsy was quickly put to rest when Pat got the business end of a few McKinney philippics.

At Bloomington North, as at most high schools in Indiana, the basketball coach tended to cut a genial figure, a backslapping quasi-celebrity who led pep rallies, was friendly with the cheerleaders and didn't expend much energy on his teaching duties. When McKinney arrived at Bloomington North in my junior year, I remember that he was shrouded in mystery. He was at once proud and detached as he walked the halls, keeping a healthy remove from everyone else. Those who had him as a teacher and expected an easy A in his history or government classes were disappointed by how rigorously he taught, running his classroom much the way he did his basketball practice. To a person, the players respected him and snapped to attention when he passed them in the halls. But he was an impenetrable, slightly aloof figure, revealing few details about himself and showing no interest in school gossip or small talk.

It took McKinney all of one year to turn the program around. His second season on the job, Bloomington North had a winning record and won the sectional title. Still, it was impossible to guess that he would turn the basketball program into a dynasty. In the ensuing fifteen years, McKinney would win the state title, routinely lead his teams to 20-win seasons, mint two Mr. Basketball winners, seven Indiana All-Stars, land dozens in college, and even send players to the NBA. Asked how he did it, what accounted for the dramatic sea change, McKinney pauses as if he had never before pondered the question. "We've had some good kids," he finally manages. "Some good assistant coaches and some good support from the administration."

It's true. But only up to a point. McKinney—a man who can't tie his shoe without deferring credit to his staff—is the single figure most responsible for the staggering success. Sure, there were some happy accidents. It was McKinney's good fortune that Sean May, an oxlike power forward who had what the scouts call "an NBA body" at age fifteen, lived in the district. And that Jared Jeffries, a smooth forward now starting in the NBA for the Washington Wizards, lived—if only by a few feet—in North's jurisdiction. And that Wal and Julia Duany left Africa in the mid-'80s and fortuitously chose to settle in Bloomington, where their three sons, each at least 6'6", would go to high school on the north side of town. But McKinney's earmarks are all over the program. He was pliant enough to change with the times, rigid enough to do so without compromising values.

McKinney is a monarch—but, unlike Knight, a largely enlightened one—whose authority is unquestioned. His *Defense über Alles* philosophy is not negotiable. At the start of every season, he gathers his players and says, in so many words, *Here's how it's going to be, and if you don't like it, there's the door.* "Basketball is not a democracy," he says. "If you have a problem with that, you might want to try an individual sport." He scoffs at the notion of the "players' coach," a new species who befriends his charges, importuning rather than demanding them to play their hardest. "I saw an article where players said they liked their coach because he was liberal and let them wear earrings," he says with disgust. "What in the world does that have to do with basketball?" He has no interest in their music or their culture or their slang or their websites. If his players' use of "phat" and "fat" connoted two different things, it was news to the coach. As he puts it, "I'm not the type of coach who's going to hold a pizza party." To him, coaching is an asymmetrical relationship, one he would just as soon not clutter by getting too chummy with his players. He takes obvious pleasure in recounting the story of a player complaining to a teammate, "Coach McKinney's unfair. He's a real asshole to me." The teammate shook his head. "No. He's fair. He's a real asshole to all of us."

For most of the '90s, McKinney's top assistant coach was Tom Bowers, a peer who moonlighted as a professor at the Indiana University Business School. The father of a son and daughter the same age as McKinney's kids, Bowers had a deep connection with the coach, and the two men killed untold hours talking deep into the night. This season, McKinney's crop of assistants—Brian Muehlhaus, Andy Hodson, Jason Speer, David Pillar and George Leonard—are hardworking and dutiful and never complain, despite making less money ($2,000 for the season) than they would if they flipped burgers or dispensed lattes. But they are bachelors and newlyweds in their late twenties and early thirties who are closer in age to the players than the coach. References in coaching meetings to Pontiac ragtops and the Rascals and G. Gordon Liddy are met with blank stares.

Though he'd recently turned fifty-six, McKinney could easily pass for a decade younger. His nimbus of hair has only a slight concentric circle of baldness, his build is that of a former athlete who still tries to stay in shape. But his looks deceive. In today's parlance: McKinney is Old School. And damn proud of it.

Old School means that he disdains cheating and can't abide taking shortcuts or exploiting loopholes that make ethically dubious behavior technically legal. Unlike other basketball coaches in the area who had a knack for filling a roster spot with a foreign exchange student—one who just so happened to play the position where the team had a deficiency—McKinney never recruited kids. McKinney wouldn't field players who lived outside the district, even as other coaches—even some within the Bloomington North athletic department—were importing kids and placing them in the homes of assistant coaches. A few years ago, the father of a player gave McKinney a check for $100, telling him to spend it however he pleased. Whiffing a bribe, McKinney returned the money. A few weeks later, the player mysteriously transferred. This is a man who, after some deliberation, considers "using the g.d. word" as his biggest vice. "I guess I am just a right-wrong person," McKinney says slowly. "I don't like injustice."

The Old School code means that you are self-sufficient. When your rivals do cut corners and bend rules perilously close to the breaking point, you don't rat them out. Instead you redouble your resolve to beat them—and take that much more satisfaction when you do. When your team's locker room needs a paint job, you don't complain to the athletic director. You buy paint and brushes and spend days quietly doing it yourself. When you could be spending your summer fishing or reading or making up for the times you didn't see your family during the season, you hold a basketball camp and work with kids who have no chance of ever playing a significant role on the team. When Nike offers to provide free basketball shoes to your players and all you have to do in return is adorn your gym with their banners, you politely decline. The assault on your dignity, the gnawing sense that you'd "sold out" would be too big a price to pay. And besides, your players are high school athletes, not corporate shills.

Old School means taking pains to be opaque. McKinney's slumped shoulders are a dead giveaway that the coach doesn't traffic in self-aggrandizement or self-promotion or self-absorption. His typical game-night getup—a cranberry sweater, black slacks, black shoes, white socks and a pen he neglected to remove from behind his ear—draws as little attention to him as possible. His postgame interviews are a relentless parade of banalities. McKinney would sum up even the most emotional victories and devastating losses by observing, "Both teams played hard." "I was happy to see we made the necessary adjustments."

Arms and the man: McKinney offers words of encouragement to forward Sean May, one of seven Indiana All-Star players the coach turned out at Bloomington North. (*Jeremy Hogan/ Bloomington* Herald-Times)

"Our guards complemented each other." (Perhaps he meant "Our guards complimented each other"—it wouldn't have made any less sense.) The team's beat writers learned quickly that a yes-no question received a yes-no answer. When you express your approval to your players, you often do it wordlessly—a firm pat on the back or a subtle nod.

Old School also means no star system, no separate set of rules for the best players. If anything, McKinney was tougher on the players with the most talent, even Jeffries and May, who were tapped as NBA prospects as freshmen. "Man, did he get on me," Jeffries told me after a shootaround the afternoon before a game at Madison Square Garden last March. "I remember games where I would be scoring points and rebounding and we'd be winning and then I'd get to the locker room: 'Jared, you didn't block out for crap.' 'Jared, I don't care how many points you have, you have to help the weak side.' Practice was the same way. Every day, 'Jared!' At the time you're like, 'Man, what do I have to do to please him?' But you know something? He was right." At this point, Jeffries stops and scans the floor to make sure that his current coach isn't within earshot. "Coach McKinney did more for my game than anyone else I've played for." May, too, was no stranger to McKinney's doghouse. In his sophomore season at North Carolina, May wrote a note to McKinney thanking him for everything he had done to help him get better, and apologizing for the times he hadn't played his hardest for him.

Still, the code wasn't immutable. For all of McKinney's establishmentarian ways, his success owes just as much as anything to an open-mindedness, a respect for differences, an ability to adjust to a changing culture. When he came to Bloomington, he recognized immediately that the international community affiliated with IU was a huge untapped resource. He embraced the diversity, reaching out to families who didn't look like him, whose names didn't necessarily roll off the tongue, and made it clear that their kids were welcome in his gym. One could say he thought globally and acted locally.

When Bloomington North won the 1997 state title, romping Delta 75–54, the rotation featured a Sudanese forward (Kueth Duany) and an Indonesian point guard (Mario Wuysang) and a center (Djibril Kante) whose father came to Bloomington from Mali. They blended seamlessly with the more paradigmatic Hoosiers, who included McKinney's son, David. Before the final game, when the state's media grilled the team on their unlikely backgrounds, Matt Reed, a buzz-cut white kid from just outside the Bloomington city limits whose twin brother, Ryan, was also on the North team, took the microphone and let loose this gem: "Hell, we're the only foreigners on the team. We're from Unionville."

As the quality of players improved (due in no small part to the infrastructure he established) and the caliber of athletes increased dramatically, McKinney was willing to adjust his coaching style. Though it ran counter to the methods on which he was weaned, he employed up-tempo offenses that gave players creative freedom and called for trapping and pressing defenses. There was still structure, and those departing from it would earn an extended stay on the bench. But there was also a willingness to adjust his strategy to fit the character of his team. One of the few tchotchkes on McKinney's desk is a plaque with a quotation from Abraham Lincoln: YOU CANNOT BRING ABOUT PROSPERITY BY DISCOURAGING THRIFT. YOU CANNOT STRENGTHEN THE WEAK BY WEAKENING THE STRONG. "That," says McKinney, "is how I look at basketball. You have to change to fit your personnel."

Likewise, he was flexible enough to make concessions to a changing culture. McKinney realized that summer leagues were an inevitability, and while he was appropriately suspicious of most AAU coaches, he worked with them, figuring that at least his players were getting some game experience over the summer. He didn't say a word when three players showed up one day with pierced ears. He bit his tongue and chalked it up to nothing more than a totem of kids still finetuning their identities. He also resigned himself to the fact that not all of his players look at the game the way he does, with his ferocious intensity or his abject hatred of defeat. The current team, in particular, is peopled with "good kids," smart and genial teenagers but ones who performed with a nonchalance that bordered on complacency. "That's who they are, and on some level maybe I need to accept that," he says. "Sometimes it's easy to forget that not everyone shares your values." He also felt strongly about "letting kids be kids," encouraging his players to compete in other sports outside of basketball season—rare sentiment among today's coaches.

Then there is the tattoo that adorns his left shoulder, a brown basketball perhaps two inches in diameter ringed with the words BHSN '97 STATE CHAMPS. The thought of McKinney getting "inked up" is no more incongruous than Harry Truman getting his navel pierced. McKinney refuses to show it off and bridles at the mention of it. "Dumbest thing I've ever done," he says, brushing the air in embarrassment and self-disgust. But there it is, both an indelible emblem of the pinnacle of his coaching career and an indelible sign that he might not be so rigid after all.

Like many Hoosiers, under McKinney's hardened carapace is a soft interior. His voice catches when talking about Errek Suhr. In his freshman year at Bloomington North, Suhr made the varsity team only to break his wrist a few weeks later. Then, a few games into the season, he learned that his sister Jenny—who had once dated McKinney's son—was diagnosed with terminal brain cancer. Jenny was a basketball fan who liked few things more than watching her little brother play. Stoic the entire time, Suhr played with a cast over his broken wrist so his sister could continue watching him play. She died a few months later. "I think I admired that as much as anything I had seen coaching," McKinney says. Did he ever convey that to Suhr? "A lot of times you have players [you particularly like], but they don't know they're the favorite and you don't want them to."

Given how McKinney speaks unapologetically of erecting emotional barriers between himself and his players, it's astonishing how many consider themselves fortunate for coming into his orbit and describe him as a transforming figure in their lives. Derrick Cross, a supremely talented guard for Bloomington North in the early '90s, came from a single-parent home and devoted so much time to basketball that classwork was an afterthought. In Cross's sophomore year, McKinney called the player into his office. "Do you still want to play college ball, Derrick?"

"Yeah, Coach."

"Well, these grades are going to keep you from doing it."

As Cross started to cry, McKinney unfurled a contract. If Cross agreed to work harder in his classes, McKinney vowed to help him in any way possible, which included picking him up at 5:30 A.M. so they could go over homework before the school day. "Once I actually sat down and tried, I saw that I could do the work," Cross says. "It was just a question of not putting it off." Cross went on to play ball at Miami of Ohio and graduated in 1995 with a B.S. in sport management and health appraisal. He went on to get a master's degree in recreational sports from Indiana University. He lives in Bloomington, dividing his time between studying for a second master's in recreational sports management and running Urban Stylz, a store that sells hip-hop apparel—brands like Enyce and Phat Farm and Sean John that, in another earmark of changing times, one doesn't necessarily associate with southern Indiana. "This is no exaggeration," says Cross. "Coach McKinney changed my life."

*T*ime was, the men stalking the sidelines were square-jawed masters and commanders whose authority was absolute. They had names like Wooden and Rupp and Auerbach and Knight and were immune both from criticism and from petty office politics. No more. Mirroring the general erosion of moral authority in society, coaches have become middle managers of sort, beset by pressure from both below and above. Neither their job security nor their sphere of influence is what it once was. Parents and fans think little of berating them. Players think little of questioning their judgment or proficiency.

Owners and athletic directors think little of terminating them for failing to meet expectations that often were inflated to begin with.

By the end of the 2003–04 NBA season, nineteen of twenty-nine teams had changed coaches within the year, some more than once. At one point in the season, Terry Stotts, a Bloomington North graduate, had coached the Atlanta Hawks for thirteen months, making him the longest-tenured coach in the Eastern Conference. "The money is unreal, but the lack of job security has just gotten to be just as crazy in the other direction," Stotts told me over dinner late in season. "You come to work in the morning knowing you could be fired in the afternoon."

And this was fairly symptomatic. Esteemed college coaches were under the gun everywhere, not least in West Lafayette, Indiana, where Gene Keady—a thoroughly decent, hardworking leader who won 70 percent of his games coaching Purdue over the past quarter-century—was on the hot seat after a few down seasons. Matt Doherty, coach of the venerable North Carolina Tar Heels, was fired after a group of disgruntled players led a coup against him. (Perversely, Sean May, the former Bloomington North star, was among the insurrectionists.) At the high school level, the coach of Indian Creek, a small school a half-hour south of Indianapolis, came under fire when his players openly rebelled against him. The acts of protest included a player throwing a pass to J. R. Angle, the son of the team's coach, Larry Angle, when J.R. was on the bench. *Hey, Coach! You want me to pass to your kid? Fine. Take that.* It was dismissed as a relatively innocent indiscretion until it came to light that adult fans, dissatisfied with the way Angle was running the team, had paid the kid $45 to perform the prank. The IHSAA banned the offending player from competing in basketball his senior season and the adult instigators were prohibited from attending games. But Angle resigned, and the ugly interlude presented another shot across the bow of the coaching profession.

Though most of it was self-imposed, McKinney was feeling a

certain amount of pressure too. There had been some personnel changes at the school and new administrators weren't according him the support he was accustomed to. Parents knew better than to confront him over the kids' playing time, but each season he got a few anonymous letters—from grandparents, he suspected—critiquing his coaching. Midway through the season, a letter to the editor of the local paper, the Bloomington *Herald-Times*, criticized McKinney for his "negativity and lack of enthusiasm or support" and for "belittling his team's success."

Sufficiently thick-skinned, McKinney could handle the criticism, writing it off as a cost of doing business. More vexing was what he saw as falling standards of accountability and the rise of apologist parents. A few days earlier, a player had arrived late for a game-day walk-through. The team rule is that players are punished for tardiness by running laps. As the kid entered the gym, his mother trailed him. "Don't make him run laps," the mother pleaded. "It's not his fault; it's mine." McKinney was unmoved. "The kids haven't changed, but the parents have," he laments. "They look for any reason to excuse their kids. I'm about sick of it sometimes."

After his thirty-four years on the job, McKinney's passion both for basketball and for teaching still burned fiercely. But the office politics and the super-sized helping of stress were becoming unbearable. For the first time in his life, he had high blood pressure. He had spent his share of weekends away from his family. A long teaching career had allowed him—slowly, methodically—to build up a nest egg, plus some rental property he and his wife managed had become a nice source of supplemental income. He had won a state title and eclipsed 400 wins for his career, generally the benchmark for Hall of Fame status. Though he told only his wife and a few confidants, he went through the season all but sure it would be his last.

In part, he kept it secret because, in the deep recesses of his mind, he figured he might have a change of heart. But the silence also precluded any sort of sentimental send-off. When he finally put away his clipboard for the last time, when he stopped coming to that dingy office before practice, what did he want written as his coaching epitaph? McKinney paused for a good ten seconds before giving the ultimate Midwest Gothic answer: "He did the job they paid him to do."

4

KNIGHT AND DAY

TO ATTEND AN INDIANA UNIVERSITY BASKETBALL GAME at Assembly Hall is to find yourself double-teamed by ritual and tradition. The Hoosiers have been playing in the building since 1971, and amazingly little about the game experience has changed since the doors first opened. The same unofficial seating policy holds, mandating that Indiana's landed gentry—big-time donors, former IU basketball players—sit on the courtside bleachers, while the common fans sit in the hard-back seats higher up. Since Day One, the team has been wearing the identical candy-cane warm-ups. The band has stuck to the same repertoire of songs. The concession stands have been serving the same hypersalted popcorn. For nearly thirty years they have had the same public address announcer, a kindly, mustachioed man, Chuck Crabb, who pronounces "sophomore" as a three-syllable word and alerts fans as to which cars have their lights left on in the parking lot. Season tickets are a form of family heirloom handed down from generation to generation, so fans often sit alongside the same families for decades. The scoreboards, the courtside tables, the Indiana decal on the floor surface have all remained unchanged.

There is comfort in the routine, and it's worth pointing out that so much ceremony was made possible by the consistent excellence of the IU teams. But with this constancy as a backdrop, it's hard to exaggerate the dimension of changes that have recently rocked Hoosier Nation. The iconic Bob Knight, a fixture on the sidelines for twenty-nine years, was replaced with a man who, put simply, is his polar opposite. Black replaced white. New School supplanted Old School. Knowledge and experience gave way to youth and enthusiasm. Profanity yielded to piety. Though he was the rare Hoosier who neither knew nor cared about Indiana basketball, my father had a pretty good analogy for the transformation. As he once explained to a friend overseas: "It's like you've been listening to classical music on the radio for all your life and decide to change stations after thirty years. Instead of easing into something, you go right to speed metal. That's what the switch from Bob Knight to Mike Davis was like."

Most fans had braced themselves for life A.B., After Bobby. But the conventional wisdom was that Knight's replacement would come from "within the family." He would keep the tradition alive and look, coach and comport himself like his predecessor. Steve Alford, a prototypical Hoosier and the hero of Indiana's 1987 NCAA championship team, fit the mold. So did Jim Crews, the former Evansville coach who played for Knight in the '70s. Even the name of Knight's younger son, Pat, who played for IU from 1990 to '94, was bandied about as a successor. Who would have imagined that the heir to the bench would be a young, handsome, African-American from Alabama, so religious that he won't schedule a practice on Sunday? "I've been on the job for four years almost," Davis said in the winter of 2004. "I know a lot of people still can't believe I have this job—and that includes me."

Davis says there are instances when he'll call time-outs during games and assemble his team; though his lips will move and he'll bark out instructions to his players, his mind is elsewhere. He'll stare up into the crimson sea in the stands, see the quintet of championship banners overhead, spy those damn television cameras that always seem to catch him at the least flattering times, hear the drums and horns of the pep band and wonder . . . *Am I really the coach of Indiana?* "Honest," he says. "I still go through that. It's like, 'Man, how did this all happen?' "

The story is Indiana's version of a Greek tragedy.

Bob Knight was already a boy wonder when he arrived in Bloomington in 1971. "Genius" has become a word thrown around the sports world with reckless abandon, applied to anyone marginally more proficient than the average Joe at a specific pursuit. But Knight was, by any measure, a basketball genius, a savant who saw the sport— its geometry, its possibilities—differently from how anyone else did. As one of his rivals once conceded, "Bobby doesn't coach the same game the rest of us do." Within five years of his arrival, Knight had guided the Hoosiers to a national title. By the time he turned fifty, he had added a second and third title, an Olympic gold medal in 1984, and was on the fast track to becoming the most successful basketball coach in NCAA history.

Knight was a figure fit for canonization. The purists appreciated the motion offense Knight birthed—all five players orbiting the court like synchronized gears on a watch—and admired the labyrinth of screens, picks and spacing he deployed to befuddle opponents. His insistence on man-to-man defense was in keeping with the spirit of Indiana, a state that puts a premium on self-reliance and personal responsibility. The Hoosiers' brand of basketball—death by a thousand cuts, so to speak—was a striking contrast to the largely improvisational NBA style of play that was coming into vogue at other college programs, like Kentucky, North Carolina and Arizona.

But Knight's real appeal—what truly made him a cult figure in the state—was what he represented. He was a bulwark against change. In an era of slackening standards, Knight was (in theory, anyway) an advocate of discipline, accountability and exactitude. In a time of spin and packaging and polish, he didn't waste time with nuance or subtlety. *Here's what I think, and if you don't like it, there's the door, you son of a bitch.* He was the face—too often a snarling, contorted one—of The Way It Was.

He picked his fights against popular opponents: referees, rival coaches, whiners and windbags in the media, pointy-headed academics who resented his dominion, Indiana University's faceless bureaucrats and administrators. (Who, after all, likes his boss?) Even his off-season hobbies—exotic hunting and fishing trips with the likes of George Bush and Norman Schwarzkopf—struck a resonant chord with the constituency. Knight's nickname, the General, was an apt one. His goose-stepping minions weren't just the twelve players he coached; the subordinates were also the state's citizenry. To say that Knight was a god in Indiana is to sell short his stature. He was *the* god.

But like a hero in the classical canon, Knight was undone by an Aristotelian fatal flaw: in his case, a potent speedball of rage, paranoia and intransigence on which he eventually overdosed. When Knight brought shame to both the university and the basketball program by, say, hurling a chair across the court, well, *that was just Bobby being Bobby.* When he used language and imagery profane enough to make a sailor blanch, well, *what coach doesn't lose it from time to time?* When he kicked his son in the shin or fiercely grabbed a fistful of a player's jersey, well, *how many national titles has Gene Keady, the comparatively mild-mannered coach for rival Purdue, won?* To an army of pliant red-sweatered enablers, Knight was infallible. But as his teams slipped a level or two and Knight's conduct became ever more bizarre, it grew increasingly difficult to defend the man. This was compounded by a series of early flameouts in the NCAA tournament. It became clear that the gilded Knight Era was not going to end gracefully.

The endgame might represent the single darkest chapter in Indiana basketball. It was an ugly, public feud that tattered the soul of Hoosier Nation. The Cliffs Notes version: In May 2000, a series of incidents imperiled Knight's job. Knight had demonstrated gross insubordination with his bosses—bosses he had often handpicked. In a fit of rage, he had once thrown a potted plant at a secretary that barely missed her head. In an attempt to illustrate graphically just how poorly the team was playing, he allegedly brandished soiled toilet paper during a locker room tirade. Perhaps most damning, a disgruntled assistant coach released a practice tape that showed Knight grabbing the jugular of Neil Reed, a feisty point guard. Suddenly, Knight, the fiercely proud man who made concessions to no one, was groveling for his job to Myles Brand, the university president. Brand gave the public appearance of bestowing upon Knight a final chance, under a "zero tolerance" policy. Friends warned Knight that "zero tolerance" was an impossible standard and that his fate was already sealed. They urged him to resign with his dignity still intact. Like Caesar, Knight ignored the soothsayers.

Three months after his reprieve, Knight was walking to his office when a freshman student passed and said, "Hey, what's up, Knight?" It wasn't necessarily the most deferential greeting, but it wasn't the most offensive one either. Knight, however, spun and, according to the student's account, grabbed him by the arm and bellowed, "Show me some fucking respect. I'm older than you." For his part, Knight maintains that he was merely trying to administer a lesson in "manners and civility," an explanation filled with more than a little irony. Whatever.

By Brand's decree it breached the "zero tolerance" policy. On September 11, 2000, Bob Knight was fired. Having stood up to the campus bully, Brand was subsequently rewarded by being named head of the NCAA, based in Indianapolis.

Especially as the team's on-court fortunes had flagged, Knight had become a hugely polarizing figure, engendering both profound loyalty and profound contempt. After his firing, the divisions deepened. Knight's critics were gleeful. The bully finally got his just deserts. Not unlike Elmer Gantry, the self-righteous preacher who turned out to be a hard-drinking womanizer, Knight's hypocrisy was laid bare. The man who demanded discipline couldn't control his conduct even with an ultimatum hanging over him. To Knight's supporters, he was a casualty of political correctness. He was not the sinner but the sinned against, and his ouster was further proof that the times were changing for the worse, the world was going to hell.

As I watched the ugliness unfold from afar, my dominant emotion was sadness. If Knight wasn't worthy of unconditional worship, he did far more good than harm. Too often, his eruptions and outright pathological behavior overshadowed his small acts of kindness. There are countless stories like the one Jon Gruden, the Tampa Bay Buccaneers' coach, tells. Gruden grew up in Bloomington and was a ballboy for the Hoosiers during the early '70s. Ten or so years after the Grudens left Bloomington, Jon's mother, Kathy, had surgery to remove a cancerous kidney. When Knight somehow heard the news, he sent Kathy an IU basketball jersey and a handwritten note of encouragement. "People don't talk about that side enough," says Gruden.

For that matter, critics are also too quick to gloss over Knight's steadfast refusal to cheat and to shortchange his mastery of X's and O's. And when the chattering class complains that only a small handful of his players made it to the NBA, they neglect to mention that half a

Knight court: Before his ugly demise, Bobby Knight won 661 games at Indiana University, putting him on track to become the winningest coach in college basketball history. (*John Iacono*/Sports Illustrated)

dozen players of Knight's went on to become NBA head coaches or general managers—and more than a dozen Knight disciples are coaching in college.

But in the end, it was clear that his bent toward the megalomaniacal had gotten the better of him. Drunk on power, detached from reality, stubborn to a fault, he himself was responsible for his spectacular crash. Still, it was a pity to see him go out so unceremoniously. He deserved better.

vernight, the basketball program resembled some chaotic Bosch canvas. Players were irate, many vowing to transfer, though it would have meant sitting out an entire season. Recruits were confused. Some high-rolling donors vowed to withdraw their support for the school that had run off a legend; others vowed to ramp up their contributions since the administration had taken a stand against a man who they felt was an autocrat. Knight encouraged his assistants to resign. By his code, the crew goes down with the ship. He even offered to pay their salaries for the following year if they quit. Students burned Brand in effigy, trashed his front lawn and held campus protests.

Lost in the emotionally charged debate was this immutable truth: Knight's effectiveness as a coach had been steadily diminishing and his resolute inflexibility in the face of a changing culture had hastened his demise. His unwillingness to adjust to these changes had doomed him every bit as much as his antisocial behavior.

There was a time when Knight's cult of personality was *the* draw of the Indiana basketball program. Midwest parents—fathers in particular—dreamed of sending their kids to Knight's program as boys and seeing them leave as men. I recall the father of an Indiana player in the early '80s lauding Knight as "the Vince Lombardi of basketball." But in his later years, Knight's aura worked to the program's detriment. Lombardi had long fallen out of favor, replaced by the permissive, nurturing "players' coach." What hotshot prospect, coddled by so many for so long, wanted to enlist in the General's boot camp and get stuck with basketball's equivalent of KP duty when he could go to any of a hundred other programs and get feted like royalty? Further, more and more players came from single-parent homes, unfamiliar with a martinet male figure administering tough love. Often deluded by grandeur, most high school prospects have their sights set on the NBA. There was scarcely a program worse suited to this end, what with Knight's insistence that players sublimate their games to the good of the team and his propensity to bench his best players for the slightest infractions. Even within the state of Indiana, a conga line of top high school players did what was once unthinkable and turned down a chance to play for Knight.

Knight also refused to deal with the street agents and AAU coaches who, more and more, were insinuating themselves into the recruitment process. At some level, this was utterly to Knight's credit: The AAU circuit is littered with some of the most unsavory characters who are not incarcerated. But, sad as it sounds, the reality is that there is a rule in present-day college basketball: If a coach wants any chance at landing blue-chip recruits, sometimes he has to dirty his hands.

The few top players Knight was able to lure to Bloomington often failed to survive four years. Knight's motivational ploys and psychological gambits that a generation ago resulted in players improving their performance now resulted in their transferring. The players who left the Indiana program during the '90s could have formed an All-Star team. And as they split town, invariably castigated for their softness and selfishness, they all had the same fundamental critique: Basketball under Knight wasn't fun. "I didn't even consider playing for Indiana," says Shawn Kemp, an all-state player at Elkhart's Concord High in the late '80s, who would turn pro at nineteen and go on to become an NBA All-Star. "You want to have a good time in college, not get your ass kicked by a grumpy old man."

Same for Zach Randolph, an NBA star who graduated from Marion High in 2000. As a junior in high school Randolph was among the top college prospects in the country, and he took a recruiting trip to Bloomington. When he met with Knight, the story goes, the coach promptly told him to show some "goddamn respect" and remove his

Split decision: After succeeding Knight in 2000, Davis has received mixed reviews from Hoosier Nation. (*Bob Rosato*/Sports Illustrated)

"goddamn hat." Randolph left the meeting goddamn sure he wasn't going to play for Indiana. It's completely reasonable to ask if Knight shouldn't be lauded for his old-school sensibilities. During Randolph's senior year at Marion, he did time in a juvenile facility after receiving a stolen handgun. He lasted one season at Michigan State before turning pro. Though he is an emerging star with the Portland Trail Blazers, he sucker-punched a teammate and was arrested for driving under the influence of an intoxicant. If he never considered playing for IU, so what? But alienating studs such as Randolph left Knight with players who, qualitatively, could scarcely compete.

During the last decade of Knight's reign, watching the Hoosiers play was like watching a horse and buggy on a superhighway. The efficacy of Knight's vaunted motion offense was neutered when the players doing the motion were a step slower than the opposition. The sharpshooters Knight recruited often had trouble freeing themselves from the opposition's defense. The man-to-man defense Knight espoused lost its potency when opponents could "break ankles" with their speed or simply elevate over the defense for a shot. The school that had won three NCAA titles between 1976 and 1987 had reached just one Final Four in Knight's remaining thirteen seasons at Indiana. In Knight's last six years, the teams won no Big Ten titles and just two NCAA tournament games. Based strictly on the team's performance, it was time for a change.

I n the fall of 2000, as *l'affaire* Bobby raged and the first day of practice was just weeks away, Davis and another assistant coach, John Treloar, were summoned to the home of Terry Clapacs, Indiana's athletic director, who was a vice president at the time. Clapacs explained that after speaking with the players, he wanted to offer the pair the job of co–interim coaches. But the last thing a program already racked by instability needed was a pair of co-coaches. To his credit, Treloar recognized as much immediately and offered to stay on as an assistant but deferred the head job to Davis.

Davis insists that he felt vestigial loyalty to Knight. It was, after all, Knight who had given Davis his break. Raised by his mother, a secretary at the local high school, in a sleepy town in rural Alabama, Davis was a good but not a great basketball player. He played four seasons for the Crimson Tide and was drafted by the Milwaukee Bucks but never made it beyond the CBA, playing for $500 a week in outposts like Wichita Falls and Topeka. When his NBA aspirations ended, he went through a rough stretch. He had never graduated from Alabama, and suddenly he needed a new source of income to support his family. He took a job as an assistant coach at tiny Miles College that paid so little he had to supplement his income selling T-shirts out of the trunk of his car. In 1990, Davis's seventeen-month-old daughter, Nicole, was killed in an auto accident that seriously injured his first wife. "Not just what happened to Nicole, but that whole period, it was very much reality hitting," he says. "As a player you think everything is always going to come easy, you're always going to be successful and make a great living, but you learn that's not necessarily true."

Davis picked up his degree from Thomas Edison College and worked as an assistant to Treloar in the CBA before landing a low-level assistant's job at Alabama. In 1998, Treloar called with an intriguing offer. Treloar, who had coached Pat Knight in the CBA and had followed Pat to join the Indiana coaching staff, knew that Bob Knight was looking to hire an assistant primarily to help with recruiting. Davis understood that this was code. The translation: Indiana had been getting beat luring top players and needed a black presence to give the program some "street cred." (Indiana hadn't had a black assistant coach since Joby Wright left in 1990.) Davis jumped at the chance. When he prayed he sometimes made it a point to thank the Lord for delivering him to Knight.

But now Knight was out and Davis suddenly had a chance to coach Indiana University, as blue chip as blue chip gets. How does a young, ambitious coach turn that down, however adverse the circumstances? And the financial considerations weren't insignificant for Davis either. He had recently swallowed considerable pride, accepting a loan from a family friend in Alabama, which he repaid only after Knight surprised the staff with $25,000 Christmas bonuses. When the offer from Clapacs came, Davis and his family were living in Indianapolis in a modest rental home. "The bottom line was that it was too good an opportunity not to take," says Davis. "I figured I would be the interim coach and then get a job at a mid-major conference after the season." So he accepted the interim job and became the first African-American head coach in the history of the Indiana University athletic department.

There was a temporary armistice. At least the wayward ship now had a captain. But Davis's appointment gave rise to new tensions. Davis's decision—compounded by his failure to confer with Pat Knight, the team's third assistant coach—enraged Bob Knight. Davis was summarily expelled from the Cult of Bobby. Davis hadn't coached a game and he was already persona non grata among the Knight loyalists. Race complicated the picture as well. "I had black players who thought I was going to play them because they were black," Davis told *Sports Illustrated.* "And I had white players who thought I was going to play only the black players because I was black. It was a mess. I just told everyone to play hard and the rest would take care of itself."

They did and it did. The team finished 21–13 and made the NCAA tournament, not a sterling year by Hoosier standards but a miracle worthy of Lourdes given the disarray that had shrouded the team when the season started. When the administration removed the "interim" tag from Davis's title, he rewarded their faith by taking the team to the Final Four and national title game the following season. Slowly, there was healing in the heartland. *Winning omnia vincit.* And the guy with the stutter from small-town Alabama who had never made the big time as a player had arrived.

Davis's first months on the job were pure baptism by fire.

Davis had never before been a head coach at any level and thus never really cultivated a management style. He wasted a few months trying to emulate Knight. On the inside Davis was fairly calm, but he emoted on the sidelines, his face contorting with intensity. "Then I realized I had to be me and not be Coach," Davis said, referring, as he always does, to Knight without mentioning him by name. "Maybe I thought there was a special way a coach had to act. But I just had to do my own thing."

Davis's "thing" is nothing like his predecessor's. Knight was a despot—sometimes benevolent, sometimes not—who operated at a healthy remove from his players. Many say Knight would go weeks without talking to them, save for some verbal dressing-down on the practice court. Davis, on the other hand, is the epitome of a players' coach, that new species that regards players as surrogate sons. Davis's charges refer to him as "Coach D.," "D." or sometimes, in their bolder moments, "Dawg." ("It doesn't matter what they call me," he says, shrugging. "They know I'm the coach.") For better or worse, he understands their slang, comprehends their dress, permits hip-hop strains to waft through the cabin on team flights. He even knows that 50 Cent is pronounced "Fiddy Cent" in authentic hip-hop locution.

Whereas Knight's doghouse was so famed that it could have been included on a tourist map of Bloomington, Davis is—depending on your point of view—decidedly more forgiving or decidedly less strict. Whether it's because he has a nineteen-year-old son of his own, because his upbringing mirrored that of many of his players, or because it's simply his nature, he can't bring himself to erect artificial barriers between himself and his team. "There's no reason to mess with people's heads," he says, a thinly cloaked reference to the man whose office he inherited. "I might get upset about the basketball, but that has nothing to do with our relationship."

Davis has a particularly close relationship with A. J. Moye, who graduated from Indiana in 2004. When Moye was a high school senior in Atlanta, Davis recruited him heavily and one day showed up at Moye's school at lunchtime. Moye suggested they go out to eat, but he recalls Davis telling him, "I'm not too good for a government meal." The two ate in the cafeteria. At Indiana, Moye's NBA aspirations were deferred by injuries. On top of that, he had a daughter out of wedlock, his father contracted cancer and the schoolwork was a challenge. "Through everything," he says, "Coach was my rock." The two were sufficiently close that Moye sometimes escaped school by going over to Davis's home uninvited, to study in peace or watch football while snacking on Davis's couch. (For a good chuckle, imagine Bob Knight returning from a day at the office to find one of his players sprawled on his sofa, having just helped himself to a sandwich.)

Like most folks connected to the Indiana program, Moye takes pains to avoid comparing Knight and Davis. But he makes no secret of his bond with Davis. "Coach D. isn't a players' coach, he's a people's coach. He's good to everyone and you can always talk to him—not just when he's in the mood. If we hadn't won a single game in all my four years, because of my relationship with him, I'd still be happy I chose to come here."

The dramatic differences between Knight and Davis are also apparent during games. Knight was a coaching Merlin who tailored his offense to the skills of personnel and had a sixth sense for changing his rotation based on the flow of the games. Suffice it to say that Davis has not distinguished himself for his bench coaching or strategic competence. It didn't take long for Davis to scrap Knight's methodical motion offense and replace it with an NBA-style system predicated on spacing and exploiting mismatches. (There is a perception that Davis's "offense" is anarchy and he has surrendered power to his players; in fact, his offense consists of seventy plays, more than Knight ever had.) Davis's offensive scheme sounds plausible when he explains it. It's just that it doesn't work, particularly not with the personnel he has at hand. It's difficult to create mismatches when your team is undersized. Spacing gambits backfire when your team shoots miserably from long range. That Indiana has played the better part of Davis's first four seasons without a reliable point guard hasn't helped either.

Perhaps the starkest contrasts between Knight and Davis are manifest in how they handle the pressure that attends what might be the most high-profile job in the state. Knight's reaction to criticism was to offer "a half victory sign," as it's called in polite circles; as he made clear during his ugly denouement, he would sooner sport a tattoo (or a tutu) than admit error. His contempt for the media—his respect for the longtime and revered Bloomington *Herald-Times* sports editor, Bob Hammel, notwithstanding—was epic. Anyone whose loyalty was doubted was excommunicated. In the end, he had turned inward and insulated himself from the masses with a small coterie of pliant friends.

If Knight answered to no one, Davis answers to *everyone*. One suspects Davis would talk to a lamppost if it had ears. His weekly radio show sometimes sounds like a confessional. He's happy to discuss lineups and forthcoming games with Assembly Hall custodians, members of the two churches he attends, even the bag boys at the Marsh grocery store near his new Bloomington home. After his occasional outbursts—most notably an epic meltdown against Kentucky in 2002—he has been tearfully remorseful. In a marked departure from the fortress Knight erected, Davis is not only accessible to the media but unfailingly candid.

If Knight brushed off criticism disdainfully like so much dandruff on a lapel, Davis is deeply affected by it. After Indiana lost in the first round of the 2003 NCAA tournament, Davis ill-advisedly complained to the media that the team was uncoachable. Bob Kravitz, the *Indianapolis Star's* columnist, wrote an essay the following day chastising him for his whining. That morning, Davis called Kravitz at his home. "I just want to thank you for having the courage to write that,"

Davis said. He's gotten so worked up over hate mail and poisonous e-mail sent to his office that his secretary doesn't bother to pass it on. "Some people," he says, his eyes suddenly burning like headlights, "they just want to take you down. It's like a sport for them." In particular, Davis burns up huge psychic energy worrying about his critics online. "When you lose, they go on the Internet and they start talking about you so bad," Davis said. "I thought my name was 'hot seat, hot seat, hot seat' and 'can't coach, can't coach, can't coach.'"

Catch Davis at a weaker moment and he'll assert that much of the criticism has a racial edge. It's hard to blame him when you surf the Web and find that a message board popular with Knight toadies—the password is "Clair Bee," a former coach whom Knight often cites as his biggest inspiration—excoriates Davis in the most vile, racist terms imaginable. During the disappointing 2003–04 season, the log-on page featured an unflattering photo of Davis (nicknamed "Da Doof" on the site) with the caption: *Why dat reeportah say I beez pear-a-noid??? Hope day doe-ahn find out about dem 900 numbers I be callin . . . No mo' 'scuses, Doof.*

While he takes pains to stress that he feels overwhelmingly comfortable in Indiana, Davis admits, "Some people have a problem with someone who doesn't look like they do or speak like they do." He has also become adept at deciphering code. "When fans say this isn't like old Indiana teams, it means *We have too many black players.* When they say, 'He can't adjust,' it means *He's stupid.* That probably gets to me more than anything," he says with an audible sigh. "I wish some of those that say, 'Davis can't coach,' 'Davis is lazy,' I wish they would come to work with me."

They would see him bunkered in his office—nicknamed "The Cave"—a dark, subterranean place in the bowels of Assembly Hall appointed in a sort of rec room gothic. Large leather couches and chairs circle a giant television, bracketed by stacks of videotapes. It is Davis's second home during the season. He regularly spends nights there between November and March and often has his wife, Tamilya, bring him lunch so they can steal a few minutes together. "The season may only go for four months—five if you're lucky," he says. "But I'm telling you, this job is nonstop."

He has a point. In the when-it-was days, Knight was famous for taking lengthy, exotic fishing and hunting trips during the summer. Surely he wasn't alone among his colleagues. Today, no coach could possibly go shooting Kodiak in Alaska or bonefishing off the coast of Brazil and expect to come back to campus employed. A day away from the office and the coach returns to a blizzard of voice mails, faxes and unread e-mails.

What's more, the occupational hazards have mounted. A generation ago, coaches didn't have to deal with agents whispering sweet nothings into the ears of players, urging them to turn pro. They didn't concern themselves with unsavory, deep-pocketed boosters. There weren't websites and webcasts, sports talk radio and a proliferation of cable television outlets that made every misstep a potential international crisis. The financial stakes between winning and losing were not nearly so high. Not long ago, coaches scouted talent within their state, poached a player or two from a neighboring state and, *voilà*, that was the recruiting season. Knight went nearly a decade before venturing outside the Midwest to lure a player. The 2003–04 Indiana team featured players from Louisiana, Oregon, Texas, Florida, Georgia, Maryland and North Carolina. And coaches didn't have to worry about players committing and then skipping college altogether. Throughout Indiana's forgettable 2003–04 season there was always a silver lining: the recruiting Davis had waiting in the wings was considered one of the best in the country. But the top player, Josh Smith, a 6'9" forward from Georgia, decided to bypass college and head to the NBA and another prospect didn't make grades. Suddenly, a banner recruiting class was merely a better-than-average one.

A fter his first year out of college basketball since the fifties, Knight landed in the folds of western Texas, coaching at Texas Tech, gone but not forgotten in Hoosier Nation. (If the sight of Knight stalking the sidelines in a black-and-maroon sweater is still jarring to some, his support in his former state is such that some of the highest concentration of members in the Red Raider Club—basically a donor list for the Texas Tech Athletic Department—can be found in south-central Indiana.) While he finally dropped a lawsuit to sue Indiana University over his termination, Knight has gone to great lengths to make Davis's job still more difficult.

He has questioned the loyalty of members of the Indiana basketball family who have demonstrated the slightest support for Davis. In a particularly galling display of manipulation, Knight insinuated himself into the 2001 recruitment of Sean May, then a star forward at Bloomington North and generally regarded as the best player in the state. Sean had made his intentions abundantly clear: He wanted to stay in Bloomington and play for IU, following in the sizable footsteps of his father, Scott, the hero of the Hoosiers' 1976 NCAA championship team. Sean told other Indiana recruits, as well as some of his high school teammates, how much he looked forward to playing for the Hoosiers.

This enraged Knight. According to multiple sources with firsthand knowledge, Knight let it be known that if Sean May were to attend Indiana, Scott May should consider himself excommunicated from The General's inner circle. Knight also allegedly conveyed to Sean's parents that their son would receive inadequate coaching and harm his chances of making it to the NBA if he played for Davis. Though Sean May had no interest in playing for Knight at Texas Tech, in the fall of 2001, he and Scott flew to Lubbock to meet with Knight, summoned by the Godfather, as it were. The following day, Sean called a press conference to announce that he was spurning Indiana and that he would instead accept a scholarship offer to play for the University of North Carolina. Three years later, Davis chomps on his lip when the episode is raised and quickly changes the subject.

There are times when it all threatens to overtake Davis. When the team is playing abominably and letters to the editor are calling him an "embarrassment" and a seventeen-year-old kid who vowed to play for him is now wavering and the booster club needs him to make a luncheon speech and the Boys Club needs a dozen autographed balls and an out-of-town reporter won't stop asking him personal questions and he hasn't seen his toddler son in days . . . it gets to him. But he has a coping mechanism. He says a prayer, reads a Bible verse, recounts his blessing and exhales. "The fact is, I would do this job if they didn't pay me a cent," he claims, an odd sentiment given that he played hardball for a hefty raise two years ago. "It's a great job and I love coaching, love being around the kids. It's just . . ."

The thought hangs awkwardly in the air, as Davis looks around his spartan office. As if the truth serum kicks in, an ironic smile comes to his face, pushing aside the three-day growth on his chin. "But man, if you don't watch out, it can get to you." Davis's larger-than-life predecessor, whose ghost still resides in Assembly Hall, couldn't have put it any better.

5

OUT OF AFRICA

BY THE TIME BLOOMINGTON NORTH PLAYED AT DECATUR Central on December 18, the night before Christmas break, the team was 5–0 and looked deserving of its ranking, No. 3 in the state. The Cougars had beaten their opponents by a combined score of 303–182, outrebounded them 211–118 and played parsimonious defense, permitting no adversary to put up more than 24 points in a half. The team was slowly evolving, a group of disparate parts starting to form a symphonic whole. From the way they playfully bumped each other during the pregame layup lines to the way they reacted to adverse calls, their collective disposition suggested that whatever insecurities the players may have had before the season had faded.

True to form, Coach McKinney bristled at the slightest suggestion that the team's early progress ought to be a source of optimism. Where the disinterested observer was impressed that the team was undefeated despite having played just two home games, McKinney waved a dismissive hand. "Our schedule is going to get a lot tougher," he grumbled. Where the neutral observer saw an unselfish team with a balanced offense, McKinney lamented that an ecumenical attack sometimes means that no player "wants to step up and be a leader." Where the unbiased observer saw a fairly complete tapestry, McKinney saw holes and frays in his team's fabric. He was particularly disgusted by the team's foul shooting. Free throws—the most elemental shot, one that all Hoosiers worth their salt can make with closed eyes—was a particular bugbear. To McKinney's outright embarrassment, his team was shooting barely 50 percent from the line.

There were other "issues and concerns," as McKinney called them: Josh Macy and Anthony Lindsey, the two senior guards, had plenty of savvy, but their lack of foot speed was apparent. Josh Norris, the talented forward, had yet to find his comfort zone. Most maddening, the players' effort, both individually and collectively, was wildly inconsistent. Like a cellular phone that would flicker in and out of "dead zones" with little predictability, the Cougars could be effective and connected one moment, distant and unreliable the next. Sure, the very concept of "consistent high school players" is almost oxymoronic. But McKinney lost sleep—quite literally—over so much erratic play.

Decatur Central High School sits due south of Indianapolis, where suburban sprawl has steadily gnawed into countryside that was once farmland. Although it draws its students from a fairly wide area, the basketball team has long struggled. The previous season the team won just two games. It had never come within 20 points of beating Bloomington North.

The varsity game hadn't begun and fans were still at the concession stand buying "walking tacos," a calorie bomb composed of sour cream, chili and nacho cheese dumped unceremoniously into a bag of corn chips. (To judge from the comestibles offered at basketball concession stands, it's no surprise Indiana consistently ranks among the states with the highest obesity rates—this even after Jared Fogle, a resident of greater Indianapolis, famously lost 245 pounds eating Subway sandwiches.) Cheerleaders were applying the last coating of base to their faces. Both coaching staffs huddled on their respective sides of the bleachers' Mason-Dixon line, going over game plans for the final time.

Even during warm-ups, a shrill voice tinged with an African accent pierced the gymnasium air. "Come on, Bloomington North!" bellowed the tall, indomitable woman with obsidian skin, wearing an orange chenille sweater, jeans and fashionable L.L. Bean–style moccasins. Her husband, an equally dark-skinned man two inches shorter with a bald head and a beard that was more salt than pepper, looked on, smiling but silent. "Let's box out and play hard early!" his wife intoned. "Hands up on defense!"

Julia Duany readily admits that she is an accidental basketball-phile, an unlikely superfan who never imagined that she'd spend much of her forties sitting (or standing) on rickety high school bleachers, getting worked up over lane violations and blocking fouls that should have been whistled as charges. But she is, without apology, a die-hard basketball fan and she figures that, counting high school, college and AAU, she has cheered her way through a thousand games over the past decade. Bil Duany, the baby of the family, is the fifth of her spawn to be a basketball star for Bloomington North. Now the end of an era is drawing near. "I can't believe it," she says. "But after all these years, I only have a few of these games left."

*I*n the office they share at the Workshop in Political Theory and Policy Analysis on the Indiana University campus, Wal and Julia Duany recite their odyssey, filling in each other's gaps. It's an adventure story they've told and retold a thousand times. And still, they recount it with passion and animation and a sense of genuine awe, almost as if describing a movie someone else is starring in. Midway through the particular account on a snowy, gray Indiana December day, they realized that it was almost twenty years to the day that their lives took a hairpin turn.

"Twenty years!" Julia shrieked. "Do you believe it, Wal?"

"I don't believe any of it," he deadpanned.

Natives of Sudan, the largest country in Africa, Wal and Julia were married in late 1972. He was a finance minister for the government; she was a student. They lived comfortably in Juba, a city of 60,000 in the southern part of the country. There had been a few hardships. Both Wal and Julia died a little when their first son, Urom, contracted a fever and lapsed into a coma after his first birthday and never awoke. And after an uprising by the opposition party, Wal was jailed in the early 1980s for nearly a year without a trial. But in a country beset by poverty unimaginable by Western standards, the Duanys lived in relative ease. There was always enough food—no small consideration among Sudanese. And after losing Urom, Julia and Wal had four healthy children within five years.

It was late 1983 when three of Wal's nephews arrived nervously on his stoop, delivering news that civil war was breaking out once again. The totalitarian, Muslim-dominated government had massacred hundreds in a town on the Ethiopian border. Former government officers were not allowed to go anywhere without first informing a national security office. Educated, politically connected, and unabashedly Christian, the Duanys were targets for the thugs. The country had already recently fallen under Shari'ah, Islamic law, which had deprived the Duanys of basic rights. Furthermore, their oldest living son, Duany, was eight, old enough to be drafted as a child soldier. The situation was only going to get worse. "Our choices were clear," says Julia. "Go to jail, get killed, or leave the country."

But where? The Duanys left Juba for Khartoum, the country's capital. They hoped to blend in among the millions, and keep low profiles as they sent their kids to school until the civil war died down. But they soon found the city's living conditions untenable, and, having given up their farm in Juba, there were now financial concerns as well. In the 1960s during an earlier phase of the Sudanese civil war, Wal had spent years in the jungles of southern Sudan and fought for the resistance movement. He didn't want his family to go through that, nor did he want them to live in exile elsewhere in Africa. Julia's brother was a doctor in London; but when she had visited him, she had met countless Sudanese immigrants who were living on the dole, having lost the motivation to work. When Wal suggested America, Julia shook her head. Unlike her husband, who had studied at Syracuse, she had never been to the United States. She looked at a bottle of Johnnie Walker scotch on the shelf of their home and shuddered as she envisioned America as a land of wretched excess, its citizenry walking around with pistols in one hand and bottles of booze in the other.

Still, Wal worked his contacts and arranged to receive a scholarship to study at a university in the obscure town of Bloomington, Indiana. ("Not India, Julia. It's called Indiana.") He was thrilled—as much for the opportunity to study as the chance to leave his country—but was wary that the government would not let him out if he took the entire family. Wal left Sudan alone, dousing any suspicions that he would never return.

So now it was up to Julia to make it to Indiana with the rest of the family. She was eight months pregnant with her fifth child at the time and found only one airline, KLM, that would sell her a ticket. The airfare was $5,000—roughly ten times the *annual* median household income in the Sudan. She bought the tickets and, under the guise of a family vacation, flew with four kids under eight to London.

In London, Julia gave birth to a son, Bil, named after her father. After she spent a few weeks convalescing, she and the five kids continued their journey to Indiana, where Wal was waiting nervously. Sitting in the lounge at New York's Kennedy Airport before boarding the connecting flight to Indianapolis, Julia watched a man rubbing his hand on the leg of his female companion; the woman sucked enthusiastically on a mint, not seeming to mind. Julia was horrified by the immodesty. In Sudan, she thought to herself, the man would be subject to thirty lashes and three months in the public prison. Maybe Johnny Walker wasn't such an inaccurate representation of the United States.

When the family finally reunited, the seven Duanys moved into a three-bedroom apartment in Tulip Tree, a crescent-shaped housing center for foreign students on the east edge of the Indiana University campus. They were in town for a few days when white flakes started falling from the sky. Their first instinct was that the cold had caused some horrible structural damage and now Tulip Tree was crumbling apart. It was the first time they had seen snow.

As Wal pursued his doctorate in public policy, Julia tended to the five kids, took some courses, and worked at the cafeteria of an Indiana University dormitory to help pay the rent. In the morning she would join the kids and watch *Sesame Street.* It was the most time-efficient way to improve her English. As a third-grader at University Elementary

School, the oldest son, Duany Duany—it's Nilotic tradition to give a first son the family name for a first name—was the tallest kid in his class. (Though Wal is only 5'11", Julia is 6'1" and had uncles eclipsing seven feet in height.) Predictably, within a few weeks, Duany was spirited to the Bloomington Boys Club and introduced to the local passion-cum-obsession: basketball. "At his first game, I sat down and one of the other mothers said, 'You can't sit there! Your boy is on the other team!'" recalls Julia. "So I moved and then the game started and all the parents were yelling and screaming. 'Shoot it!' 'That was traveling!' 'Put my son in the game, Coach!' I spent that game not watching the basketball but watching all the other parents."

Wal cuts her off. "Now, of course, she's the loudest one!"

Owing to a large population of foreign students, Bloomington was awash in so-called "internationals." The family's neighbors at Tulip Tree were Turks and Koreans and Brazilians and Israelis and Pakistanis, each with their own tales of displacement and transition and visions of hope. At school, there were plenty of other kids who spoke in tongues other than English at home and had no hope of ever finding their names on the key rings sold at gift shops and amusement parks. There were even other children from Africa. Throughout their years at Bloomington North—surely the only high school in Indiana to cull its student body from seventy different countries—various Duanys shared the basketball court with teammates from Mali, Kenya and Nigeria.

The Duanys found an ineluctable sense of warmth and comfort among the locals. It can be hard enough integrating your family into a new community. Imagine doing so as African refugees with onyx-colored skin, traditional dress and thick accents in the heart of the heartland. But in Bloomington, the Duanys' "otherness" was embraced. The kids had no trouble making friends and fitting in at school. The older Duany daughter, Nyagon, was even voted Bloomington North's homecoming queen in 1996, the same year she graduated as valedictorian with a 4.0 GPA. "What that symbolized to me, I'll never forget it," says Julia. Naturally outgoing, active in their church, they had no trouble insinuating themselves into the community. But as Julia puts it fairly poetically, "Sports is how I really got to meet Indiana." She learned that when your five kids play multiple sports and you don't miss a game, you tend to form bonds with a lot of other people.

Before any of their three sons had played a basketball game for Bloomington North, Julia and Wal befriended Tom McKinney and his wife, Judy. The McKinneys were both products of southern Indiana and, at first blush anyway, appeared to share little common ground with a Sudanese couple. But the more they talked, the more overlap they found in their values and aesthetics. One morning over breakfast, Wal took a swig of coffee and asked Tom, "Julia and I travel a lot. If anything happens to us, would you and Judy take custody of the kids?" The response was fast in coming. "I'd be honored, Wal."

As the five kids took their star turns on the basketball court over the course of a decade, Julia and Wal were somewhat ambivalent. They were proud of the trophies and recognition and they realized that basketball could be a vehicle to a better life. But Wal, especially, bristled at the thought that his kids were contributing to what he saw as a poisonous stereotype. "Too many people think that black boys, young black men, use their bodies and not their brains." The Duany Academic Policy was a simple one: "Schoolwork first, sports second. And if anyone's grade point average dipped below 3.0, they were ineligible." Only one kid ran afoul of the rule. Kueth once brought home a C in English. "Of all subjects!" Julia said disgustedly. "English is how you communicate!" With McKinney's blessing, Wal and Julia yanked their middle son off the team until he got an A on his next paper.

To say that the Duanys have achieved the American dream is to traffic in staggering understatement. Duany, the oldest, was a basketball star at Bloomington North but also a conscientious student who didn't shy away from the hardest courses. He went to Wisconsin on a basketball scholarship, played in the 2000 Final Four and graduated with a degree in behavioral sciences. He now plays professionally in Europe and has designs on going to law school. Kueth, a polished swingman who led North to the state title in 1997, went to Syracuse on a basketball scholarship. In his final game, he played a central role when the Orangemen won the 2003 NCAA title. Having earned two degrees, in information science and political science, he is now playing overseas as well. One daughter, Nok, went to Georgetown on a basketball scholarship, graduated with a degreee in marketing, and is playing professionally in Portugal. Nyagon played basketball for Bradley and is currently a student at Indiana University Medical School. If Bil could earn a college scholarship, the Duanys, it is believed, would be the first family in U.S. history to send five kids to college on basketball scholarships. "That's some serious pressure, huh?" says Bil.

As for Duany *père*, Wal received a joint doctorate in Public Policy from the Department of Political and Environmental Affairs at Indiana University in 1992 and now works for the Workshop in Political Theory and Policy Analysis, an academic think tank at IU. Julia earned a Ph.D. in higher education from Indiana University and is also a research associate at the Workshop. She specializes in gender studies and conflict resolution in developing countries. A few years ago, a coworker casually mentioned to Julia that she ought to write a book about her saga. She said, "Why not?" and in 2003 published a 250-page autobiography titled *Making Peace & Nurturing Life.* "Not a day goes by when I don't think about the opportunity this country has given my family," she says. "We feel very blessed to be here." And it's not just a sound bite. Before the Decatur Central game, the p.a. announcer asked that the fans rise "to honor this great country and the brave men and women who defend it." The couple from the Sudan shot out of their seats as if propelled from a cannon and, a cappella, belted out

"The Star-Spangled Banner" as loudly and lustily as any of the other 1,500 fans.

Yet the family's fondness for the United States, for Indiana and for Bloomington is edged in sadness. Had the situation in their homeland improved, they likely would have returned. But the Sudanese civil war and the oppression by the Muslim government continued to rage. The war has resulted in more than two million casualties, the deadliest conflict since World War II, if one generally ignored by the Western media. A quarter of the country has been displaced. In the rural south of Sudan, 80 percent of the children are malnourished. The country has been militarized beyond recognition. "The infrastructure, the culture, whole generations, they're being destroyed," says Wal solemnly. "The Muslims want to make Sudan an Islamic country. We believe in democracy, so it's a bad situation." A prominent leader-by-proxy of the South Sudan Liberation Movement, Wal regularly returns for months at a time, counseling the southerners, trying to broker peace. Julia flies home regularly as well, making humanitarian visits, distributing nonprescription medicine, seeing her family, her friends, her country in a state of chaos.

By any measure, it is an astonishing success story. But even in progressive Bloomington, admiration for the Duanys hasn't been unconditional. There are some Hoosiers who consider it their sons' right of birth to play high school basketball. When their kids get cut from a team that includes taller, more athletic kids born on another continent, it offends their sense of fairness and creates a certain cultural tension. Something sacred has been taken away by outsiders. To a vocal minority, this is an extension of the demographic shifts and social policies like affirmative action that have left them feeling marginalized and disenfranchised by the times. In a world that they sometimes struggled to understand, basketball was a familiar touchstone. Now that too seemed to be rigged against them.

During a December haircut at the Razor's Image barbershop, the patron in the chair next to mine complained bitterly when talk turned to Bloomington North's team. "All them Africans they brought in at [Bloomington] North," he groused, implying—wrongly—that there was something unsavory in their recruitment. "They *should* be winning big." The father of a Bloomington North football player, who spoke to me on the condition that his identity not be revealed, was similarly embittered. "My son can play ball," he says. "He was one of the best kids on his eighth-grade team. He went to camps. All that. But how's he supposed to compete with kids from Africa who are like seven feet tall? I don't blame the coach. Hell, I'd want that on my team too. But, maybe, I don't know, you know? It doesn't seem right to the Indiana kids who work hard. Know what I mean?" Another father, aggrieved that McKinney had cut his son from the varsity, once charged McKinney with "overseas recruiting" and threatened to take his complaint to the state high school athletic association. (He never followed up, perhaps because the "overseas" players in question had been living in Bloomington since before they were in kindergarten.)

This resentment isn't lost on Wal and Julia. "A lot of times people will say nice things—'Good game'—to you but you see in their face that they don't mean it," says Julia. Adds Wal, "No one has ever come out and said it, but I think some people feel maybe we've taken something that is theirs." Just as thousands of Indiana jobs have been "outsourced" overseas, slots on the basketball team are now being filled by "outsiders." These parents, unable to mask their disappointment, see themselves as the losers in globalization.

*I*ndiana may be the crucible of basketball, but the sport has, unmistakably, gone global. Walk down the streets of any foreign city from Berlin to Bangalore and you'll see a fashion show of Duke bas-

Bil come due: Finally healthy, the youngest of the Duany clan soared in
his senior season. (*Jeremy Hogan/Bloomington* Herald-Times)

ketball caps, Kentucky T-shirts, and replica LeBron James jerseys. More than half the hits on the NBA's websites come from fans outside the United States. The NCAA and NBA have procured billions in television rights and merchandising and sponsorship revenues outside the United States. On a recent trip to Beijing, I was stopped on a pedestrian street by a kid maybe fourteen years old who wanted to practice his English. When he asked where I was born and I responded "Indiana," he grew wide-eyed. "I like Reggie Miller!" he enthused. In his book *Michael Jordan and the New Global Capitalism*, Cornell political scientist Walter LaFeber notes that Jordan, a more widely recognized international figure than the pope, emblematizes the global economy, is a brand that relies on technology and marketing to cross borders and generate multinational commerce.

Americans relish exportation, getting the world to buy our products, enlist our services, watch our movies. But free trade is a two-way proposition, even in basketball. And while sport is being exported worldwide, now the imports are arriving in the form of labor. So many "internationals" have flooded the basketball marketplace that a Rand McNally Atlas can be as vital a reference as a media guide. More than seventy players born outside the United States played for NBA teams during the 2003–04 season. Of the fifty-eight players selected in the 2003 draft, twenty hailed from abroad, including No. 2 pick Darko Milicic. As it stands, there are Poles in Memphis, Kiwis in Miami, Croats in Milwaukee, Serbs in Sacramento, Frenchmen, Argentines and Turks in San Antonio. As for the college game, most Division I teams have at least a few players on their roster who hail from outside the United States. In the 2004 NCAA final, the pivotal matchup pitted Connecticut's Emeka Okafor (the son of Nigerian parents) against Georgia Tech's Luke Schenscher (an Australian). In UConn's previous Final Four game, Okafor had to get past Duke's Luol Deng (from Sudan).

The trend will only accelerate. To generalize, overseas players—who grow up deprived of *SportsCenter* and all it represents, bereft of avaricious AAU coaches, shorn of a sense of entitlement—are more skilled in the fundamentals, more easily coached, more inclined to team play and ball movement. This was laid bare at the 2004 Athens Olympics, where the United States was embarrassed by the international competition. "The Europeans have it right," no less than Larry Bird told the *Indianapolis Star.* "Over there, they practice twice a day, and in the morning session, all they do is shoot. Shoot and shoot and shoot." Plus they tend to hail from middle-class, two-parent households and their "character" (an NBA neologism roughly translated as "They won't make the arrest logs or alienate fans and sponsors with antisocial behavior") is usually beyond reproach.

Just as the trend of globalization has an underbelly (widening chasms between the haves and have-nots, plummeting environmental standards, outsourcing of jobs, to name three), so too is basketball's global trend not without its problems. Some go so far as to push for protectionist measures. While the NBA has no trouble slathering its logo and beaming its games all over the world, when the labor market goes international, there is backlash. John Thompson, the former Georgetown coach, now an NBA commentator, recently explained, "Guys should feel threatened. These kids from other countries can play. . . . Players here need to wake up and smell the coffee: eventually, the league could go Euro." Other critics bemoan the foreign athletes in college sports, asserting their recruitment deprives the offspring of hardworking, taxpaying Americans of scholarships.

The influx of foreign-born players has also created a marketing challenge. Basketball has thrived thanks to the cult of personality, the ability to sell Michael Jordan and Shaquille O'Neal to Mainstream (that is, white suburban) America, packaging the players not merely as superior athletes but likable cyborgs fit for Disney cartoons. Allen

Iverson and other "New Jack players," with their perpetual scowls and their copious tattoos and deep familiarity with the legal system, are obviously tougher sells. Fair enough. But are fans any more likely to form a bond with, say, Nené, the Denver Nuggets' one-named forward from Brazil? Though Nené is a perfectly skilled player, and his English (and our Portuguese) is less than perfect, he returns to Brazil in the off-season and he didn't play for State U. It makes for an interesting "race versus culture" discussion, but are fans any more likely to identify with him than they are with, say, Iverson? Likewise, the NBA takes pains to define cool and market the avant-garde hipness of its product. The mainstream consumer has made it clear that the LeBron James jersey has sufficient currency, that it's worth the $120. Whether the consumer is willing to dispose of cash for a jersey reading "Ilgauskas" or "Milicic" or "Tskitishvili" on the back is less of a sure thing.

The ambivalence toward "global basketball" was manifest at the World Basketball Championships held in Indianapolis in the summer of 2002. This was the premier international competition before the Athens Olympics and yet the crowds rivaled those at a Hoosier high school intrasquad game. Scarcity in number was compounded by apathy. Teams expecting to play before the world's foremost basketball cognoscenti were stunned. "I'm struggling with what people around here think this is," New Zealand coach Tab Baldwin said. "I think it's the World Championship. People need to come out."

The Indiana Sports Corporation lost more than $2.5 million on the event and explanations were abundant. Even in hoops-mad Indiana, fans take a break in the summer. A National Hot Rod Association drag-racing event up the road was siphoning fans. The American team was missing most of the A-list stars; and interest really declined once the team was eliminated from gold medal contention. Still, it was hard to escape this conclusion: There is a reason why hockey and soccer and the U.S. Open tennis tournament bend over backward to promote homegrown talent. The popular Indiana bumper sticker exhorting us to "Buy American" applies to sports as well.

In Indiana, towns named after more famous international locales are, almost defiantly, pronounced alernatively. So Milan, home to the basketball team that spawned the movie *Hoosiers*, is pronounced "*My*-lun." Versailles is "Ver-*sales*." Terre Haute, the site of Indiana State University, is "Terra *Hote*." Brazil is "*Braz*-uhl." Cole Porter's hometown of Peru is "*Pay*-ru." It's usually passed off as nothing more than another of the state's endearing quirks. But I wonder if it doesn't bespeak a certain cultural unease with matters foreign—an unease that extends to foreign basketball.

*D*uring the jayvee game, the Bloomington North varsity players sat on the Decatur Central bleachers with measured cool, their legs spread over three rows. They occasionally yelled encouragement— "C'mon, Sam! Play big!" they barked at Sam Russo, a curly-haired sophomore who was 6'4" but had yet to fill out his coat-hanger frame— but it was mostly an exercise in marking time before the 7:30 tip-off. During a lull in the jayvee action, Kyle Thomas, the son of a white mother and African-American father, asked Bil Duany about his name. Thomas had seen his buddy's name misspelled "Bill" innumerable times and knew it was not short for William. What exactly *was* the origin?

"It means a white spot on a black bull," Bil explained.

Pause.

"For real?"

"For real."

This tidbit was passed around to other team members and made for a source of amusement for a good five minutes. "It's a metaphor,"

Bil said, helpless to stem the tide of grief he was getting. "Or a simile. Whatever. It's symbolic."

There is, of course, an abiding irony to the symbolism. In Indiana he is the precise converse of a white presence on an otherwise black canvas. But Bil doesn't really see it that way. Sure, there are reminders that his looks stand out in the heartland—invariably, the team photographer uses the wrong exposure and Bil's face is unrecognizable in team portraits. And sure, there are morons at visiting gyms who mockingly chant "U-S-A, U-S-A" when he draws a foul. True, he was conceived in Africa and born in Europe. But ultimately he is a thoroughly typical, corn-fed Hoosier who speaks in a thick Indiana twang and is fluent in Hoosierese: a bag is a "sack" and he'll wait "on" you, not for you, after practice. Like so many other Indiana kids, he speaks lovingly of his car, a black Rodeo, and suffice to say he does his share to contribute to the baggy jeans microeconomy. He likes the rapper 50 Cent, he has sacrificed untold hours at the altar of PlayStation2, and he is inherently distrustful of big cities. "I'll travel for AAU or something and even then I get homesick for Indiana," he says, running a hand through his braids. "Maybe people are surprised because of how I look or because of my hair, but you know I'm just a normal Indiana kid. Like hanging with my friends. Try to get good grades. Love to play basketball. I don't know, just normal stuff."

It's a familiar double-edged sword for immigrant families. They want nothing more than for their kids to assimilate, to make a seamless transition to a new culture, cultivate a sense of place, explore their identity. For the Duanys, they were thrilled when their kids brought home new friends, new slang, new fashions. At the same time, there was something disconcerting about their Americanization. When each of her five kids went through the rite of passage of getting a driver's license at sixteen, Julia always marveled thinking that at the same age, Sudanese boys are initiated into manhood in a ceremony involving spears and lion skins. Likewise, Wal sometimes did a mental calculus when his kids demanded the latest trends. *Those Nikes cost $135, which would feed a Sudanese family for a year.* As their peers in Africa were fighting in the military or starting families, the Duany kids were in graduate school or talking on their cell phones with their agents about playing basketball for teams in Europe.

In the case of Bil, the cultural assimilation is particularly pronounced. He is a bright, self-possessed, delightful teenager with charm to burn. But to him, Africa is almost as foreign as it is to any other Indiana kid. At the 2003 Final Four, Kueth—whose Nilotic name, fittingly, translates to "courage caused by political strife"—used his platform to speak eloquently about the devastation and the serious human rights violations in his Sudanese homeland, about the Muslim regime that, without exaggeration, could be called genocidal. Ask Bil about the Sudanese civil war and his eyes start to dart around as if to say, *Um, can we get back to talking about PlayStation and basketball?* Unlike his siblings, who were born in Sudan, he doesn't speak or understand Nu'er, the local dialect. "I always say that Bil is American, not African," says Julia with a trace of sadness. "He knows about cars but not about cows."

Duany ("Doc") Duany and Kueth Duany, who remember the traumatic exodus from Sudan and were raised in a small apartment, played basketball with a sense of urgency. The game was great fun for them, but they also recognized at an early age that it could be a means of improving their lives. By contrast, Bil has no recollections of despair. By the time he was in middle school, the family was able to move out of Tulip Tree to a modest home on Bloomington's west side, not far from the IU campus. Unlike his brothers, Bil has his own bedroom, his own car, his own cell phone. "Spoiled rotten," Doc says with a smile. And surely it's no coincidence that on the basketball court, Bil lacks the internal drive of his older brothers. Doc was a silky shooter who spent countless hours practicing alone on the erratically surfaced Tulip Tree court, his jumper tracing a perfect parabola through the net. Kueth, the best athlete of the bunch, was a slasher able to manufacture offense. Bil is a smoother, more versatile and more athletic player, but his outside shot is suspect and, lacking a consistent release point, it has clearly been neglected in practice for sexier parts of the game. His free throw shooting had been abysmal so far: Heading into the Decatur Central game, he hadn't even made half of his attempts. Though only eight years separate the three brothers, they are clearly of different eras.

The success of his older siblings has also inflated Bil's basketball ego. Before the season, a handful of college teams—Davidson, Bradley, Creighton—had proffered scholarships to Bil. If these aren't "big-time" programs that play on national television every week or send boatloads of players to the pros, they are more-than-respectable Division I programs at schools that are strong academically. But reality can be elusive and wisdom can be hard-won when you're eighteen—particularly when your brothers played in recent Final Fours—and Bil declined the offers. He figured he would tear it up during the season and attract the attention of a school the likes of North Carolina or Oklahoma. To the outsider, it sounded crazy. If his knee injuries hadn't scared schools off, anything less than a banner senior year would. Here he had a choice of scholarship offers; by season's end, who knew whether he'd still have any birds in his massive, bony hands. "It's his choice," Wal said resignedly. But in a perverse way, Bil's boldness was yet another indication that the Duany family has made it. He had a safety net.

As the season progressed, his decision to turn down the scholarship offers looked increasingly iffy. This was never more apparent than in the Decatur Central game. The Hawks were young and undersized; no player stood taller than 6'2". After a sloppy start, Bloomington led 29–22 at halftime, to the delight of Julia and Wal as well as Nok and Nyagon, who were in Indiana for the Christmas holiday. Bil had his way with a smaller defender and rebounded aggressively, which brought vocal encomiums from Julia. "Keep swinging the ball!" she yelled as the Cougars departed for the locker room.

But in the second half, Bil went into basketball's version of the witness protection program, completely disappearing from the game. Behind a hot-shooting sophomore, Devon Dumas, Decatur Central went on a 17–0 run, improbably turning a 41–29 deficit into a 46–41 lead. On possession after possession, Bil seldom touched the ball. When he did, he deferentially tossed it back to a guard. As both a senior captain and the best player on the court—and one who had a half-foot height advantage over his defender—he would have been well within his rights to glower at his teammates and bark: "Get. Me. The. Bleeping. Ball." But he made no such overtures, betraying only the smallest traces of frustration as his team's lead evaporated.

It didn't help that the officiating was poor. In a theme that would repeat itself throughout the season, the referees seemed to take pity on Bloomington North's industrious, decidedly smaller opponents and their guerrilla style of ball. North players would stand completely stationary and block shots and still get cited for fouls. On the other end of the floor, the Hawks would clutch and grab like outclassed prizefighters without consequence. At one point in the first half, the Cougars' center, Reed Ludlow, went up for a shot and the Decatur Central defender, in an unsuccessful attempt to block it, slapped the backboard. The entire stanchion shook wildly, causing Ludlow's point-blank shot to miss. It was blatant goaltending. In unison, the North players yelled to the refs and pointed to the fixture, which was still swaying. "I didn't see it!" the zebra shrugged. McKinney took the high road. When multiple players retreated to the bench at a time-out and complained about the officiating, the coach wasn't hearing it. "They're not beating us," he barked. "We're beating ourselves."

In a pell-mell fourth quarter, North had the ball and a two-point lead with 30 seconds left. Seeing a seam in the defense, Anthony Lindsey, the gallant point guard, drove to the basketball and was laid out by a defender, absorbing as much contact as any tackle he had endured during football season. Amazingly, no whistle was forthcoming. As Lindsey lay on the ground, incredulous, Decatur Central rebounded the ball, headed downcourt and called time-out. With 10 seconds remaining, Decatur Central ran a double-screen to free Dumas, their best player. It was a thoroughly predictable play, the success of which depended solely on whether the Bloomington North defenders would fight through a bramble of bodies with sufficient effort to defend the shooter. "Here's what we're trying to do," the Hawks essentially said. "Try and beat us."

Bloomington North couldn't. Decatur Central ran the play, and as expected, Dumas's man, Josh Norris, was obstructed by a thicket of screens. Duany and Macy responded as though they had been shot with tranquilizer guns and provided no help. Dumas, unconscious for the entire half, caught the ball at the top of the key. In one fluid motion, he turned and fired a three-pointer that found a home at the bottom of the net. The crowd went nuts and, as North called time-out, Dumas ran to the student section to exchange delirious high fives.

North was trailing by only a point and had the ball at halfcourt with two seconds to play. Again, it should have been Duany Time. Throw him the ball in the paint and he'd use his height and reach advantage to retrieve the pass. Though the refs had made it painfully clear that they wouldn't be calling a foul, you had to like his odds of making a shot from within ten feet. Yet when North set up for the final play, Duany made only a halfhearted effort to extricate himself from the defense. The inbound pass went to Lindsey, who had played a strong all-around game but had shot tepidly all evening. He took the pass well beyond the three-point line, dribbled once and heaved a thirty-footer that bounced innocuously off the rim. Ballgame. Decatur North 52, Bloomington North 51.

That Bloomington North had lost for the first time all season was one thing. That they had lost to a markedly inferior team that had simply expended more effort infuriated McKinney. "We're going to have to make changes, find guys who show more pride wearing the Bloomington North uniform," he said dejectedly as he leaned against a wall outside the locker room for support. "Once you're up ten, twelve points, you have the opportunity to put somebody away, and we didn't." In keeping with an annual tradition, McKinney and his wife were going to spend the following week of Christmas break in Naples, Florida. As the bus eased out of the Decatur Central parking lot, McKinney knew his vacation had already been ruined.

The stat sheet would suggest that Bil had played a whale of a game: 16 points and 14 rebounds are the kinds of numbers that might catch the eyes of Division I recruiters. But any scout or assistant coach who had watched the game would have said the same thing. Whether Bil fully knew it or not, he should have had 30 points and 20 rebounds. Julia was philosophical afterward. "They should have won that one, but they're still 5–1," she said. Trite as it sounds, who knows better than she that there are a lot worse fates in life than losing a high school basketball game. After a pause, she added: "We should have won, should have played better defense in the end. But those refs, they were *baaaaad.*"

6

THE NBA'S BIG $HOW

IS THERE A BETTER METAPHOR FOR THE CURRENT STATE OF basketball in Indiana than Conseco Fieldhouse? Stylish, self-confident and well-proportioned, the home of the NBA's Indiana Pacers sits between Delaware and Pennsylvania streets in downtown Indianapolis, a 750,000-square-foot talisman of the awkward tug-of-war between basketball's past and future. Though it opened only in 1999—a youngster, even given the comically meager half-lives of contemporary sports arenas—the structure pays homage to the state's basketball history.

Take one step inside and it's easy to transport yourself back to the 1950s. Nicknamed "The Barn," the place looks from the outside like a classic Indiana high school gym on steroids. Inside, there are old-time scoreboards and rickety seats and a russet motif and steel beams and bare-bulb lighting. The practice court is built to resemble a typical bandbox gym, à la Hickory High in the movie *Hoosiers*, replete with brick walls and a manual scoreboard. The corridors are lined with sepia-toned photos of Indiana teams. You half expect to find egg creams on the menu at the concession stands. No touch is too small: the condiments in the court-level restaurant are stored in plastic replicas of canvas basketball shoes. There is also significance in what's missing. There are no gaudy lights or garish marquee out front, promoting the Matchbox Twenty concert later in the month; no cheesy figurines or corporate logo on the side of the building; no mammoth parking lot, no neon. "This place is all retro," says Jermaine O'Neal, the Pacers' best player. "It's classy in the throwback way, know what I'm saying?"

Sort of. For all the historic touches, there are abundant reminders that this isn't the 1950s and that the Fieldhouse is very much a product of today's sports-industrial complex. For one thing, revenue generators lurk at every turn. There are the requisite corporate suites, those isolation boxes where the landed classes can rub elbows and eat overpriced shrimp cocktail—often with their backs turned to the action on the floor—without mingling with the great unwashed below. Most of the courtside real estate is adorned, sometimes tastefully and sometimes not, with advertisements—"signage," to use the sports locution. There are courtside placards that rotate electronically, an RCA logo on the stanchion, a half-dozen corporate emblems on the overhead scoreboard. The Pacemates dance team is brought to you by Pepsi. When they're through gyrating, the McDonald's Prize Patrol plies fans with T-shirts. The quaint practice floor has a Gatorade insignia slathered near midcourt. Perhaps the ultimate sign of the times: in the lobby of this classic building, without a trace of irony, sits a Starbucks.

Even the name of the place, the core of its identity, is at once quaint and unremittingly modern. "The Fieldhouse," of course, is a nod to the prosaic all-purpose gyms. At the same time, the franchise has followed the trend of siphoning extra revenue by selling the naming rights. The Indianapolis-based financial services firm Conseco ponies up $2 million each year for the right to attach its name to the building. That Conseco flirted with bankruptcy after the stock market crash in the late '90s and has fallen prey to the corporate sin du jour of flimsy accounting . . . well, it's somehow fitting, too.

The building that was effectively replaced by the Fieldhouse, Market Square Arena, was something of an acquired taste. Sandwiched a few blocks north of the plot the Fieldhouse now occupies on the east side of downtown, MSA abutted a public market—hence the name—and reeked of the well-intentioned-but-terminally-tasteless '70s. Somehow it was fitting that the building was christened on September 15, 1974, with a Glen Campbell concert. "It looks like a huge turd" is how the father of a childhood friend of mine once described MSA. To my mind, MSA always looked like a futuristic space station blighting the Indianapolis skyline. The exterior was ominously black and bedizened with an awkward dome. When he played for the Pacers, George McGinnis was asked to sit atop the roof for a promotional photo shoot and pose with a basketball in his monstrous hands. McGinnis, who grew up in Indianapolis, declined out of fear that he might slide off the dome and land on the macadam below.

What MSA lacked in architectural charm it made up for in impracticality. The basketball floor was, illogically, three stories above street level, creating snarling traffic in the elevators and walkways before and after events. The various tunnels and catacombs inside the building were curiously narrow; there are stories of bands taking the stage without vital pieces of sound equipment that couldn't be squeezed through the passageways. There was one women's restroom in the entire building. The Pacers complained that the home locker room in MSA was less commodious than the visitors' quarters in other arenas.

Still, the place was not without its charms. A few blocks from the geographic middle of the state, MSA was in many ways Indiana's literal epicenter, our Coliseum, and it helped make the state's citizens feel as though we were living in a place of some significance. Wayne Gretzky, playing in the ill-fated World Hockey Association, scored his first goal as a professional hockey player in the building. The building achieved a true measure of immortality on June 26, 1977, when Elvis played his last concert there.

But the venue made its name as a basketball gym. It came into existence largely because the Indianapolis mayor at the time, Richard Lugar, was embarrassed that Bloomington—and not the state's capital city—had the honor of hosting the high school basketball championships. So MSA was built and Indianapolis promptly wrested back the tournament finals. Soon "getting to Market Square" was the coin of the realm for any team that could run a three-man weave. To the delight of IU alumni in Indianapolis, the Hoosiers played an annual preconference tournament in the building.

Above all, MSA was the longtime home to the Pacers, the cream of the wild and woolly ABA and often the dregs of the NBA. The games were seldom pretty, and frequently the home team was responsible for the lesser of the two integers on the scoreboard. But the fans never much seemed to mind. At least until the Colts left Baltimore under the cover of darkness and came to town in the mid-'80s, the Pacers were the only pro game in the entire state. (Not for nothing have they always been the Indiana, not the Indianapolis, Pacers.) The tickets were priced reasonably and the ushers were famously lax about letting kids gravitate from the nosebleeds to the vacant seats—of which there were usually plenty—closer to the court level. On their way to the locker room, a parade of affable players would unfailingly stop and sign autographs: Darnell Hillman and his cumulus cloud Afro, Billy Knight, Steve Stipanovich, the terminally underrated Vern Fleming and my favorite, Clark Kellogg, an oxlike forward who could have been an elite NBA player had he not been felled by knee injuries. "In other cities we would have gotten booed off the floor," says Kellogg, currently a broadcaster for the team and college games on CBS and online columnist for Yahoo! Sports. "But people came and had a good time watching the basketball and there was a real college atmosphere."

Despite growing success on the court, by the mid-'90s it was abundantly clear that if the Pacers had any hope of remaining in Indiana, the team was going to need nicer digs. The paucity of charm was the least of it. MSA's real defect was a lack of "revenue streams." There were no luxury boxes to speak of, no club seats, few advertising opportunities courtside and on the scoreboard. The vast majority of the other NBA teams had moved to sleek new buildings with every conceivable amenity. (The Miami Heat lasted in their first arena for just twelve years before moving to a new home that boasted a cedar cigar bar overlooking Biscayne Bay.) Three hours up the road from Indy, the Bulls razed dowdy Chicago Stadium, in its place building the mammoth United Center. The Michael Jordan statue outside notwithstanding, the arena has all the soul and intimacy of an airplane hangar. But it has a whopping 216 luxury suites. If the team can lease each for an average of, say, $200,000 a season, that's more than $40 million in additional annual revenue.

For the Pacers, the rub was this: The NBA salary cap is tracked to overall revenues around the league. In the mid-'90s, the league revenues were growing at a rate worthy of Jack's beanstalk. This was partly due to the league's burgeoning television contract, but it was also because so many teams dramatically fattened their coffers after moving to upscale venues. The Pacers were getting burned at both ends. With no suites or club seating, the franchise all but took a vow of poverty. Even with growing attendance, the club ranked in the bottom third in revenues. At the same time, ownership was being forced to disburse more and more in salaries each year because of the growing salary cap.

"There was just no way to make it work," says team president Donnie Walsh. "The reality of the NBA is that unless you're the Knicks, you can't survive in an older arena without the amenities."

There was also the thinking that MSA was starting to put the team at a competitive disadvantage. With no practice court or significant weight-training facilities in the building, the players spent inordinate amounts of time in their cars, driving to various practice centers. Whereas other franchises had film rooms with high-tech video equipment where the team could gather to watch tape (and then hold video game contests on the big screen), the Luddite Pacers were forced to wheel a VCR into the locker room. Deprived of beaches, 300 days a year of balmy weather, a lively club scene, Indiana was already somewhat hobbled when it came time to recruit free agents. It didn't help that other teams could take a prospective player to their arena and show off the equivalent of a palatial estate while the Pacers were forced to try to talk up their modest split-level.

The arena project fell largely into the lap of David Kahn, a young, hard-charging Pacers executive who had come to the team after working at a high-powered New York law firm. Kahn quickly became an expert on sports venues, traveling to every NBA arena, embarking on a barnstorming tour of Indiana high school gyms—Anderson, Muncie, New Castle, Seymour, Columbus North—and taking meticulous notes on structural assets and liabilities and the small touches that made the facilities unique. "What you don't want is for fans to feel like this could be anywhere in America. You want the place to speak to them, to who they are and to what makes them special. We also didn't want some multipurpose venue. We wanted them to associate the Fieldhouse with the Pacers and vice versa. When you think of Fenway Park, you think of the Red Sox. And when you think of the Red Sox, you think of Fenway Park. That's what we wanted here."

After securing nearly $200 million in funding with a creative public-private partnership that provoked little outrage from the locals—no small feat, that—the Fieldhouse opened to rave reviews in the fall of 1999 and is now the benchmark for new basketball venues.

Overnight, the Fieldhouse had a staggering effect on the Pacers' bottom line. In the team's first season in its new home, revenues tripled from approximately $40 million to more than $120 million. To be sure, some of that was owed to its share of the ever-increasing national television contract. But the largest causal effect was the new 18,345-seat arena and its sixty-nine suites (average price of more than $100,000 per season), sufficient club seats and advertising opportunities. The team that had ranked in the bottom third of the league financially was suddenly in the top quarter. Even today, as the team's on-court fortunes have waxed and waned, the Pacers are firmly ensconced in the top third in revenue, no mean feat given that Indianapolis is the NBA's fifth-smallest market. Better still, the suites and club seats mean that teams can afford to reduce prices for the common fan. The Pacers offer balcony-level seats—which would be nosebleeds anywhere else, but aren't at the Fieldhouse because of the extraordinary sight lines—for as low as $12, roughly the price of a movie. In an ESPN.com poll, the Pacers ranked No. 12 among the 188 major professional sports franchises in overall fan satisfaction.

As for the notion that the retro vibe is somewhat sullied by Starbucks and the corporate name and all the contemporary touchstones that reduce the game to a bit player in the overall attraction, Kahn is unapologetic. "Look, we're all romantics to some extent. But not so much that we can afford to do things that are fiscally irresponsible. Part of the tradition of Indiana basketball is that Hoosiers expect their teams to be competitive. If you're forgoing revenues, you're limiting your ability to be the best team. That's just the reality of the NBA in today's world and today's marketplace."

Before Market Square Arena was reduced to atmospheric particles and turned—literally—into a parking lot, one man was selected to take the final shot in the building's history. Fittingly enough, the honor was conferred on Bobby Leonard, who never scored a point for the Pacers but, at least in Indiana, is the figure most closely associated with the franchise. After the Pacers' final practice in the building, Larry Bird threw a pass to Leonard, who was under the basket. Then sixty-eight, Leonard didn't bother to jump, but his shot kissed the backboard and trickled through the net. "Boom, Baby," said Leonard, invoking the catchphrase he uses in his current job as the team's beloved radio broadcaster.

Known universally as "Slick"—a nickname coined when he was playing for the Minneapolis Lakers and beat the team's player-coach, George Mikan, in a series of gin rummy games—Leonard has been with the franchise throughout its dramatic evolution. He was the coach of the Pacers' dynastic teams in the swashbuckling, red-white-and-blue-balled ABA of the 1970s. He would moonlight as the team's traveling secretary, scout, media relations manager and occasional bus driver. His wife, Nancy, was the de facto general manager and CFO. The team played its games in the Coliseum at the Indiana State Fairgrounds. When the air was often perfumed with "eau de livestock" from the nearby stalls, it fell on Slick to affix air freshener in the arena and change the manure-stained carpeting, too. "So," he says, cackling, "you could say I was the part-time maintenance worker, too."

The 1976 merger—"the massacre," Leonard calls it—between the ABA and NBA nearly sounded the death knell for pro basketball in Indiana. The small-market franchise with modest ticket pricing struggled to keep up with big-city teams who could more easily afford star players. By the early eighties, the city's mayor, William Hudnut,

NBA's New School: Pacers forward Ron Artest was dismissed by some Hoosiers as a New Jack NBA Star even before he entered the stands to fight Detroit fans during a November 2004 game, earning him the longest suspension in NBA history. (*John Biever*/Sports Illustrated)

appeared on public service television spots, beseeching Hoosiers to support the Pacers. Leonard took part in telethons, singing "Back Home Again in Indiana," as the phone number for the season ticket office flickered on the screen. Eventually, Mel and Herb Simon, Brooklynite brothers who had made their fortune in commercial real estate, stepped up and bought the franchise for $11 million. Even so, the tough times persisted. "It wasn't a shoestring budget we were on," says Leonard. "It was a Velcro budget." Adds Reggie Miller, who joined the team in 1987 and never changed uniforms: "I remember when I first came here they put up these big, black curtains to hide all the empty seats. There were high school teams that outdrew us."

The NBA as a whole wasn't much better off. A league-wide drug problem and the dearth of magnetic, must-see stars conspired to make the NBA a major league sport in name only. Most franchises bled money and played to huge pastures of empty seats. The low point may have come in the late '70s when the NBA Finals were, amazingly, broadcast on tape delay.

The differences between then and now are, of course, staggering. The NBA is a global, multibillion-dollar enterprise often held up as *the* model sports league. Players are paid so lavishly their salaries are almost an abstraction. Consider: As a member of the Washington Wizards, Jared Jeffries, the former Bloomington North star, will make more for one game than the average American will earn in a year. And he is no star. Tricked-up charter planes with Internet access and catered spreads and flat-screen televisions have replaced the team buses and commercial flights.

The Pacers reflect this growth, too. The first earmark of change is the cheerful woman answering the phone at the main switchboard who greets callers by saying, "Pacers Sports and Entertainment!" Now a multitentacled organization, it has burgeoned to include more than a hundred employees and multiple levels of executives who watch games from swank offices. The players wear items of jewelry—diamond earrings the size of tenderloin sandwiches and sausages of gold around their necks—worth more than the entire franchise not all that long ago. The Simons were rewarded for their loyalty: Analysts estimate that their investment has increased more than twentyfold, to $240 million. "The jerseys still say Pacers and I still get a check from them twice a month," says Leonard. "Other than that, everything has changed."

Take the experience of attending a Pacers game. The goals are still ten feet off the ground and ninety-four feet apart. But everything else is different. Almost unrecognizably so. Games are a typically contemporary conflation of, well, sports and entertainment. Like all NBA contests, Indiana's come with all the modern-day trappings, the cloyingly splashy pregame introductions, the earsplitting hip-hop music, lasers on the ceiling and—no doubt to the horror of the local fire marshal—indoor fireworks. Subtlety and quiet are dual affronts. Suffice to say, we've come (or gone, as the case may be) a long way from the days when the ABA Pacers begged local high school marching bands to perform during halftime.

Purists justifiably hate it and complain that the Vegas-style ambience detracts from the basketball. But this slick packaging has been at the core of the NBA's success. When David Stern took over as NBA commissioner in 1984, there was a perception—an insurmountable one, many thought—that the league was "too black." It is Stern who devised the marketing strategy that was either ingenious, exploitative or both. On his watch, the league took the—pick your euphemism—urban/inner-city/black culture from which most players come and presented it to a white, suburban audience in a hip, edgy and non-threatening way. With the help of complicit shoe companies and other image-makers, the league created a class of crossover stars who had the requisite authenticity to peddle overpriced sneakers to black kids but also had currency with white audiences. Magic Johnson, with his Showtime game but also million-watt grin and winning personality, was the prototype. He begat Michael Jordan, a matchless player but one who also recalled a CEO with his cigars and his $5,000 suits and his golf game. Kobe Bryant was not only heir to Jordan with his anti-gravitational game but was equally polished—*he speaks Italian!*—and unthreatening. Or so we were led to believe. (You can imagine the consternation in the league headquarters when one star stands trial for rape and another for manslaughter, and a popular team broadcaster is revealed to have fourteen children by six women—all of which pocked the 2003–04 season.)

One former NBA official once explained to me that the NBA aspires to the chord struck by the comedian Chris Rock—who, perhaps not coincidentally, is featured in various NBA promotional campaigns: "You have enough street credibility for the black kids and at the same time, you have the white audience think they're cooler than they really are."

So the musical selections are hip-hop even if the intended audience is decidedly not. Dance troupes shimmy to the latest urban moves with maximum pheromonal impact. Cool-sounding inner-city vernacular creeps into league telecasts and ads for league sponsors. At some level, it has worked brilliantly. The NBA is something of a funhouse mirror: predominantly white crowds cheering predominantly black players. But the discomfort is minimal. One black player told *Sports Illustrated*, "You go diving into the stands after a ball, and you land on some investment banker's cell phone. Meanwhile, the fellas you grew up with can't afford a ticket to get in. Yeah, you think about those things." But a more common reaction resembles something Baron Davis of the New Orleans Hornets told me: "Long as people are spending that much money on tickets, I don't care what they look like."

Perhaps all the savvy marketing and diversionary bells and whistles are necessary. Perhaps you need fireworks when the games themselves often feature little in the way of pyrotechnics. Today's NBA is a bit like playing the slots. A lot of the action is the equivalent of a cherry, a bar and a lemon—which is to say, utterly forgettable and devoid of value. Too often, three players sit on the perimeter as idle as lawn ornaments while a guard and a big man pass back and forth until one sees the shot clock dwindling and hoists the ball basketward. With a slogging style, a clot of missed shots and a talent pool diluted by overaggressive expansion to thirty franchises and an increasingly younger, less-polished workforce, professional basketball too often lands on the wrong side of watchability.

Yet, like the slots, a few times a night—just as your patience is wearing thin and you're thinking about flipping the channel to that Teddy Roosevelt documentary or the Iron Chef eggplant-mincing demonstration—you hit the bar-bar-bar jackpot. Even at a time when webcasts and ceaseless highlight shows have raised the awe threshold to dizzying heights, a typical game still features a half-dozen sequences that cause eyes to pop and jaws to drop in equal measure, comic book plays performed by human superheroes.

On a bitterly cold Wednesday in the middle of December, the Pacers played the Orlando Magic in one of those ho-hum games that lard up the eighty-two-date schedule. Midway through the third quarter, Pacers guard Ron Artest trapped Orlando star Tracy McGrady near the half-court equator. McGrady tried to grift Artest by going left, but the player didn't budge. Artest swiped at the ball, pried it loose and headed downcourt. He took three dribbles, then elevated. In one fluid motion he kept McGrady at bay with his left hand, curled around the rim in midair and dunked violently with his right. It was a sensational play, one that spanned just a few seconds but encapsulated almost every attribute necessary for basketball success: cunning, strength, speed, athleticism, power, grace, poetry in movement.

Naturally, this occasioned another round of deafening hip-hop over the p.a. system.

From a well-appointed office at the lip of the court, one man watches the Pacers with a mix of emotions. At times, Larry Bird can't help but marvel at the raw skills of today's players, their midair flights of fancy, their ability to defy prevailing laws of physics. Other times he winces and curses and kicks his fancy leather loafers on the coffee table as he beholds the boneheaded plays, the laissez-faire defense and, most of all, the ghastly shooting. "I think about it all the time," he says, clucking in disappointment. "The fundamentals are lacking."

Even in his late forties, more than a decade removed from his last game, Bird remains the archetype for Indiana basketball. After burning out on coaching the Pacers and leaving the public eye for three years, he returned to the franchise in the summer of 2003 as president of basketball operations. While he is still so popular that he can't watch games from the stands—"Hard to evaluate your team and sign autographs at the same time," he says—he is no mere figurehead. When we spoke last winter he had just returned from a scouting trip to Europe. He was barely on the job for a month when he made his imprint, terminating the team's coach, Isiah Thomas, a longtime nemesis whose surfeit of style and deficit of substance is anathema to Bird. Thomas was replaced by Rick Carlisle, an organized, no-nonsense coach, a teammate of Bird's on the Boston Celtics and a fellow purist who shares his basketball values.

Jarring as it is to see Bird, erstwhile "Hick from French Lick," clad in a trendy herringbone sportcoat, sucking down bottled water as he reclines on a leather couch in a suite, he remains without pretense. Asked about the state of today's NBA, he minces no words. "I realize this is what guys from the '70s were saying about us, but we've got problems. I mean, in our league it's hard to find a guy who can hit a midrange jumper. It's embarrassing, frankly. They all want to take it to the rim, which is not a bad thing. But once they get there, what are they going to do about it? I've seen point guards break traps, break presses, but they can't make a fifteen-footer to save their lives. Well, you can take the ball anywhere you want, but if you can't hit a fifteen-footer what good is that?"

Inasmuch as the game has devolved, Bird blames the usual suspects. Highlights glorify dunks and three-point shots and little in between. "There's always a 'Jam of the Night,' or whatever," says Bird. "I'd like to see a 'Midrange Jumper of the Night,' or a 'Good Defensive Possession of the Night.'" The explosion of AAU ball means that kids forsake practicing in the summer and instead play a series of games, many of them featuring less defense than lunchtime gatherings at the YMCA. Bird recalls that he and his French Lick High School teammates would work on their games during June and July. Then, in August, they would play full-court games against the starting five from the rival team from West Baden. "No coaches, no refs," he recalls. "You didn't play defense? You had four guys on your ass."

Bird also bristles at the trend of talented teenagers skipping college and bounding straight for the NBA. "Today, you have kids in seventh grade saying, 'I'm going to play in the NBA,' and I think that's bad," he says. "We had such a different mind-set. I was just like anyone else that came through the ranks. I practiced a lot and my goal was to start on the varsity team in high school. After my senior year, I got to go to college, but I just wanted to fit in there. In college, I didn't hardly think about the NBA until I got drafted. It's mind-boggling we let our game get to this. It hurts our game. It hurts the college game. It hurts the high school game."

He's hardly the Man of La Mancha waging a lonely crusade. The trend of players forgoing college and heading straight from high school to the NBA is the current hot-button topic in basketball. Though the first player to make the jump, Bill Willoughby, did so in 1975, this career path has become particularly modish in recent years. It has caused all sorts of consternation, engendered all sorts of spirited debate, and is held out by the purists as Exhibit A when talk turns to why the NBA is headed to hell. Donnie Walsh, the Pacers' estimable president, calls it "the biggest challenge that basketball faces on all levels."

What's odd is that a similar career path is standard operating procedure in other sports. For years, the tennis circuit has been saturated with sixteen- and seventeen-year-olds traveling the world trying to make it big. For decades, baseball players have signed contracts the day they graduated from high school and promptly shipped off like GIs to Omaha or Ocala, the first stop on the way to the Show. No one claims the sky is falling because these athletes aren't toting backpacks to Biology 101 or reading Faulkner on the quad. (Or, more realistically, drinking beer from a funnel while playing poker and listening to illegally downloaded music until sunrise.)

Why the righteous indignation in hoops? One explanation is that Operation Bypass College has wrecked the symbiotic relationship between the NBA and NCAA. For years, the college game provided the NBA with a subsidized minor league that enabled players to polish their games and their personas in equal measure, before becoming professionals. Also, the NBA is a star-driven league and the college game helped make luminaries—when Bird, Jordan and Barkley were drafted, they were already entrenched in the public consciousness. As for the college game, in the halcyon days when the best high school players matriculated to State U., the on-court product was better, recruiting was easier, fans could form deeper attachments to familiar teams. (It's no coincidence that television ratings for the NCAA Tournament have tanked in recent years.) Then, once a player completed his tour of duty and left for the pros, State U. could puff its chest and boast that it was the alma mater of this or that NBA player.

It was a terrific deal for all parties except one: the class of talented eighteen-year-olds who were enriching universities to the tune of millions while shouldering huge opportunity costs by deferring the NBA's lucre. Worse still, the current NBA salary structure is such that a player is constricted by a graduated rookie wage scale that precludes even the best player from getting a truly fat contract until he has played five years. A college graduate who enters the NBA at twenty-two might not be eligible for "max money" until he is twenty-seven. After that deal lapses he will likely be in his mid-thirties and play for a "veteran exemption" salary. An eighteen-year-old who turns pro will get his max deal at twenty-three and then possibly another at twenty-eight. Get NBA owners to go "off the record" and they'll concede that the extra big contract is the real reason they want to see an age limit imposed.

But what about the college degree they're passing up? say the Chicken Littles. You can't put a price tag on that. Perhaps, but look closely at how few college basketball players—particularly with NBA potential—are actually graduating. For instance, at the University of Cincinnati, a top program that has routinely sent a boatload of players to the NBA goes years and years without graduating a single African-American team member. Likewise, a staggering forty-four of the sixty-five basketball programs that competed in the 2004 NCAA tournament graduated less than 50 percent of their players since 1990.

What about the manifold social benefits of college, its role as a safe canal between the turbulent seas of adolescence and adulthood? One could easily make the case that college *prolongs* adolescence and arrested development. NBA players might be coddled and cosseted, but they have to fill their days, pay their bills, negotiate office politics. In the infantilizing world of college sports, a player's entire schedule is planned. Athletes often board in all-jock dorms. Provided coursework isn't being done for them, athletes work at study tables open only to fellow members of the jockacracy. The infinite loop of games, weight training and practice takes up forty or fifty hours of their week. The notion that "student-athletes" playing college ball are sitting in the dorm lounge ruminating about Sartre or why good things happen to bad people—it's as passé as canvas shoes.

Fine, but what about the cautionary tales, the kids who—guided by delusions of grandeur and/or bad advice—fail to make it and are suddenly out of luck, having squandered their chance for a college scholarship? Is it worse than the fate of an NBA prospect who passes up millions by going to college and promptly blows out his knee or pops a disk in his back? And unlike in other sports, the basketball job market is sufficiently large that an eighteen-year-old who doesn't make an NBA roster can still earn a nice living playing overseas.

Reduced to its essence, one wonders if the cause célèbre of high school kids peregrinating straight to the NBA doesn't come down to this: To many folks, there is simply something distasteful about uneducated teenagers—most of them black—disrupting the status quo and making millions.

Consider the case of Jonathan Bender and it's hard to make a moral case for age limits. Bender is one of four players on the Pacers' roster never to have spent a day on a college campus. Even in warm-ups, you can almost see the nervous energy and insecurity radiate off his rangy frame. Bender is in his fifth year as an NBA player, almost inconceivable given how boyish he looks. He has a baby face and a head so disproportionately small for his body that his elasticized headband often slides down into his eyes. Bender speaks so softly that the reporters leaning in to hear what he's saying look as though they're trying to kiss him. His body is pure scaffolding, so skinny you can see cables of muscles thrusting with every move. His game is a work in progress as well. Though his knee was scoped a few months ago, he throws down ferocious dunks and effortlessly tosses reverse layups laced with back-spin that offer a tantalizing glimpse of his vast potential. But then he badly misfires on ten-foot jumpers and betrays only vague comprehension as assistant coach Chuck Person leans in to offer a pointer.

Bender grew up in Picayune, Mississippi, where his childhood was the diorama of tough times typical of NBA players. A town of 11,000 near the Louisiana border, Picayune—true to its name—is a sleepy, depressed place. The median per capita income is $15,798 for an individual and $26,958 for a household. If the Bender household eclipsed the average, it wasn't by much. When Jonathan was thirteen, his father died. His mother worked long, hard hours as a nurse and went back to school to get a degree in community health. Jonathan was a dazzling high school player, a lithe and versatile forward. At the 1999 McDonald's All-American game he scored 31 points, grabbed 10 rebounds and worked the scouts in attendance into a lather with a string of no-way-in-the-world dunks. Steered by a team of advisers, some more creditable than others, Bender spurned offers from top programs and entered the 1999 NBA draft. In a move that tidily summed up the degree to which drafting players is a crapshoot, the Pacers agreed on draft day to trade Antonio Davis, a reliable veteran center, to Toronto in exchange for the rights to Bender, the fifth pick. Davis went on to become an All-Star in Toronto. Bender routinely goes an entire game without molting his warm-ups; he has never averaged more than seven points in a season.

Nevertheless, he currently makes $6 million a year and is close to qualifying for an NBA pension that could pay him a six-figure annual income for the rest of his life. He's been able to buy his mother a house and send thousands of dollars to cousins and friends and friends of friends who need the help. At twenty-three, he has already amassed a big pile of chips; even if he never fulfills his vast potential, with any modicum of responsible financial planning, he will retire a rich man.

That knee injury that has hampered his progress? Had he stayed in school, it would have occurred after his junior season. Think he still gets picked No. 5? Picked at all? Hard to assert that he would have been better off in school.

And he is not even the best-case scenario. For that, you'd have to look across the Pacers' plush locker room. Though he is a hulking presence at nearly seven feet tall, Jermaine O'Neal is often difficult to find—his diamond earrings refract prisms when illuminated by the overhead lights, obscuring his face. After his senior year at Eau Claire High School in Columbia, South Carolina, O'Neal jumped directly to the NBA and was selected in the first round by the Portland Trail Blazers. While he languished on their bench for three seasons, he was handsomely remunerated. Traded to the Pacers in 2000, he's flourished to become the best big man in the Eastern Conference and a perennial All-Star. In the 2003 off-season, at the age of twenty-four—barely the age of a rookie a generation ago—he signed a contract worth $126 million. "Not going to college obviously worked out for me," says O'Neal, thoughtful and well-spoken despite having ended his formal education after twelfth grade. "But even in Portland when I wasn't playing, I didn't have any regrets. To be honest, if you can get drafted, college just doesn't make sense."

The Pacers' 2003–2004 roster was right out of central casting for a contemporary NBA team. There were emerging stars. Reggie Miller was the detached veteran, a shell of his former self but still a dangerous clutch shooter whose professionalism and quiet dignity subtly rub off on his younger teammates. There were the off-the-rack journeymen, the likes of point guard Anthony Johnson and forward Scot Pollard, who were acquired less on merit than to accommodate the salary cap. There was a European project, Primoz Brezec, a shy twenty-two-year-old forward from Slovenia who readily admitted that he had yet to find comfort or a sense of place in central Indiana. Apart from his wife, Brezec had no friends or family in Indianapolis and frittered away most of the time between games watching DVDs and racking up hundreds of dollars each month calling home on his cell phone. (He since decamped to the Charlotte Expansion franchise.)

The most intriguing player on the team was swingman Ron Artest, a peerless defender who performs at an All-Star level but is also regarded as one of the league's First Team head cases. The NBA is as much the-ater as it is sport. It needs villains as well as heroes. Owing to his pen-chant for technical fouls—which cost him 12 games in suspensions in 2002–03—and emotional outbursts, Artest wears a black hat. He is often depicted as the second coming of Dennis Rodman or, as one sports magazine sensationalized, "The Scariest Man in the NBA." Pacers fans, not surprisingly, are divided, many having written him off as a typical "New Jack" player. (Artest burnished this reputation in 2004 when he—unsuccessfully— asked for time off from basketball to fin-ish recording a rap album.)

The abiding irony is that Artest's game is more "Hoosier" than anyone else's on the Indiana team. Though he's endowed with plenty of athleticism, Artest plays like he's from another era. He competes with nonstop intensity, almost as though his very salvation is riding on the game's outcome. While he scores more than 15 points a game, he takes much more pride in his defense. Plus he's a hoops junkie, known to stop on the way home from Pacer practices to play pickup at the park near his McMansion in the Indianapolis suburbs.

And therein lies another reason to like Artest. There's an endearing guilelessness to him that ought to play particularly well in Indiana, a state that values authenticity above all. In an age when celebrity ath-letes are either opaque or aloof, when there often exists a wide chasm between public and private personae (see: Bryant, Kobe), Artest is the straightest of straight shooters, wonderfully tone-deaf to the nuances of public relations. Ask him a question, he'll look you in the eye and answer it. Yell his name from the upper reaches of Conseco Fieldhouse and he'll turn to acknowledge the voice, incapable of pretending not to hear it. Earlier in his NBA career, Artest had a friend who worked at a Circuit City electronics store. Figuring that if he, too, worked at the store, he'd be able to spend more time with his friend, Artest applied for a job. Naïve? Definitely. Eccentric? No doubt. The Most Dangerous Man in the NBA? Hardly.

In a classic Old School–New School clash, Artest picked up a technical in the 2003 preseason when he pretended to throw a ball to the ref and then took it back. "He's not from the park," Artest said of the ref. It was precisely the kind of antic—innocuous on the surface but stupid and ruinous to team chemistry—that Artest got away with under Isiah Thomas. Carlisle immediately benched Artest. "If I'm going to be taken out for stuff like that, I'd rather not be in the game," Artest complained. "I'd rather be with another team."

The next day at practice, Bird pulled Artest aside. "How long do you think I'm going to fuck around with you?"

Artest was stunned. "What?"

Bird locked eyes with him again. "How long do you think I'm going to fuck around with you? Pull that shit one more time and I'm trading your ass."

Artest recorded five technical fouls the rest of the season. If he didn't completely lose his black hat, he endeared himself to the fans. They came to appreciate his defense and admire his passion. Even his outbursts were recast. His technical fouls weren't occasioned by fighting or ref-baiting or trash-talking. No, they were exercises in self-flagellation coming when he was dissatisfied with his own play. Sure, he could blow a gasket when the game wasn't going as well as he'd like.

But wouldn't that describe Bird, Scott Skiles, Damon Bailey and hundreds of other Hoosiers? "To be honest, Ronny reminds me of me," says Leonard. "He just needs to overcome some immaturity and find his way a bit. Then he'll be fine." The same could be said of the league as a whole. (Alas, Artest did not overcome his immaturity. On November 19, 2004, after being doused with a cup of beer during a game against the Pistons, Artest charged into the stands, inciting a near riot and drawing a record suspension from the NBA.)

The NBA is currently in the throes of an adjustment period. And many of the current problems are owed to the immaturity of players, more and more of whom are skipping college altogether. But at the core, professional basketball will be fine. It features the best basketball practitioners in the world, and for all its flux, that isn't likely to change.

Against Orlando, the Pacers played a sloppy game but still had a chance to win. Down by a point, Al Harrington had a wide-open fifteen-footer from the wing that barely grazed the iron. On the ensuing possession, Orlando missed a free throw but Harrington neglected to block out his man. Orlando retrieved the ball and closed out the game. It was almost allegorical, a tidy summary of today's NBA: a young player's inability to execute fundamentals costing his team. But it was just one game out of eighty-two. As fans filed out of the arena— many of them employing better block-out technique than Harrington had exhibited on the game's decisive play—there was little sense of outrage. They had come for entertainment and, by and large, they'd been entertained.

As the masses approached the main concourse, they were greeted by a promotional banner. Part of an ongoing NBA public relations campaign, the placard originally read, "Why Do I Love This Game?" Amid the stampede to the exit, however, it had been ripped. It now read, "Do I Love This Game?" The question was a good one. *Do I Love the NBA?* I suppose like most Hoosiers, my answer is yes. Just not unconditionally.

7

THE NUMBERS RACKET

ANY DISCUSSION OF BASKETBALL'S SHIFTING TECTONICS would be incomplete without discussing the role of technology. Sex may have been the first divertissement to find a rapt audience in cyberspace; but, at least in Indiana, basketball wasn't far behind. Time was when hoops fans would sit on barber chairs or barstools, hover near the water cooler, and hold court on the fortunes of the local team. Today, the opinions are often just as passionate, the disagreements just as vicious, but the forums have moved online. Fans seeking to commiserate with the like-minded need only log on to the site of their choice.

Take peegs.com. Mike Pegram, a middle-aged father of two, was working in the corporate finance department of Arvin Industries when he started his eponymous website. It was the late '90s and he began tooling around on a message board devoted to Indiana basketball. Once a swimmer for Doc Counsilman, the late and legendary Indiana University coach, Pegram used his *nom de net* "Peegs," logged on, and ranted about IU's recruiting wars and passed on tidbits he had picked up following the team and talking to sources. Over time, he developed a cult following. With the Internet bubble still in its inflation stage, he quit his job to launch his own online destination devoted to all things Hoosier basketball.

He could scarcely have timed it better. The Bob Knight contretemps erupted a few months later and the site emerged as *the* forum for fans to articulate industrial-strength opinions. From all points on the globe, hundreds of thousands of citizens of Hoosier Nation were logging on daily and posting rants. Given that Pegram was not only charging subscribers a fee but receiving from advertisers as much as $2 per thousand-page views, the going was good. Working from the basement of his Columbus, Indiana, home, Pegram was on the verge of becoming wealthy—as well as one of the state's most influential basketball "journalists."

The tech bubble, of course, burst, and business has slowed for Pegram. But his site continues to generate all sorts of traffic, drawing more eyeballs than the sports sections of all the state's major newspapers combined. Sites like peegs.com are godsends for hard-core fans. They're either free or inexpensive, they're easily accessed and there are no geographic limits. You can be in Calcutta and it can be two in the morning, but so long as you have a browser you can get your fix of news, gossip and opinion on Indiana basketball.

But the real appeal of message boards is the "interactive" component. Why read or listen to the opinions of an expert when *you* can be the expert mounting the online soapbox? Saw a player violating curfew after a game? Post your "news" online and thousands of fans will read it. Ran into a coach at a bar and clicked a photo with your digital camera? Nothing to prevent you from posting it in the public domain.

Because of both the immediacy and the lack of a censor, these sites have put pressure on traditional media outlets. When former Iowa State basketball coach Larry Eustachy was caught on film drinking and kissing coeds, the image was first posted on a University of Missouri Athletics message board. Only later did more legitimate and traditional outlets such as the Des Moines *Register* report the story. In Indiana, peegs.com routinely "breaks news" pertaining to Indiana basketball— recruiting commitments, personnel changes, injury updates. Among other "scoops," it was the first outlet to run Knight's infamous apology letter after he was fired.

This autonomy comes at a price. The message boards are known as web communities; but a vital component of any community is accountability. When the local columnist or host of the sports radio station expresses an opinion—however objectionable—they're doing so with their name attached. When the information or assertion in question is provided online by StudBoy11 or IH8Purdue, it's another matter altogether. Plus, there are no censors for taste or civility. The site firemikedavis.com, for instance, is a repository for cheap shots and withering personal attacks on the coach.

These online destinations are another example of the segmentation of society. But they are here to stay, as much a part of the rooting experience as call-in radio shows were a generation ago and fan clubs a generation before that. And the sooner the subjects concede as much, the better. Davis routinely gets the piñata treatment on these boards but still had the good sense to show up at a recent peegs.com golf outing and slap some backs. "Here's how I look at it," he says philosophically. "If there's a new place where people can go to talk about Indiana basketball and be passionate, ultimately that's a good thing. When they don't care is when I get worried."

The proliferation and popularity of message boards present just one of the innumerable ways technology has changed the culture of basketball. The NBA beams two games a week to China, where 300 million nascent fans watch hoops. Players with knee injuries undergo laser surgeries and return in a matter of days rather than months. Even high school teams sell tickets and merchandise on their websites. But, until recently, the onslaught of technology had little direct impact on the actual game. To use the current vernacular, basketball has never been a "data-driven business."

Through the decades, coaches have used the same primitive grease boards for designing and sketching plays, even using the same primitive letters X and O to designate offense and defense. Players consider few statistics other than points, rebounds and assists. Notwithstanding the two-way pagers that have become the *de rigueur* accoutrement for NBA players, teams invested little in electronic equipment. Some of this is simply practical. Basketball teams at every level play three and four games a week, hardly allowing enough time to devote attention to dissecting tape or significant hi-tech scouting. But there's also a more abstract explanation. Basketball, not unlike jazz, is largely about improvisation and instinct. Basketball, the thinking went, is a sport for the soul, not for cold, rational numbers. At some level, it's the classic confrontation between science and the humanities.

Tom McKinney, for one, doesn't much mess with technology. Cellular phones, he maintains, are "a Communist plot" designed to destroy human interaction. He's kidding. Maybe. He is only able to access his e-mail account when he uses the high school computer system—and if his players competed at the same speed at which he responds to messages, they would be benched in perpetuity. The game tape he watches is grainy footage usually shot from a single overhead camera.

Charts and graphs and statistics are of minimal use to him. "My mind doesn't work like that," he says flatly.

He's in good company. A Hall of Fame player, Jerry West has become equally well known for an uncanny ability to judge basketball talent. West is currently the president of the Memphis Grizzlies, and by his second year on the job he had transformed a dreadful collective into a playoff team. One of his office walls is consumed by a giant magnetic board bearing the name of every player in the NBA as well as the prospects available in the next NBA draft. Asked whether it wouldn't be infinitely easier to store the information on a hard drive, he shrugs. "Never really considered that." Asked whether he uses statistical analysis or a cognate of SABRmetrics—a complex mathematical analysis of players that is all the rage in baseball and the subject of the bestselling book *Moneyball*—to assess players, West waves his hand through air. "Nah, I don't need that stuff. They're not going to tell me who makes the big plays under pressure, who is a good teammate, who is a leader, who is injury-prone. I trust these," he says, pointing to his eyes. "They tell me everything I need to know."

But that's starting to change. Like the Luddites who finally give in and grudgingly open an e-mail account, basketball is beginning to embrace technology and quantitative analysis. Which is good news for Wayne Winston and Jeff Sagarin. A professor of decision sciences at the Indiana University Business School and a professional sports statistician, respectively, Winston and Sagarin are the co-creators of WinVal, a convoluted model for rating the effectiveness of NBA players. If the math behind WinVal is impossibly complex, the philosophy behind it is blissfully simple. Loosely based on hockey's "plus–minus" ratings, which credit a player for being on the ice when his team scores (and penalize him when the opponent puts the puck in the net), WinVal answers the most basic question: Is the team better off when Player X is in the game?

It's generally safe to assume that a player who reaches double figures in points and rebounds has played capably. Conversely, a player
who goes 0-for-11 from the field and accumulates six fouls has, in all
likelihood, not played a banner game. But the traditional box score
tells us only so much. Until WinVal, statisticians had yet to figure out
how to credit the player who made the vital pass that came prior to the
assist. Or the player who planted himself like a bridge abutment as his
opponent came haring through the lane, drawing a crucial charging
call. Or the proletariat drawn to loose balls. "Most of basketball is
made up of things for which there are no stats," says Winston. "You
know how announcers always say, 'He does the intangibles'? WinVal
makes the intangibles tangible."

Sucking data directly from the NBA's official courtside computers
immediately after each game has ended, WinVal uses quantitative analysis to create what the progenitors call "the most complete statistical
profile possible for the NBA's 300-plus players." Which players play
well against certain teams? What lineups score the most points or play
the worst defense? How does a certain player perform on the road, or
on the second night of back-to-back games or against an opponent
from a city starting in a vowel? WinVal tells all. "The data speaks for
itself," says Dallas Mavericks owner Mark Cuban, who pays $100,000
annually to use WinVal and claims never to sign a player or make a
trade without first consulting the relevant WinVal data. "It's a great investment to keep on searching for the models that can be a better or
best predictor of performance at the team and player level."

Winston and Sagarin are the Felix Unger and Oscar Madison of
sports statisticians. They first met nearly thirty years ago as
MIT undergraduates. Both suburban New Yorkers—Sagarin from

Long Island, Winston a Jersey guy—they lived in the same dorm and bonded watching their Bostonian classmates suffer over the fate of the Red Sox. After graduation, they both gravitated to Indiana, thinking it a mere pit stop before returning to civilization, Sagarin to attend business school, Winston to become an assistant professor. Neither left.

A silver-haired father of two teenagers who swims two miles a day, Winston is, rather decidedly, the less eccentric of the pair. Affable and irrepressible, he speaks at the pace of an auctioneer, the thoughts seeming to pass through his cortex faster than he can articulate them. Specializing in applied probability, he has published articles with daunting titles like "Optimal Pricing for a Monopolist Facing Rational Customers—Operations Research: Applications and Algorithms." Before cocreating WinVal, his claim to fame was an appearance on *Jeopardy!* that netted him $16,800.

Sagarin—how to say this?—cuts a less conventional figure. He lives alone in Bloomington in a house overwhelmed by sports books and computer printouts, and he has carved a reputation as *the* rankings laureate of the sports world. Through a series of high-math equations—the secrets of which he guards as if it were the formula for Coke—he has figured out a way to rank teams based not only on wins and losses but also the quality of the opposition. Without revealing too much, he is happy to describe the theory behind his thinking. But more often than not, he loses the listener with a Berlitz assault of "geometric mean" and "logarithmic function." Sagarin is a charter member of the controversial BCS, and his college football rankings are largely responsible for determining which teams play in which bowl games. His college basketball rankings are used by the NCAA's selection committee when determining seeds for March Madness and are carried by most major newspapers. It's no exaggeration to say that he's among the most powerful figures in college sports. Which amuses him as much as anyone else. "I've basically made a good living doing what I would have done for free when I was eleven," he says.

After their first go-round with WinVal, they realized a fatal error in their model. If the world's most skilled defender and indefatigable hustler played for a sad-sack team the likes of the Los Angeles Clippers, his WinVal rating would nonetheless be low. (Says Sagarin, "We realized that if you took four guys out of a bar and teamed them with Kevin Garnett, he'd still wouldn't do well.") Conversely, if Gary Coleman were the fifth member of the Lakers alongside Kobe Bryant, Shaquille O'Neal, Gary Payton and Karl Malone, he'd still have a decent rating simply by dint of his teammates. The flaw was corrected easily enough. Sagarin and Winston added a variable that took into account both the quality of the team and the quality of the opposition. If Player X is on a team that is usually outscored by 11 points a game, but is outscored by only eight points when he is on the court, his rating would be a plus-three. They've since tinkered to weigh "crunch time" more heavily than "garbage time," when the game's outcome is no longer in doubt.

WinVal often confirms the obvious. Garnett, the versatile Minnesota Timberwolves forward, was voted the NBA's MVP for the 2003–04 regular season. His WinVal rating was, not surprisingly, an off-the-charts +16, meaning that over 48 minutes he was worth 16 points more than the average player. Likewise, Shaquille O'Neal is a terrifically valuable player even on the flush-with-talent Lakers. Same with Kobe Bryant. Ron Artest, the Pacers' defensive stopper, has a strong WinVal rating mostly because the team surrenders more points in his absence. (See the chart on pages 142–143.)

There are, however, a number of counterintuitive results. According to WinVal, Allen Iverson is not a particularly valuable player and is a liability on defense. Huh? Doesn't he consistently lead the NBA in steals? "Yes," says Winston. "But you don't see the times he gambles for steals and misses and the other team scores. We think Eric Snow and Aaron McKie are more valuable to Philadelphia." WinVal also determined that Miami's Dwyane Wade was the best rookie in 2003–04, far superior to both Cleveland's celebrated LeBron James and Denver's Carmelo Anthony. Anthony's WinVal was −6: +5 for offense but −11 for defense. "*SportsCenter* shows his offense, his awesome dunks, not the times he gets beat on defense," explains Winston. WinVal was vindicated when Wade led Miami into the second round of the playoffs, playing while James and Anthony were on summer vacation.

As Sagarin and Winston have dissected small forests' worth of printouts, they've made a number of compelling "collateral findings." Plotting WinVal ratings on a graph, they deduced that the mean NBA player reaches his peak at age twenty-nine before his WinVal rating— i.e., his effectiveness—begins to drop. ("Unless it's a total no-brainer I'd be really careful to trade for anyone over twenty-nine," says Sagarin.) They determined that the San Antonio swingman Manu Ginobili is a terminally underrated player. But above all, they have concluded that most NBA coaches have no idea which lineups are effective and which are lousy. They single out the New York Knicks, who often played a lineup with a cumulative rating of −17 and rarely played one that was a cumulative +53. They also note that the Knicks have a tendency to lavish long-term contracts on players with WinVal ratings that are trending downward. "Owners say to us, 'What do we need your data for?'" says Sagarin. "We feel like saying, 'Gee, maybe if you didn't sign one bad guy at $30 million, you wouldn't ask that question.'"

WinVal would be a windfall for any basketball agent worth his alligator-skin loafers. Armed with the necessary—and easily manipulated—data, they could make a compelling case for their clients at the bargaining table. *Sure, Johnson's points and rebounds have dropped off since last season. But WinVal shows that the team performs 13 percent above the season average when he's on the floor. What are you rewarding here, individual statistics or winning?* But Sagarin and

Winston are in agreement about the subspecies of agents—"The scum of the earth," they say in concert—and have a pact that they'll never sell agents the data. They have been asked by financial services companies, hedge fund managers and risk arbitrageurs to devise similar programs, but, again, no dice. They're math nuts, but they're also basketball nuts. Half the fun rests in the fact that they're working for NBA teams.

In the summer of 2003, the pair made a WinVal sales call to Donnie Walsh, trying to get him to bite on the six-figure investment. The Pacers' CEO and consigliere, Walsh is an old school "basketball guy" so wrapped up in his team's fortunes that he divides his time during games between the action on the floor and stepping outside for a nerve-calming cigarette break. When Sagarin and Winston met with Walsh at his Conseco Fieldhouse office, they deconstructed the Pacers' dismal first-round playoff loss to the Boston Celtics. Unsheathing their WinVal data, they pointed out that the Pacers' lineup of Austin Croshere, Al Harrington, Ron Artest, Jermaine O'Neal and Jamaal Tinsley was terrific in Game One. The quintet's WinVal rating was a remarkably high +50. In the second game they were almost as dazzling, logging a +44. "What about Game Three?" Walsh asked, taking the bait. Winston and Sagarin gleefully pointed out that that particular combination of players was not again used for the rest of the series. The architecture of Walsh's face collapsed. Sagarin interjected. "Hey, don't blame the coaches. There's so much going on, no one could know this stuff off the top of their heads," he said. "Look, Donnie, basketball should be a data-driven business. When it's not, you're just costing yourself."

Sensing skepticism, Winston and Sagarin then turned their presentation to the value of Jermaine O'Neal. A star-on-the-make, O'Neal was about to enter his prime and the Pacers had to decide whether to lavish him with a "max money" deal, NBA-speak for a bank-busting contract bestowed on the team's designated "franchise" player under the parameters of the league's salary cap. In O'Neal's case, he stood to make slightly more than $125 million over seven years. Yes, O'Neal had been named to the All-Star team and his bona fides were established. But there were lingering questions about his true value as well as his maturity. (A quintessential postmodern moment: A few months earlier, as the Pacers were fighting for a playoff position, O'Neal spent a day shooting a Nike commercial in the Bronx and his charter flight didn't return to Indianapolis until 3:00 A.M. Not surprisingly, he played a subpar game that night.) Little things like that had made some of the Indiana brass gun-shy. Plus, even using the Monopoly-money standards of the NBA, $125 million is a colossal investment.

Sagarin and Winston treaded lightly but titillated Walsh with more data. Without much argument, they assumed that O'Neal, center Brad Miller and Ron Artest were the team's three best players in 2002–03. Without Miller in the lineup, but with Artest and O'Neal on the floor, the Pacers played at a +3 level. Without Artest in the lineup, but with O'Neal and Miller playing, the Pacers were a +4. The team's rating without O'Neal but with Artest and Miller? +14. "Bottom line," Sagarin said matter-of-factly. "He's not that key a player." Walsh looked on. Poker player that he is, it was hard to discern if he was fascinated by all of the empirical information in front of him. Or disdainful of the two mathematically inclined pinheads who were wasting his time trying to pollute art with science.

It may not be easy to get the typical sports franchise to spend $100,000 on a computer program. But Mark Cuban stands at the opposite pole of anything typical. In many ways, Cuban is the standard-bearer for the postmodern sports tycoon. Not just because he is young, outspoken, wears flip-flops and jeans and is brash enough to make fun of David Stern's nose hair or storm the court to tackle an effigy of a referee as an April Fool's joke. There was a time the owners of sports franchises were wealthy captains of industry (or their lucky scions) and treated the business like a toy. Cuban treats the toy like a business. For all his "new economy" casualness and self-styled hipness, he knows his team's finances better than any other owner. His Dell computer all but surgically attached to his lap, he is forever analyzing his team's spreadsheet, obsessing over value, efficiency and profitability. His preferred mode of communication is e-mail, which enables him to respond at thunderclap speed. Because every second counts, he doesn't use punctuation or capital letters in his e-mails.

Cuban's success has been predicated on a trinity of sports and technology and entrepreneurial spirit. As a freshman at Indiana University in the late '70s, Cuban had sweet-talked his way into Winston's graduate-level statistics class. (As Cuban put it, he wanted to take as many challenging classes as he could before he was old enough to get into Bloomington's watering holes.) At IU, he was an inveterate sports fan and rugby player; but he made extra beer money by giving (no joke) disco dancing lessons and selling powdered milk. A story that is now firmly embedded in Bloomington civic lore recounts that Cuban and some buddies opened a bar near campus named Motley's Pub that was a wildly popular haunt where undergrads with anything vaguely resembling valid identification could come in and drink until they sprained their bladders. That is, until Motley's held a wet T-shirt contest and the *Indiana Daily Student* ran a picture of one of the contestants who happened to be a sixteen-year-old already on probation.

Cuban finished up his coursework at Indiana and returned to his native Pittsburgh to take a bank job. While he liked puttering around on the office computer, he soon realized that he was entirely too manic to sit behind a desk. He returned to Bloomington to rejoin his running buddies but soon announced that he was decamping to Dallas to enter something called "the high-tech sector," selling something called "software."

Naturally, it was a marriage of sports and technology that made Cuban a billionaire before he turned forty. Already a millionaire after selling MicroSolutions—a program that linked companies' computers to networks—to CompuServe in 1990, Cuban grew frustrated when he couldn't listen to live simulcasts of Hoosiers games from Dallas. In 1994, he and another IU friend, Todd Wagner, rectified that by founding Broadcast.com, a means of using a newfangled contraption named the Internet to stream live radio through computers. One station signed up, then a few more. Within a year, there were eighty. Suddenly, anyone with a browser and Internet access could use Broadcast.com, and, with a few clicks, hear the sports, news, weather, even watch streaming video of a Victoria's Secret fashion show. In 1999, Yahoo! bought Broadcast.com for $5.7 billion. Cuban's take? Roughly $2 billion. In 2000, he bought the Dallas Mavericks for $280 million.

By all outward appearances, Cuban was just an aging frat boy who won the high-tech lottery and was living out a fantasy. Why did he have any better idea how to run a pro team than the Joe Sports Heads calling into the sports radio show and pontificating about utterly impractical trade suggestions? But the Mavs' success—both on the court and in bluebook value—has caused other owners to rethink their business model. In the decade before Cuban bought the team, the Mavs won barely 30 percent of their games, one of the worst records in all of sports. Since Cuban took over, they have been to the playoffs every year and, as important, have all sorts of cachet. Cuban's $280 million investment in 2000? Forbes recently valued the franchise at more than $400 million.

As an owner, Cuban's m.o. has been to pay for anything or anyone that can, conceivably, give his team an incremental advantage. The towels in the visitors' locker rooms are the fluffiest in the league. A few might get stolen, but the owner figures that players might remember that small touch when deciding where to sign as free agents. The Dallas players are each equipped with laptops to make communication as easy as possible. He sends his scouting minions all over the globe in pursuit of players. In a business where one extra victory is worth more than $100,000 in additional income, he figures those are sound investments. Predictably, he was smitten by WinVal—and not simply because he knew the founders personally. "It's not much different than stocks," he says. "If you find the right guidelines to help you buy and sell, you can make money. With the NBA, the investment to capture the data is tougher from a time and accuracy perspective than from a dollar perspective. But an investment of even $1 million can easily repay itself many times over by helping you more efficiently price contracts or make the right decision on a player. Again, it's not the only data element that goes into the decision, but all other things being equal, it can be the one that hopefully helps you make the right decision."

Cuban logs on daily to a personal WinVal account and accesses the data on his ubiquitous laptop. He tends to focus on his team, but he will also run spreadsheets on the opposition, particularly during the postseason, when Dallas will play another team as many as seven straight games. If a particular statistic catches his attention, he will print it out for his coaching staff. If the coaches aren't equal to the task of poring over spreadsheets during games, at least particular bits of information—a certain player performs better on the road, another shoots poorly against teams that play a zone defense—can float into their consciousness.

Cuban, though, is not beyond calling either Winston or Sagarin and asking them what to make of a particular piece of information. Says Sagarin, "The good executive looks at the data but balances that with a common theme, a human element, when he does interpretation. Is a player's WinVal average low because he is physically unable to play any better or jump any higher? Or is it low because he is in a contract year and is saving all of his energy for the offense and doesn't care if the team wins or loses? The answer might be the difference between giving him a big contract and not."

At Cuban's urging, Winston and Sagarin also use WinVal to chart the tendencies of the league's corps of referees. The thinking: If the Mavericks have empirical evidence that refs have certain tendencies, the players will adjust their play accordingly. Says Cuban, "When you see that one official hasn't called defensive three seconds in months, that's a flag that we can use. When you see that another calls charges three times the league average, and blocking three times less than the league average, you can tell the players to be careful. 'This crew is going to give the benefit of the doubt to the defense—so try to take the charge, but be careful on the other end.'" In his long-running crusade against referees—"The Cuban Whistle Crisis," as it were—he's been known to stare down an official and yell, "That call is going to look real good on your printout."

Cuban fancies himself a broadband owner in a dial-up world. But for all his tech-driven ways, for all his willingness to innovate and push the envelope, his team remains a work in progress—if not regress. The Mavericks endured a disappointing 2003–04 season and lost in the first round of the playoffs. It's clear that Cuban has become a "Rotisserie League owner" who makes too many data-driven decisions and, afflicted by a sort of managerial ADD, putters and tinkers too much. He consults reams of spreadsheets but fails to account for unmeasurable qualities like chemistry and compatibility. As Jerry West puts it: "There's such a thing as being too reliant on technology and statistics."

Indeed, not long after Sagarin and Winston made their pitch to the Pacers' brass and explained how Brad Miller was so indispensable given the WinVal data, he was traded to Sacramento, largely to clear cap space. As for Jermaine O'Neal, the young forward Sagarin and

Winston "proved" was not worth the big contract? A few days later, the team lavished him with a seven-year $126 million "max money" contract, making him the highest-paid player in team history.

WINVAL TOP 20

2003–2004 RANKED BY ZSCORE

(a combination of points and impact rating)

RANK	PLAYER	TEAM	POINTS	OFFENSE	DEFENSE	IMPACT
1	Vince Carter	TOR	13.1	10.5	-2.6	39
2	Shaquille O'Neal	LAL	12.2	5	-7.2	41
3	Kevin Garnett	MIN	16.3	5.3	-11	34
4	Hedo Turkoglu	SAN	12.1	7.7	-4.4	34
5	Manu Ginobili	SAN	11.9	11.7	-0.2	31
6	Brad Miller	SAC	13.2	4.3	-8.9	26
7	Yao Ming	HOU	7.4	6.8	-14.2	56
8	Andre Kirilenko	UTA	9.7	5.8	-3.9	25
9	Dirk Nowitzki	DAL	10.7	7.9	-2.8	22
10	Rasheed Wallace	POR	11.3	7.5	-3.8	21
11	Brian Cardinal	GS	6.8	3.6	-3.2	31
12	Carlos Boozer	CLE	7	4.3	2.7	25
13	Eddie Jones	MIA	6.2	5.2	-1	29

RANK	PLAYER	TEAM	POINTS	OFFENSE	DEFENSE	IMPACT
14	Kurt Thomas	NYK	6.8	2.4	-4.4	25
15	Baron Davis	NOH	9.2	7.8	-1.4	19
16	Ben Wallace	DET	7.5	-7	-14.4	22
17	Andre Miller	DEN	6.6	5.1	-1.5	22
18	Ray Allen	SEA	7.8	8.6	0.8	19
19	Nené	DEN	8.4	-1	-9.4	17
20	Zach Randolph	POR	5.7	6.4	0.7	23

8

RIVAL AGENDAS

THERE ARE NO HARD, FAST METHODS FOR GAUGING THE INTEN-sity of a rivalry. But when the game has its own special billing, odds are good that the feud is authentic. The annual Bloomington North–Bloomington South basketball game, nicknamed "The Catfight," fits the description. It's less an athletic contest than it is a civic event. For one night, anyway, both teams step out of the penumbra of the Indiana Hoosiers and hijack Bloomington's attention. Alumni from both schools come in droves, more than a few squeezing lumpen physiques into letter jackets earned in years past. In a rare departure from their usual ironic disaffect, students betray school spirit and ar-rive at the game wearing face paint and wigs, armed with megaphones and banners. The game almost takes on the dimension of a theme party: Fans cram into a warm gym on a cold winter night and pretend they're rooting for a small-town Indiana high school during the Eisenhower administration.

A little history: The city of Bloomington was incorporated in 1818, two years after Indiana became the nineteenth state in the Union. Settlers were culled from other parts of the state as well as from Ohio and Kentucky, lured by the hilly topography and abundance of salt springs. By 1820, Indiana University—first known as the State Seminary and then Indiana College—was christened a few blocks south of Bloomington's downtown area. Since then, it's been a college town, its identity and soul tied inextricably to the university. One often talks of town-gown relations between a community and the college situated there; but in Bloomington the gown more or less *is* the town. Bloomington's year-round population is on the order of 65,000; when school is in session, that swells to more than 100,000.

For the first 150 years of the town's existence, there was only one secondary school, Bloomington High School. In the early 1970s, BHS underwent a sort of mitosis. Roughly half of the students remained in the BHS facility—of no small significance, the BHS Panther mascot stayed as well—and became the student body of what would be called Bloomington High School South. The rest of the kids were shipped off to a new facility hard by State Highway 37 on the north side of town and were now students of Bloomington High School North.

An intense intra-city rivalry took little time to gestate. This wasn't just a case of two schools in one town vying for bragging rights. From the start, Bloomington North harbored an inferiority complex. The city's homegrown power brokers at the time were Bloomington High School alumni, and they continued supporting the Panthers, even if the school's name had changed. Bloomington South also lies directly across Walnut Street from the local newspaper, so, perhaps inevitably, there were claims of favorable press coverage. It didn't help that the paper's longtime Bloomington South beat writer is legendarily partisan,

not above banging his fist on the press table and vociferously express-
ing his displeasure when calls go against "his" team. What's more,
Bloomington South long had superior athletic facilities, including a
practice gym for the basketball team. Even the choice of Bloomington
North's team mascot—the Cougars—felt derivative. "There was always this sense that we were sort of Bloomington's stepchild," recalls
Terry Stotts, until recently the coach of the NBA's Atlanta Hawks and
a member of Bloomington North's graduating class of 1976. "It's one
thing being in IU's shadow all the time, but we felt like we weren't
even the most important high school in town."

Solidly middle class, Bloomington has no "wrong side of the tracks"
and the pockets of poverty are small. The bulk of the IU faculty families live on the east side of town, while the west side is decidedly more
working-class. Bisecting the town east-west would have created two
very different high schools; but cleaving it north-south created two
schools that, in many respects, are mirror images. Bloomington North
and South are roughly the same size, employ similarly qualified teach-
ers and have roughly the same makeup of students—a mix of faculty
brats, scions of professionals, rural kids and assorted other "townies."
According to the latest Indiana Department of Education Data, the
average SAT score for a Bloomington South student was 1079. At
North, it was 1077. All the symmetry has only served to fuel the North-
South rivalry. Which only stands to reason: A rivalry, by definition,
implies a certain level of parity. If one school were consistently superior, passions wouldn't be aroused. With so few material differences between the two schools, the playing field is level and excuses for losing
are hard to come by. It has all the right ingredients for friction.

What is by nature the most emotional regular-season game of the
year was freighted with additional significance in 2004. Among nearly
100 high school basketball teams in Indiana's Class 4A division, the
two from Bloomington were neighbors in the rankings polls, North at

No. 7 and South at No. 8. Bloomington South's team was endowed with quickness but lacked size and bulk. Bloomington North's had a bruising front line but wasn't going to win many sprints. A team filled with sophomores and juniors, South played with energy and the mix of insouciance and cluelessness that attends youth. North, stocked with seniors, had experience on its side but could play *too* deliberately at times.

Recent history was the final squirt of lighter fluid on an already combustible pyre. North was still licking its wounds from the stunning loss to South in the 2003 sectional finals. More than a trace of bitterness lingered from that debacle ten months earlier. On the other hand, barely two months previously, the Bloomington North football team had beaten Bloomington South, 38–20, for the first time in fifteen years.

As the teams warmed up two hours prior to the game and the North gymnasium was already crackling with 2,500 fans—the 4,200-seat capacity would be met midway through the jayvee game—the chants from the Bloomington South student section began. "Last year's sectional! (Tap, tap, tap-tap-tap.) Last year's sectional! (Tap, tap, tap-tap-tap.)" The Bloomington North student section responded in kind: "Cougar Football! (Tap, tap, tap-tap-tap.) Cougar Football! (Tap, tap, tap-tap-tap.)"

So often in sports there is an inverse relationship between the pregame hype and the quality of the subsequent game. On this night the game would live up to the considerable buildup. Bloomington North started slowly, as though fully conscious that this was their—and quite possibly McKinney's—last chance to beat South in a regular-season game. Every pass was made tentatively, every shot was laced with fluttery hesitation. The two guards, Josh Macy and Anthony Lindsey, committed a welter of ballhandling errors. McKinney even took the drastic step of inserting a freshman (a freshman!), Gant

Elmore, to stanch the flow of mistakes. By the end of the first quarter, Bloomington North had tallied as many turnovers as points. McKinney glowered at his players. "You. Must. Protect. The. Basketball."

Bloomington North played with more poise in the second quarter, but South's quick, sharpshooting guards helped push the lead to as many as 12 points. In particular, Drew Adams, a Bloomington South guard who had played for the North freshman team before abruptly transferring, was filling up the stat sheet. South led 29–20 at halftime. As the North players lumbered into their dressing room with shoulders slumped, McKinney let his team have it. For all his protestations that this was "just another game," McKinney desperately wanted to win. His charges knew it. That they were getting thoroughly beaten not just by South, but largely by a group of sophomores and juniors, infuriated him. He was, without putting too fine a point on it, as pissed off as he would be all season.

The coach generally traffics in the collective *you*—"You need to get after it better" is a favorite McKinneyism—letting the players internalize the message and decide for themselves whether they're included or exempted from the harangue. But this time, as McKinney addressed the team in the locker room at halftime, he fixed his gaze on senior swingman Josh Norris. His back pressed against the blackboard, McKinney was seething. "Josh, none of your teammates will say this, but I will. You're letting everyone down. You've barely scored. Your man is lighting you up. You've turned the ball over. What have you done for us so far tonight? I mean, what have you done to help the team win?" Norris stared back at McKinney, his mentor turned tormentor. A blank expression on his face, he nodded like a bobble-head doll. "Nothing," he answered sheepishly. The answer lingered for a few seconds, but, typically, McKinney ended on an up note. "You're the best athlete in the school, Josh. Now play like it!"

McKinney had coached kids from every conceivable economic

background, kids from a variety of countries, kids who were destined for the NBA and kids thrilled just to have made the varsity team. Getting through to Norris posed a unique challenge. Though he was a two-year starter on the basketball team and a fearless star safety on the Bloomington North football team, Norris was most passionate about his role on the Faith Team at his father's church.

A gentle man who speaks in a voice full of sincerity, Kim Norris is the head pastor of the Cherry Hill Christian Church, perched a block from the Indiana University football stadium. Kim describes his congregation of 250 members as "Pentecostal Charismatic" and his services are demonstrative, intense sessions filled with screaming, singing, healing, dancing and speaking in tongues. Josh's mother is an assistant pastor, as is an older brother. His uncle is an administrative pastor. Josh, usually clad in a dress shirt and khakis, plays bass guitar on a platform near the altar during Sunday-morning services and is a regular at Wednesday Bible study. "Faith is really the center of everything in our lives," he says. "A spirit-filled church is like the heartbeat."

The Pentecostal faith is often portrayed as one of Christianity's stricter sects, forbidding makeup, immodest dress and, in some cases, playing sports. But Kim's church has no dress code, and, as Josh puts it, "Some women cake on the makeup and that's cool." As for sports, basketball runs in the Norris family. Josh's grandfather, Woody Norris, played at Butler University for the legendary coach Tony Hinkle and then briefly for a professional club team in Indianapolis. Kim played basketball at Brebeuf, a prestigious Indianapolis prep school, during which time he was born again. Basketball always came easy to Josh, the youngest of four siblings. But so did football, baseball and just about everything else he tried. McKinney was hardly exaggerating when he characterized the kid as the school's best athlete. Quick and agile at 6'2", 180 pounds, he is a slashing player with a reliable midrange jumper but a preference for driving to the hole. The summer before his senior season, he had played on two AAU teams and more than held his own against some of the best high school players in the country.

Immersed in the jock culture that—even at the high school level—has seldom been confused with a bastion of rectitude, Norris nevertheless moves easily between the spiritual and the material worlds. After his final football game, a 32–28 loss to Mooresville, he walked dejectedly to Kim and the first words out of his mouth were, "Dad, I was cussing out there. Sorry." It all but goes without saying that he doesn't drink. "I just don't feel I need to be doing that," he says with a dismissive laugh. On a few occasions he pulled aside some of his wilder football teammates and tried to explain that there was a better way for them to lead their lives. His biggest vice? "Sometimes," he says sheepishly, "I talk about girls in a derogatory way."

At the same time, he likes to listen to hip-hop—"but not the new stuff, because it's kind of wack." The joystick on the PlayStation he got for Christmas is nearly worn out. He's one of the few players on the basketball team to have a girlfriend and is popular among his teammates, most of whom have accepted his invitation to attend a service at his Pentecostal church. "J-No is totally cool," says Bil Duany. "We respect where he's from—he respects where we're from."

Norris's faith can manifest itself awkwardly on the basketball court. Perhaps because he believes the game's outcome is ultimately in the hands of a higher power, he tends to lack a sense of urgency. He is a fluid athlete, one who can dunk with ease and play any of three positions capably. But there is an emotional vacancy to his game. As one of the Bloomington North assistant coaches explained: "He could be playing a pickup game at the park and he could be playing in the state finals and he'd approach the game the same way." Invoking, almost verbatim, the line that others applied to Duany, the coach added, "He likes to play. I'm not sure he likes to compete."

Now, with Bloomington North getting comprehensively waxed by its hated crosstown rival, McKinney was asking Norris to do just that—compete.

Even during halftime, the crowd was deafening. Police, in fact, had been summoned to bar the door of the North gym, determined to turn away late-arriving fans, thus preventing the place from becoming any more of a fire hazard than it already was. The crowd was announced at 4,200, but there were an additional 800 bodies standing three-deep, happy for an obstructed view of the court. Predictably, the crowd behavior was something other than decorous. During time-outs, North football players walked near the sidelines brandishing a banner reading "38–20," the score of the last North-South football game. South fans responded with a cheer: "North Football Sucks!" At one point, Duany was whistled for a charging foul, eliciting the chant of "Bullshit, bullshit" from the North quarters. "We don't do that at North," bellowed p.a. announcer Richard Ritz, a longtime French teacher at the school. Later in the game, South fans tore down the silk banners commemorating North's 1997 state title and runner-up finish in 2000.

Taking their cue from the teams' two head coaches, who sat together and talked cordially during the jayvee game, the players competed honorably. The action was physical, and no shot or rebound went uncontested. But there was scant trash-talking, no cheap shots, no technical fouls. In Indiana, it is up to the home team to supply the officiating, a practice that lends itself to abuse. Aware of the game's magnitude, McKinney requested the services of Bob Anderson and Ray Tebbe, two well-regarded veteran refs who had both worked the state championship game in prior years. Unlike so many other games during the season, the officiating on this night was beyond reproach.

Having been chastened by their coach, North scored two quick baskets after halftime. Jogging downcourt, North's center, Reed Ludlow, looked up at the scoreboard and shouted to no one in particular, "We got a ballgame!" The rest of the game was terrific theater, filled with thrusting and parrying, subtle momentum shifts but no team seizing command. Every possession—every dribble—was laden with significance. The shooting by Bloomington South, so hot in the first half, cooled off. Bloomington North, meanwhile, began to impose its height and size advantage. Duany helped bring the ball upcourt against South's fleet-footed defenders, but then camped near the basket, where he scored on fluid moves. Positioned on the other side of the goal, Kyle Thomas, the 6'4", 250-pound dreadnought, used brute force to score and rebound.

As for Josh Norris, McKinney's blistering halftime "pep talk" had its desired effect. Like medicine kicking in, he finally asserted himself, canning a series of short jumpers, flying through the lane to grab rebounds, slaloming through picks and screens to make sure that his man couldn't be liberated for an open shot. He scored seven points in the fourth quarter—none more important than a pull-up three-pointer that gave North its first lead of the second half.

With 11 seconds remaining, North ahead 47–46 and the fans on both sides in an absolute lather, South fouled Lindsey, North's senior point guard. Free throw shooting was Bloomington North's season-long bugbear, and now the team faced a one-and-one under the most pressurized circumstances. But the opposition could scarcely have picked a worse player to foul. Physically, Lindsey might have been the most limited player on the team. Neurologically, he was on another level. When he wasn't playing point guard, he was the star quarterback of the football team and the starting shortstop of the baseball team. He was a throwback; a stoic, hard-nosed kid, inoculated from pressure. In many ways he was cut from the same cloth as his coach. A slave to superstition, he had a number of pregame quirks that included eating a six-inch turkey sandwich from Subway. But once the games started, he was bloodless. Never more so than on this night.

After the ref handed him the ball, Lindsey took a few dribbles, at once alone and in company of thousands. He gave the rim a Medusa stare and then casually hoisted a shot as if it were an exercise no more taxing than retying an unlaced shoe. Studded with a bit of spin, the ball passed through the center of the basket. Swish. The second shot was dead-solid perfect as well. On the bench, McKinney's face was frozen, registering nothing that could be called emotion. "That," McKinney said flatly afterward, "is what a senior is supposed to do."

On Bloomington South's final possession, the North defenders ricocheted off screens—much as they had failed to do in the loss to

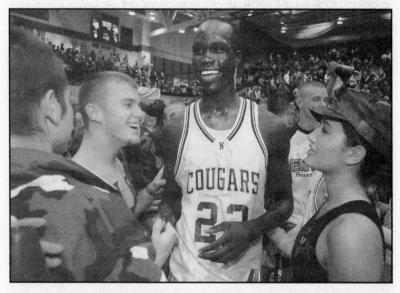

Center of attention: After Bloomington North dramatically defeated crosstown rival Bloomington South, Bil Duany was mobbed by classmates. (*Chris Howell/Bloomington Herald-Times*)

Decatur Central a few weeks earlier. A desperate three-pointer fell well short as the final horn reverberated through the din, marking an end to what was, by any measure, a thoroughly enthralling high school basketball game. North 49. South 46. The two coaches couldn't even bridge the ten yards between them to shake hands before North students spilled onto the floor and mobbed the players.

McKinney was uncharacteristically giddy in the locker room. He tried mightily to suppress a grin as he spoke to the team. "I'm really proud of you guys," he said, swiveling his head to make eye contact with each player. "You impressed me tonight. You really did. That was a heck of a basketball game and a heck of a win for the seniors." He then joked that he was sure he would pick up the next day's paper and read a quote from South's coach, J. R. Holmes, downplaying the game's significance and asserting that the real game would be the teams' looming encounter in the sectional. "Let me tell you something," McKinney said calmly. "The real game will be in March. But tonight was a real game too." The players cheered.

In another era, members of the winning Cat-fight team would be feted like victorious gladiators. They were the alpha males who stalked the school halls, dated the prettiest cheerleaders and didn't suffer from any of the adolescent awkwardness that beset the rest of us. When they won—and often when they didn't—there would be postgame parties at the home of some upperclassman whose parents had made the fatal strategic error of leaving town that weekend.

That was then. Bloomington North players are no longer accorded this exalted status, certainly not on the level of my day, when players signed autographs for fellow students. (The irony, of course, is that today's players are far superior to forebears who were deified.) Having been hit with a burst of diversity, the Bloomington North student body has become less stratified and there is no sign of a Columbine-esque ruling class of jocks. It's clear that proficiency in sports—or, for that matter, mere adequacy—is no longer a prerequisite for popularity. Sure, most of the current North players flirt with the prettiest girls and seem to have achieved the apotheosis to the "popular crowd." But it's because they're engaging or smart or felicitous. And not simply by dint of their playing on the basketball team.

Several times during the season, it struck me that the Bloomington North team was like a Chip Hilton book with more multicultural characters. On this night, there was no victory bacchanalia. After the game, the players showered and most zipped over to Taco Bell for a late dinner. A few headed home, but six seniors converged on the Duanys' modest home for the customary triathlon of eating, hanging out and competing at PlayStation2. "Just the usual chillin'," Norris explained with a shrug, almost apologetic that he couldn't describe a bawdier postgame celebration. One by one, they eventually crashed on various pieces of furniture in the Duanys' living room.

For all the modern-day hand-wringing about defiled innocence, kids growing up at warp speed, underage drinking, social coarsening, teenagers' inflamed libidos, adolescent shiftlessness and selfishness, you wonder if the Chicken Littles haven't exaggerated it all a bit. Here it was, a Friday night in basketball-mad Indiana, hours after a half-dozen seniors had just won a momentous rivalry in front of 5,000 fans. The game would get front-page coverage in the next morning's Bloomington *Herald-Times* and be the subject of chatter all over town for weeks to come. And these handsome, vigorous, college-bound eighteen-year-olds celebrated their victory by . . . throwing a slumber party.

9

THEY GOT NEXT

LIKE MOST EVERYONE WHO GREW UP IN SOUTHERN INDIANA, I always considered Purdue the Evil Empire. The school's ominous, brooding color scheme, black and gold, reinforced this image. The team's nickname—the Boilermakers—was appropriately cold and industrial. Even the school's basketball venue, Mackey Arena, always seemed to resemble nothing so much as a dungeon, a bleak, subterranean space uniquely suited for the hated rivals.

I was, at once, heartened and disappointed to learn that Purdue isn't so bad after all and that Mackey Arena is in fact a warm place that crackles with energy on game day. On this afternoon in the dead of winter, Mackey was the site of a high-stakes college basketball game between Purdue and Minnesota. The pregame tableau was fairly typical for a Big Ten battle. The band belted out enthusiastic numbers, the silly, faintly sinister Boilermakers mascot roamed the court, abnormally peppy cheerleaders smiled. A well-fed tuba player belted out the Boilers' fight song, "Hail Purdue." The smell of grease from the hot dog rotisserie wafted through the narrow concourse.

In the tunnel near the court's entrance, the Purdue team clustered, piled their hands and yelled "Together" in unison. More than 10,000 fans—many of them young families; many of them silver-haired seniors—had braved the cold and filled the seats. In keeping with its pregame ritual, the home team bounced giddily off of an inflatable train at the entrance to the court. As the players emerged from the tunnel, the fans' yelling rose in a crescendo. "Ladies and gentlemen, the defending Big Ten Tournament Champions," the public address announcer intoned. "Your Purrrrrrrdue Boyyyyyyyyyyyyy-lerrrrrrrrrrrrr-mayyyyyyyy-kkkkkkkkkers."

And with that, Katie, Carol, Emily, Lindsey, Beth, Indi, Sabrina, Erin, Ashley, Aya, Erika, Sharika and Shereka took their place in the layup line.

With respect to matters of gender, Indiana has never been an especially progressive state. It's not quite "Get your biscuits in the oven and your buns in the bed" backward. But will it ever be confused with a feminist hotbed? Um, no. At the Indianapolis 500, the unofficial slogan is not "Gentlemen, Start Your Engines" but rather "Show Me Your Tits," a catchphrase that is embroidered on all manner of shirts, caps, buttons and, naturally, beer cozies. The Little 500 bicycle race, the cornerstone of what Indiana University grandiosely calls the "World's Great College Weekend," added a women's race a few years ago. Before that, coeds competed in the Mini 500, a demeaning tricycle race held on the eve of the men's race.

Basketball was similarly late to the party. Textured and rich as Indiana's hardwood history is, it is almost exclusively a male preserve. Oscar Robertson and Larry Bird and Damon Bailey and Steve Alford and Shawn Kemp and Rick Mount and George McGinnis may be Indiana icons, treading on fame since before they were able to drive. Their female counterparts? Until recently they didn't exist. There are thousands of Hoosiers able to tick off the names of every Mr. Basketball since the honorific was first presented in 1939. Ask the same fans to name a single Miss Basketball—which was christened only in 1976—and, invariably, they'll draw blanks.

For years, fans called in sick from work and curtailed family vacations to catch the local boys' games. The following evening, the girls' team would take the same court and play in front of a few dozen family members and close friends. And this extended to college too. For decades, the Indiana University men's team has been the toughest ticket in the state. More than 15,000 fans crammed into Assembly Hall to watch the team *practice.* Their female counterparts—often offering *free* admission, no less—were lucky to draw 500 spectators. Allegedly, Bob Knight once snorted that players on the IU women's team had better not leave any menstrual blood on the practice floor.

But the wheels of change have started spinning, and today, Indiana has become a citadel for women's basketball. The Indiana Fever of the WNBA has a loyal support base. The women's teams at both Purdue and Notre Dame have won NCAA titles within the past five years. The Boilers have 7,500 season-ticket holders. At a time when the boys' high school game is losing some of its appeal and cultural significance, the girls' high school game thrives. From North Vermillion to Fort Wayne, girls' games are so well attended that they often get to use the gym on the weekend while the boys play midweek. Even at Bloomington North, the girls' team, the so-called Lady Cougars—an afterthought in my day—draws hundreds of fans. The team's best player, Whitney Thomas, the younger sister of Kyle Thomas, has attracted interest from major Division I programs. "The women's game," says Purdue's coach, Kristy Curry, *"matters."*

This surge in popularity is easy to grasp. For hidebound types, those purists who feel as though basketball has deserted them, that everything noble and beautiful has been bleached out of the game in its current incarnation, the women's game offers a refuge. All those eternal basketball verities are in evidence. Those basketball gerunds so many of today's NBA players find so altogether unpalatable—hustling and passing and helping on defense and moving the ball—are the coins of the realm in the women's game. The backboard serves a purpose in addition to supporting the rim. No less than John Wooden agrees. "If you want to watch the purest form of basketball, don't watch the guys," he maintains. The women's game, the iconic coach says, "is the only true basketball left."

The women don't dunk, don't get from half-court to the basket in two dribbles, and don't retrieve rebounds with their elbows at rim level. But there exists an unwritten contract between the players and the fans. Here's the deal: The women play the "right" way, throwing bounce passes, blocking out, competing as if their very salvation rides on the outcome of every loose ball. They won't talk trash (not much, anyway), neglect playing defense, or cruise around in customized $120,000 cars with $50,000 worth of stereo equipment, a pistol in the glove box and a joint in the ashtray. Over the past three years, more than a hundred basketball *arrivistes* left college early or bypassed it altogether to enter the NBA draft. Not a single WNBA player has charted this course—the WNBA even has a rule expressly forbidding it. What's more, if you want to catch a game in person, you won't have to break into your 401(k) to afford seats. In return, the fans overlook the botched layups and the questionable artistic merit of the games, the sports bras that poke out from under the jerseys bearing hyphenated names on the back.

*I*t was a collision of factors that helped popularize women's basketball to the point that two professional leagues were born in the late '90s. (The soulful ABL was unsentimentally crushed by the ironfisted WNBA and folded after barely one season.) Title IX, the landmark legislation banning sex discrimination at institutions receiving public funding (i.e., college athletic departments), was enacted in 1972. By the mid-'90s, a generation of girls who had grown up in an era in which women's sports were funded—if not altogether socially accepted—had come of age. What's more, in the early '90s, ESPN, the all-sports television network to which males are attached via a psychic umbilical cord, began to televise and promote the Women's NCAA Final Four. Network executives will sheepishly admit that the decision was owed to the fact that the women's tournament was cheap and abundant programming. Still, it did wonders for legitimizing the sport and creating stars. The 2004 women's championship pitting the University of Tennessee against the University of Connecticut and their incomparable star, Diana Taurasi, was the highest-rated televised basketball game—male or female—in the network's history.

But ultimately the revolution was won at the local level. It was Lisa Leslie in California and Sheryl Swoopes in Texas and Chamique Holdsclaw in New York obliterating stereotypes, performing with enough flair and grit to prove that you can have a pair of X chromosomes and still be a hell of a basketball player. In Indiana, the Joan of Arc figure was Stephanie White. It was the late '80s, and as a girl in West Lebanon, a town of 800 off the I-74 exit ramp near the Illinois border, White was a self-described "tomboy." She raced dirt bikes, played baseball—"Not softball," she's quick to point out, "baseball"—and her knees were perpetually scraped. But it was the basketball goal outside the family's home that had a magnetic pull on her. Problem was, she couldn't find a girls' team (much less a girls' league) to join, so in fourth and fifth grade, she played for a boys' team at the YMCA. Any funny looks she received subsided when she took on all comers in H-O-R-S-E and more than held her own in the games.

On Sunday nights, White played in adult pickup games with her father at the high school gym. More often than not, she was the best player on the floor. Kevin White, who worked for Quaker Oats, needed no one to tell him that he had a prodigy on his hands. Kevin put Stephanie through a battery of complex drills and schooled her in the finer points of basketball: planting at the free throw line when running the fast break, boxing out bigger opponents, stepping out on a pick and then recovering defensively. Finally, as an eleven-year-old, she joined a sixteen-and-under AAU team. Five years younger than her teammates, she was the star.

Like countless boys in the state, White worshipped the standard holy trinity of basketball players: Michael Jordan, Larry Bird and Steve Alford. "I don't think it was anything conscious," she says. "It's just that women weren't publicized. I knew that Purdue had a good team, and I guess that I knew about Vicky Hall. But they weren't on television, you didn't really read about them in the paper, people didn't really go around talking about them."

By the time White entered high school, word of her basketball virtuosity had seeped out. Once lucky to draw a few dozen fans, the girls' team at Seeger Memorial was suddenly packing their bandbox of a gym. By White's sophomore year, fans were purchasing jerseys with her name on the back. As her coach, Tom Poll, told *Sports Illustrated*, "When people who had never seen a girls' game saw Steph play, they decided they liked girls' basketball and came back for more." White was not only Indiana's Miss Basketball, but the national high school player of the year in 1995.

It wasn't just that White played well. What made her a transcendent figure in the state was that she played "right." One game, she would put on a shooting exhibition and drop in 66 points, an Indiana high school girls' record. In another, she would fight to grab 25 rebounds. A game or two later, she would set up shop on the perimeter and distribute 18 assists. Her gender notwithstanding, she was the embodiment of "Indiana basketball," a deadeye shooter who rebounded and passed and played defense and wasn't above swabbing the court with her body to pursue loose balls or leaving skid marks after taking charging fouls. White was conferred what was, at the time anyway, high praise in the Indiana basketball lexicon: she was the Damon Bailey of the girls' game.

When White decided to stay close to home and play for Purdue, it was an end in itself. She figured that after she graduated she might play overseas or do a little coaching. But a college scholarship had always been the carrot. Then, even before White piloted Purdue to the 1999 NCAA title, there was another career option. In the summer of 1997, the NBA launched a sister league for women, the WNBA. "It's hard to explain how motivating that was," says White. "All of a sudden, you have the chance to play professional basketball for a living. In the United States. I remember the first week of the season I called some of my teammates when the games were on television and we were all like, 'Is this for real?'" In the summer of 2004, she entered her fourth season with the Indiana Fever—she not only plays in the WNBA, she didn't even have to leave the state.

Meanwhile, a new generation of stars followed the path blazed by White. Katie Douglas was a high school dynamo in Indianapolis, starred for Purdue and now plays for the WNBA's Connecticut franchise. Kelly Komara, a sharpshooting guard from Schererville in Indiana's northwest corner, was crowned Miss Basketball in 1998, headed to Purdue and played professionally. Shyra Ely, an athletic interior player from Indianapolis's Ben Davis High and Miss Basketball in 2001, spurned Purdue for the University of Tennessee and is a star in the making. The following season, Shanna Zolman of Syracuse, Indiana, broke White's career high school scoring record and joined Ely at Tennessee.

The latest in the lineage is Katie Gearlds. A 6'1" strawberry blonde with a smile all but welded to her face, Gearlds may well have overtaken White as the most celebrated high school player in Indiana girls' history. As a senior, almost single-handedly, she led Beech Grove High School to the Class 3A state title, scoring in excess of 30 points a game and winning Miss Basketball. As a freshman at Purdue in 2003–04, she was a regular in the rotation and, on a team stocked with seniors, she transitioned seamlessly from high school to the top-notch college ranks. In the course of the season, she played every position except center, and averaged 10.6 points a game. "No one on the team makes better decisions," says Curry, the coach. "She's only a freshman, but she is already a complete player."

In stark contrast to White less than a decade earlier, Gearlds never had to look hard to find a game. She was traveling around the Midwest with various AAU teams when she was barely out of elementary school. Before Gearlds had entered Beech Grove High she had already pierced the public consciousness. Curry recalls that when she was offered the head coaching job at Purdue in April of 1999, one of her first orders of business was signing Gearlds as a recruit. The player was in eighth grade at the time. By the time she was a freshman in high school, scouts from college teams would attend her games.

During high school, Gearlds was a bona fide Indiana celebrity who soon grew desensitized to seeing her picture in the morning paper and couldn't go to the nearby Greenwood Park Mall without being hit up for an autograph. A sign welcomes visitors to Beech Grove, "Home of Katie Gearlds"—"I make my parents honk at it every time we drive by," she says—and her face adorns billboards. Fans who missed her high school games could get a rundown on www.katiegearlds.com. Her exalted status continues in West Lafayette. She lives not in the dorms but in an apartment with teammates. She eats most of her meals not with other undergrads but at a special training table for athletes.

None of this is to suggest that Gearlds is a pampered diva or lacks a sense of self. Quite the contrary. She is unfailingly polite, reflexively modest, conscientious about both her academics and her faith. Though Purdue usually plays home games on Sundays, she takes pains to make it to Mass at St. Thomas Aquinas Catholic Church in West Lafayette. On both her shoes, she's scrawled the twin messages "Phil 4:13" ("I can do all things through Christ who strengthens me") and "Have Fun." Gearlds is of an era when gender doesn't much matter. A basketball star is a basketball star is a basketball star. And in Gearlds's case, she is accorded the status and fringe benefits—and also the pressure— that in the past had gone only to schoolboy stars.

It may be Purdue's Coach Curry who provides the most striking example of just how far the women's game has come. Curry came to Purdue in 1999 after her predecessor, Carolyn Peck, led the Boilermakers to the NCAA title and then bolted for a well-paying WNBA job. Then a thirty-two-year-old assistant coach at Louisiana Tech, Curry emerged from a national search to land the job. Her grandfather and father were both longtime coaches in Louisiana. Now it was her turn to run a program. Including income from shoe contracts, summer camps and other bonuses, her salary pays her well into six figures. Given the economic landscape and the current market, it's a reasonable salary. But for perspective, it wasn't that long ago that the women's coach at the University of Texas, Jody Conradt, signed a contract for $19,000, leading to this headline in the next day's paper: "Woman earns a man-sized salary."

Perhaps the ultimate sign of changing times: Curry's top assistant is her husband, Kelly. Married in 1996, the Currys were both assistants on the Louisiana Tech staff. When Kristy was offered the Purdue job, Kelly figured he wasn't going to commute from the bayou to West Lafayette, so he accepted his wife's offer to work for her. A basketball "lifer," Kelly recruits and scouts and helps his wife break down game tape. He is also tasked with the majority of the childcare duties that attend the couple's two young daughters, Kelsey and Kendall.

Kristy is quick to volunteer that "he wears the pants at home," suggesting that some might find it emasculating for a man to work for his wife. But both Currys insist that it's the best of both worlds. They even use their arrangement as a recruiting tool to underscore the importance of family. "I also feel that I'm showing them that you can have a demanding career, be a good wife and be a mother all at once," she says. "It really is all possible."

*T*he differences between the men's and women's games are not particularly nuanced. The most obvious contrasts are physiological: There are few women on the planet who resemble Shaquille O'Neal, a seven-foot, 360-pound behemoth. Likewise, there are few women who are endowed with vertical leaps so prodigious as to obviate the

Girl power: As a freshman, Purdue guard Katie Gearlds
lived up to considerable hype. (*Tom Campbell*)

need to learn to shoot properly. Plus, no woman in the WNBA has the
physical superiority to be a complete ball hog. A player who stands
6'1" would be the tiniest of point guards in the NBA; in the WNBA
she could be an effective post player. Blame or credit evolution.

But the deeper divisions between the men's and women's games are
cultural. Even the most talented, sought-after female players aren't
imbued with a sense of entitlement. There are no shadowy street agents
combing middle school gyms for prospects. No shoe companies lav-
ishing big bucks on high school programs that wear their brand. No

coaches excusing their star player's antisocial and/or criminal behavior. No college boosters slipping players cash under the table and no college coaches pressuring faculty members to pass their stars so that they stay eligible to compete. At the college level, female basketball players graduate at 77 percent, nearly twice the rate of their male counterparts. At last check, no WNBA players were beating their spouses, or brandishing guns, or birthing children they had no intention of ever seeing again. In short, the material gains that have stained the male model do not taint the women's game. Not yet, anyway.

Quite apart from the fact that female players won't make the police blotter, the WNBA's superior collective moral character is apparent on the court. Theirs is a democratic game, marked by ball movement and integration. "In the men's game, it's like one guy makes all this money, he's going to say, 'I'm the Man,' and demand to shoot twenty-five times a game," says White. "That would never happen to us."

Whether the contrast owes simply to the absence of big bucks or to innate gender differences makes for a spirited debate befitting a late-night discussion on the back of a team bus. Are women inherently more inclined to sharing and teamwork and forging a sense of community? Are males—particularly the alpha males who excel at sports—more prone to aggression? Discuss this with WNBA players and most will assert that women are simply wired differently. Says White, "The female psyche and personality, it's just different. That's not to say we don't get frustrated or make mistakes, but we're not going to go knock someone out. Just saying it sounds ludicrous. It's not who we are. And even if it was, we couldn't get away with it." Put another way, there is no female equivalent of the lazy refrain "Boys will be boys."

A function of just how many fans have been alienated by the NBA's poverty of morals and wretched excess, the WNBA makes the wholesomeness of its employees a major selling point. Players are required by league rules to make a dozen unpaid appearances in the community each season. League rules also mandate that two players from every home team stick around after games to sign autographs and mingle with the crowds. Come game time, players stand with dignified posture for the national anthem, and seldom complain about officiating (which is often abysmal) or talk trash. After the final horn, both teams quaintly line up and quaintly exchange high fives in the manner of Little Leaguers. The Indiana Fever even have a rule banning cell phones in the locker room because, as center Natalie Williams explained, "they are rude." If one of the WNBA's 150 or so players gets arrested over the course of the season, it's shocking. "We know we're in a position to make or break this league, and we want this to be successful so little girls can keep dreaming about being WNBA players," says White.

The WNBA, however, has to grapple with an entirely different set of issues. For one, its allegiance with the NBA is a Mephistophelian bargain filled with philosophical and practical tensions. When the WNBA launched in 1997, it was immediately able to tap into the NBA's preexisting relationship with television networks and blue-chip sponsors such as Coke and McDonald's. Teams generally play in NBA arenas, flush with fancy scoreboards, state-of-the-art training facilities, practice gyms and cutting-edge video technology. "We wouldn't have started the league under any other model," says former WNBA president Val Ackerman. "It's been a great advantage for us to capitalize on the NBA's infrastructure." In the case of the Fever, the team plays in Conseco Fieldhouse, perhaps the world's premier basketball venue. The players can avail themselves of the Pacers' video equipment and training facilities and have siphoned the services of assistant coaches. White spent hours last summer working out with Chuck Person, a Pacers assistant coach and longtime NBA player. (Pointedly, the Fever is not allowed to use the Pacers' team plane or the team's plush locker room.)

But the access comes at a price. Like a venture capital firm that underwrites a start-up business and then demands the majority of voting seats on the board, the NBA wields considerable influence over its "sister league." Salaries are predetermined by the league with virtually no free agency or leverage in contract negotiation. Though the players have a union, it has been cowed by the NBA's omnipotent commissioner, David Stern, who has intimated that if the players stage a walkout, he'll simply pull the plug on the league. The WNBA severely restricts players' off-court income—during the season, when their marketability is highest, they are prohibited from endorsing products and companies deemed to conflict with the league's sundry corporate sponsors. "It's like everything we're allowed to do and not allowed to do has to be cleared by the league first," says Sheryl Swoopes, long one of the WNBA's top stars. "That gets old, real fast."

For feminists, in particular, this is all unsettling. The WNBA markets itself as an outgrowth of Title IX, a pioneering league predicated on female empowerment and gender equity. (This sentiment has only intensified with the folding of WUSA, the professional women's soccer league.) Yet reminders abound that the WNBA is a junior sibling indebted to—and riding the coattails of—its male counterpart. Who knows for sure whether the sponsors are genuinely supportive of the WNBA. Or are they there because of the NBA's considerable leverage? Symbolically, the season can't begin until the boys vacate the gym. Many teams' names are even derivative of the preexisting men's franchises. Some cynics go so far as to suggest that the WNBA serves as a "loss leader" for the NBA, luring a new demographic of basketball enthusiasts not with hopes that they will one day buy tickets for the Fever or Liberty but rather for the Pacers or Knicks. That the WNBA steadfastly refuses to share financial information doesn't exactly douse cynicism.

The league's low wages are also troubling. According to the league's Players' Association, the average salary is less than $50,000 for the four-month season. The league claims it's close to $57,000, as it factors in the $850,000 allotted in year-end bonus money for sixteen stars the league handpicks. Regardless, using either estimate, it's insufficient to sustain players for the entire year. So after each season, there's a mass migration overseas, where players supplement their WNBA incomes—often dramatically—by playing in South Korea or Poland or Israel or any of a dozen other foreign countries with women's pro leagues. Other players moonlight with more plebeian jobs. White, for instance, spent off-seasons as the girls' coach at Logansport High School near Lafayette and as an assistant coach at Ball State in Muncie.

Talk about any of a number of issues with WNBA players and, to a person, the women are insightful and engaging. When the subject of wages comes up (and inevitably it does), hot emotion replaces cool analysis and there seems to be a remarkable blindness to economic reality. An unprofitable league can hardly break the bank on salaries. "I think it's one not necessarily good effect of Title IX," a female executive of the WNBA's New York Liberty told me. "These girls came of age in an era of federal funding for women's sports, so it never occurs to them that all the empty seats and the [feeble] TV ratings have a bearing on how much we can pay them."

Still, the players are, understandably, torqued when they compare their salaries to the wages of team coaches and executives. For instance, WNBA coaches generally make between $150,000 and $200,000, which may not be extravagant by the standards of professional sports but is more than double the salary of the teams' highest-paid players. Another example: The Washington Mystics, allegedly the league's lone profitable team, pay lionized University of Tennessee coach Pat Summit a "consulting fee" of $200,000. The players are quick to make the point that they're not asking for the stratospheric salaries of their NBA brethren. But it's hard not to sympathize (at least a little bit) when they point out that if *every* player in the league were given a 50 percent raise, it would cost owners less than the $5 million median salary for *one* NBA player. Another arrow in their quiver: The NBA disgorges 55 percent of gross revenues on salaries. In the WNBA, salaries make up just 16 percent of gross revenues.

A far thornier issue that hobbles the league is sexuality. For reasons both intellectual and visceral, the WNBA has become a rallying point in local lesbian communities. Some teams—the L.A. Sparks and the now-defunct Miami Sol—have recognized gay women as a core demographic and marketed to them accordingly. Other teams have been less comfortable. At a New York Liberty game, ushers confiscated a banner brandished by a group calling themselves "Lesbians for Liberty." The group responded by staging a "kiss-in" during time-outs. Likewise, the Sacramento Monarchs declined to permit a group called the "Davis Dykes" to be listed on the scoreboard with other groups that had bought a block of tickets. (Management later apologized.)

As for the Fever, there is a conspicuous contingent of lesbian fans. The cognoscenti on press row recall the time a Fever player overthrew a teammate with an outlet pass, prompting a fan to yell, "Not so butch next time!" There are also a good number of straight families. This is all part of the strange alchemy of a fledgling sports league, but it is nevertheless a source of tension. Traditionalist ticket-holding families have complained to management about the presence of lesbian fans. Yet when the team takes pains to market itself as "family-friendly," it is clearly code that makes some lesbians feel unwelcome. According to one team source, the Fever high-ups constantly walk a tightrope, addressing the concerns of families without alienating the homosexual fan base.

The women's game is bereft of dunks—there's been only one jam in the WNBA's eight-year history, a fairly meek throwdown by L.A.'s Lisa Leslie—but the league is steadily, if slowly, conforming to the same trends that beset the men's game. Every season the game gets a little bit faster, a little quicker, a little flashier. When the league's supporters speak of the "vast" qualitative improvements and the "rapid advancement" in play from season to season, they are referring to the heightened athleticism of players, to an increase in plays suitable for replaying on *SportsCenter* highlights. In the spring of 2004, a high school phenom named Candace Parker broke a sign-of-the-times barrier when she beat the male field and won the dunk contest at the McDonald's game. "There's definitely more freestyle," says White. "Is it ever going to get to the point where there are reverse slams and showtime? Probably not, especially in Indiana. But things are starting to change and the game is getting faster."

White knows this firsthand. She is sufficiently talented to earn a roster spot in the highest level of basketball league—so she really *isn't* the female Damon Bailey. But her basketball fate has traced a similar arc. She was untouchable in high school, a star in college, but she doesn't even start in the WNBA. Her modest athleticism and a deeply ingrained set of basketball values that militates against "flash" conspire to work against her. That's readily apparent watching the Fever, a team whose best player, Tamika Catchings, is everything—athletic, urban, decidedly "New School"—that White isn't.

The daughter of former NBA journeyman Harvey Catchings, Tamika might well be the prototype for the next generation of female basketball star. As a young girl, she had a hearing disorder that required her to wear hearing aids. While she learned to read lips and forced herself to speak in class despite a speech impediment, the experience had a profound effect on her personality, at once deferential and intense. This is a player who responded personally to each of the 200 colleges that recruited her. When Van Chancellor, the Houston Comets' colorful coach who oversaw the last U.S. women's national team and 2004 Olympic team, once barked to Catchings that "great players get back on defense," she wrote him a note thanking him for deeming her a great player.

Despite this veneer of deference—insecurity, even—Catchings competes so inveterately that coaches have had to pull her aside and tell her to "dial it back." In one game, she was running upcourt when her contact lens popped out of her eye. She picked it up, put it in her mouth and played on, unable to see out of one eye, until the next time-out. "Bar none, she is the most fierce competitor I've ever coached," says Nell Fortner, the Fever's former coach. "No one likes to lose, but Tamika *hates* to lose." That much was apparent at the 2003 WNBA All-Star Game when Catchings, who played well despite wearing a cumbersome mask to protect her broken nose, broke down in tears afterward. Tears at an All-Star Game? Her team had lost and she felt "like crap."

Telescoping Catchings and White at a Fever practice, it's easy to see that one is an All-Star, the other a run-of-the-mill player. It's like comparing dial-up Internet service to DSL: they do the same thing, just at appreciably different speeds. They compete with comparable intensity; even in practice, they both orbit the court like windup toys and wear a mask of fury during scrimmages. It's not just that Catchings wins every footrace for a loose ball, and leaves White in the dust on defense. In the game I watched courtside against the Liberty, Catchings dropped 31 points in 36 minutes and grabbed a half-dozen rebounds. She scored her points on a battery of shots that included a thirty-five-foot just-for-fun heave as the final buzzer sounded. White made one of her five attempts and was often a liability on defense. "Catchings, friggin' Catchings," muttered New York's coach at the time, Richie Adubato. "I've never seen a player like her." Adubato, who once coached the Dallas Mavericks and the Orlando Magic, never qualified his remarks by adding "for a woman."

Players in the mold of Catchings will soon consign to dinosaur status players in the mold of White. One day soon, evolution will be such that superior athleticism will be an occupational requirement—not merely an indispensable asset—for playing in the WNBA. Perhaps defense will become optional, and behind-the-back passes and hubristic one-on-one moves will displace team basketball. There have recently been some brawls during games. One former player for the L.A. Sparks, Latasha Byears, has effectively been blackballed for her alleged role in a sexual assault on a teammate. Perhaps it's just a matter of time. Perhaps the heightened stakes and exposure will cause the women's game to cultivate the same underbelly and wayward moral compass that plagues men's basketball.

But today, the immediate future of the women's game is redolent with promise. Throughout Indiana—from the inner city of Gary to the rural rec centers of Evansville—more girls than ever are shooting the rock. Girls' AAU teams are abundant. Even after the scourge of class basketball, attendance at the high school girls' state tournament is nearly double what it was a generation ago. But the real earmark of progress is an acceptance that has seeped into the culture. It's okay to wear a basketball jersey with the name "Catchings" or "White" on the back. The girls' basketball star is no longer marginalized, as White was. The tomboy now doubles as homecoming queen and Miss Popularity. The football team turns out en masse to cheer on the girls' team. Girls who are varsity athletes, without thinking twice, proudly clad themselves in letter jackets.

As White drives home from games, no matter how she felt she played, no matter how thin her line score might be, one sight reflexively causes a smile to register on her face. "I look out the window and it doesn't matter what time of day it is," she says. "In a driveway or in a park or even on a goal attached to a tree, I can see little girls shooting buckets. How cool is that?"

10

A TOWN WHITEWASHING
ITS IMAGE

IT WAS HARD TO GET WARM, EVEN AS THE HEATERS HUMMED on the bus transporting the Bloomington North team to Martinsville, half an hour up State Road 37. A searing cold conspired with a slicing wind to peg temperatures well below freezing on this, the last Friday in January. Outside the bus, there was so much snow it looked as though all of southern Indiana had, not unlike a tenderloin sandwich, been battered in white breading. Their teeth chattering even as they were swaddled in multiple layers of clothing, the players were making the short trip to play one of their most spirited rivals. Even more so than usual, the bus was shrouded in silence.

Though Martinsville is the adjacent town north of Bloomington, it is a million interplanetary worlds away, divided by far more than some cornfields and the Morgan-Monroe County Forest. A heavily traditional, heavily religious, working-class town of 12,000 or so, Martinsville has a long and textured basketball history. John Wooden is a native son who was baptized at the First Christian Church, starred on the high school team in the 1920s and briefly coached at the school before moving on to bigger and better things. A saint of a man, now in his nineties, Wooden still has memories—as fond as they are vivid—of growing up in Martinsville. His introduction to the game came when his mother fashioned a "ball" made from a sock stuffed with rags and his father affixed a tomato basket—"We didn't have peaches in Indiana," he explains—to a wall on the family barn. "I remember when you could leave your shop unlocked during a Martinsville game and you wouldn't have to worry about getting robbed because you knew everyone in town would be at the gym," he says. Though he's lived in Los Angeles for decades now, Wooden returns to Indiana at least once a year and even keeps a book of poems by Hoosier James Whitcomb Riley next to his bed. His hometown hasn't forgotten him, either. A life-sized wax rendering of Wooden sits in the lobby of Martinsville High. "They made me look old!" he jokes.

Martinsville's next-most-famous native son is Jerry Sichting, a former star at Purdue and a Boston Celtics teammate of Larry Bird. Speaking of Bird, across the highway from Martinsville High School, sits Larry Bird Ford, surely the only car dealership in America that features a parquet floor and two regulation-sized basketball goals in the showroom. "If there's a town that's crazier about basketball," says Wooden, "I sure haven't seen it."

And yet a passionate devotion to basketball is only part of Martinsville's civic distinction.

*I*nasmuch as one of the state's top teams can face a "must-win" predicament prior to the state high school tournament, the Martinsville game presented one for Bloomington North. Since returning from Christmas break, McKinney had continued his reflexive downplaying of his team's potential, but it was getting increasingly difficult to take his demure evaluations seriously. The Cougars had sprinted to an 11–1 record and reached the fifth spot in the state's poll. Had it not been for the one sloppy period of basketball against Decatur Central, Bloomington North would have been undefeated and perhaps the top-ranked team in the state. The team had figured out how to camouflage its deficiencies—most notably footspeed at the guard position and, exasperatingly, free throw shooting. The front line was big and agile, the team shot well and the core of seniors had a sixth sense for doing what they needed to win.

In the twelfth game of the season, Bloomington North played terrifically against Wallace High, a tough school in Gary, Indiana, the city with the country's highest homicide rate eight years running. Wallace's team drove more than three hours to get to Bloomington. In a pell-mell game that resembled summer league basketball, Bloomington North shredded a full-court press, scored dozens of fast-break baskets and won 89–51. Given that a high school game comprises four eight-minute quarters, putting up 89 points is no small feat. Oddly, Gary's fan section—made up almost exclusively of African-Americans—cheered raucously for flashy plays, with little regard for which team made them. At one point Anthony Lindsey, of all players, executed a nifty juke to get by a defender. Even the Gary jayvee players behind the bench whooped and hollered. "Man, that was fun," exulted Bil Duany, who turned in a triple double of 25 points, 15 rebounds and

12 assists. "I don't know how Coach McKinney felt, but as players, that was great, running and gunning like the NBA."

Any delusions of grandeur—or, for that matter, delusions of mediocrity—exploded the following night. McKinney warned his minions that Indianapolis's Perry Meridian High School had a dangerous team. Perry's gym could make for a difficult environment and the team's star senior forward, Brandon Ray, was "a horse" of an inside player. Blinded with hubris, Bloomington players saw that their opponents had a modest 5–6 record, rolled their eyes and chalked it up to a psychological gambit by their carping coach. Hey, they were 11–1. High school kids being high school kids, they didn't just believe they were good. They believed they were invincible.

Bloomington North was palpably flat to start the game against Perry Meridian. They had no synchronicity, but managed to stay close for the first few minutes. Then the deluge. The team appeared to have suffered a sort of collective amnesia, forgetting how to execute the simplest maneuver. And on this night there would be no recovered memory. Shots didn't just fall short of their intended target but sometimes missed the entire basket fixture. Passes landed in the stands. Dribbles ricocheted off knees and out of bounds. Block-outs were forsaken. So, more generally, was defense. Perry Meridian shot torridly, but it hardly mattered. A consortium of decent middle school players would have beaten Bloomington North on this night. Testament to just how symbiotic a game basketball is, the players' futility was infectious. As soon as one player looked hopelessly adrift, they all were.

For a drought spanning 13 minutes—nearly half the game—Bloomington North didn't score a single point. In the third period alone, Perry Meridian outscored the visiting team 17–0, part of a 28–0 run. For good measure, the Cougars also surrendered runs of 9–0, 8–0, 7–0, and 6–0. Whatever had overcome Linda Blair in *The Exorcist* seemed to have befallen the Cougars. When the game came to a merciful end, the final score was 67–28. Just to repeat: The score was 67–28. Again: 67–28. And it *still* managed to understate the game's lopsidedness. For perspective, Ray single-handedly outscored Bloomington North, 32–28.

In the press seats, Brian Reitz, the team's young and perspicacious beat writer for the Bloomington *Herald-Times*, scrambled to place the loss in some historical context. He concluded that it had been the most comprehensive defeat of McKinney's tenure and one of the worst beatings in school history. "It was just one of those nights when everything went right for us and everything went wrong for them," summarized Perry Meridian's coach, Mark Barnhizer, with an exaggerated shrug. But to McKinney it was more than a cosmic accident. His team had faced adversity for the first time all season and they didn't merely fail to meet the moment; they beat a hasty retreat. How had Bil Duany, the team's best player who was performing a season-long audition for a big-time college program, managed to attempt just three shots? How had Bloomington North missed six of seven free throw attempts? How had they played so scared and betrayed so little pride? "I wish these guys had the passion, the same will to win that I do," McKinney lamented. "Maybe I just need to a do a better job accepting that they don't."

McKinney was humiliated. Personally, it represented a failing. He felt that the team's ill-preparation, its inability to self-correct, its mystifying absence of courage, reflected poorly on his coaching. Though he had made up his mind that this would be his last season, this defeat and the abiding sense of shame it occasioned all but cemented the decision. Truculently proud, he cringed at the thought that his colleagues would see the box score revealing the kind of margin that suggests that the players had quit. In some deep recesses of his mind, he wondered whether this wasn't some sort of personal Waterloo. He didn't sleep the night after the game, and by Monday morning he was still so dispirited that he walked the 3.1 miles in the snow from his home to school to clear his head. The profound embarrassment shared shelf space with feelings of fear. Getting drilled by 40 points is the type of demoralizing loss from which some teams never manage to recover.

McKinney gave little thought to shuffling the lineup and benching some of the starters. Everyone had been equally abominable. He banished any notion of reconfiguring the offense. The sets were singularly tailored to the skills and weaknesses of the players. Unless the guards magically improved their footspeed or Kyle Thomas developed a reliable jump shot overnight or Duany added thirty pounds of muscle within the week, there wasn't much to change. The "country asskicking," as Hoosiers call it, at Perry Meridian wasn't a failure of execution; it was a collective mental meltdown. At Monday's practice, McKinney made only elliptical, oblique references to the game. "How did that make you feel the other night, guys?" he asked. The players didn't answer, thinking it was a rhetorical question. But the coach was genuinely curious: Did they care?

One benefit of basketball's galloping schedule of games: It provides little time to dwell on defeats or bask in victories. Bloomington North had four days to prepare for its next game, a throwdown against the rival Martinsville Artesians. The game marked the six-year anniversary of one of the ugliest episodes in the history of Indiana basketball. While the wounds were no longer raw and open, they weren't completely healed either.

When Bloomington and Martinsville squared off in 1998, both were among the top teams in Indiana. The Cougars were the defending state champs and Martinsville had its best team in years, decades maybe. The buildup for the game was enormous, and by the time the North bus pulled up to Martinsville's gym, the intensity was nearing a fever pitch. As the multihued Bloomington North team deboarded and entered Wooden Gymnasium, a small group of Martinsville students yelled witticisms that allegedly included "Here come the darkies." Others were said to have swung their arms and mimicked the sound of apes.

The junior varsity game was hotly contested, so much so that a Bloomington North player was *bitten* by a Martinsville defender. Not surprisingly, accounts vary, but when one of Bloomington North's players pointed to his teammate's arm and appealed to the referee, a Martinsville player purportedly responded, "Stop whining, baboon." Another Martinsville junior varsity player had scrawled the letters KKK on his shoes. By the time the varsity game started, the current of tension was palpable and fans on both sides had a feeling the situation would turn uglier still.

Early in the varsity game, Kueth Duany, North's best player, was looking downcourt when a burly Martinsville forward elbowed him in the stomach. It was a blatant cheap shot, and Duany walked to the side of the court to retch. As Duany was doubled over on the sideline, a fan yelled, "That nigger's spitting on the floor! Get his ass off the floor!" Incredulous, Clay Ludlow, a player in the junior varsity game, spun around to see where the slurs were originating. "I'll never forget it," he says. "It was an old lady, maybe eighty years old."

Kueth Duany eventually went back into the game, a thriller that went to double overtime before Martinsville prevailed, 69–66. As the Bloomington North team departed, the Martinsville faithful again circled the bus. "You're not safe in this town," a Martinsville fan reportedly yelled. A Bloomington parent responded by elevating his middle finger and shouting, "You people are all alike. You'll never change." Julia Duany still shakes her head and has to collect herself when she replays that night. She was high up in the stands, and while she was unnerved to see her son doubled over in pain, she was more outraged by the tenor. "It was so nasty," she says. "I wanted to run on the court and say, 'This game cannot go on until we talk about this! We are all human beings. We all bleed red blood and breathe the same air. We have to get along with each other!'"

In keeping with his "speak softly" code, McKinney had hoped to handle a combustible situation internally. Bloomington North's principal at the time, Sue Beerman, was having none of it. The school filed a complaint with the Indiana High School State Athletic Association and Beerman was not shy about generating media coverage. "Somebody had to say, 'Enough is enough,'" she told me at the time. Meanwhile, the Bloomington North girls' team, captained by Kueth Duany's sister Nok, was scheduled to play a sectional game the following week at Martinsville High. More as a form of protest than in fear of reprisal, the team stayed home, thus ending their season. "These girls—some of them were seniors who might never get to play again—would rather stop playing basketball than go back to Martinsville," says Julia Duany. "That tells you a lot."

Martinsville's athletic department had already been in hot water. The football team, in particular, had a reputation for dirty play. After receiving Beerman's complaint and viewing tapes of the game, Conference Indiana, the league to which Martinsville and Bloomington North belong, promptly banned Martinsville from hosting conference games for one year—a punishment that ended up costing the school in excess of $50,000 in lost revenues. It remains the most severe penalty in the history of Indiana high school sports. The Indiana High School Athletic Association placed Martinsville on probation for a year and warned that a future incident would result in the suspension of the entire athletic department. The athletic department was also ordered to develop programs to foster sportsmanship and racial tolerance.

Martinsville was livid. Now a premed student at DePauw in Greencastle, Indiana, Clay Ludlow has classmates from Martinsville who still maintain that nothing happened that night. There are others who concede they heard a few racist remarks—or had heard enough in the past to assume safely that some were hurled at the visitors from Bloomington. But most Martinsville residents felt that they had gotten a raw deal. Quite apart from feeling as though the punishment vastly outstripped the crime, they held a deeper sense that the media-savvy, politically correct liberals from the college town were flexing their muscles at Martinsville's expense, eroding what little power they had. It wasn't just sporting events they were losing. It was a culture war.

To many in Bloomington, the incident confirmed what they had long suspected: that Martinsville was a racist hotbed. For as long I can remember, stories abounded of African-Americans getting harassed and threatened as they drove through that town. Bloomingtonians were instructed to fill up their tanks before heading to and from Indianapolis—stopping for gas in Martinsville would mean risking trouble as well as putting money in the Ku Klux Klan's coffers. "K-K-K, K-K-K," we would cheer derisively when our teams played against Martinsville. And this perception was widespread. Now an assistant coach with the NBA's Minnesota Timberwolves, Jerry Sichting recalls that when he went to Purdue and his black teammates got wind of his hometown, he had to convince them that no, he did not wear a sheet over his head after practice.

In truth, there is scant evidence to suggest that the reputation is accurate. Some incidents may have been rooted in truth but were greatly embellished in the retelling. Other stories were simply myth. Yes, Martinsville was the site of a Ku Klux Klan rally in the 1920s, but that was no singular feat. The KKK was a popular movement throughout the state at the time. In fact, Indiana was so supportive of the Klan that roughly one in three white males was a member, and the Grand Dragon, D. C. Stephenson, became one of the wealthiest and most powerful men in Indiana. "I am the law in Indiana," he remarked at the height of his power in the early '20s. (In 1925, Stephenson fatally bit a woman while raping her aboard a train; he was convicted of second-degree murder and the power of the Klan in Indiana dissipated as quickly as it had flared up.)

A rumor I can recall hearing while I was growing up is that most of the Klan's highest-ranking personnel hailed from Martinsville. This is absolutely bogus. There were—and, lamentably, are—Klan leaders from Indiana, but the majority are from the northern half of the state. In another instance, critics cited a racist incident that occurred in Martinsville, conveniently neglecting to mention that it happened in Martinsville, Tennessee, not Martinsville, Indiana. And the urban (rural?) legend that families in Martinsville tied ribbons around their mailboxes and gates denoting Klan membership? Unequivocally false.

But it almost didn't matter. Martinsville's image was that of a fertile basin for intolerance and hate. Incidents like the Bloomington North game only reinforced a perception that was fast becoming reality.

The unseemliness that Martinsville residents still call the "Bloomington North thing" was far from the only time African-Americans were made to feel less than welcome in a Hoosier gym. Indiana's generally rich and proud state history is mottled by episodes of racism that include lynchings and the popularity of the KKK in the 1920s. Perhaps, then, it's not surprising that the treatment of black players and schools represents the biggest mar on an otherwise proud basketball past.

Black players from decades past talk of hearing the "N-word" at games and getting jobbed by corrupt officiating. But as is often the case in matters of race, the worse sins are not of commission but omission. Even a cursory study of Indiana's basketball history quickly reveals that it is largely a white history, its romanticized teams and players all looking and playing a certain way. For the first half of the twentieth century, black players, teams and coaches were thoroughly marginalized from Hoosier Hysteria. Even as they entered the mainstream, and eventually came to figure prominently, too often they were overlooked. As in many states, Indiana's high schools were segregated until the *Brown v. Board of Education* decision in 1954. Until 1942, teams from black high schools were not even allowed to play in the state high school tournament. As early as the 1920s, representatives from black schools tried, to no avail, to plead with the Indiana High School Athletic Association. Arthur Trester, a notorious autocrat who ran the IHSAA in the '20s, employed the most tortured logic, asserting that since the black schools were not public schools open to all students, he was powerless to include them. Why, employing the same "logic," the all-white schools weren't similarly ineligible he never quite made clear. (Ironically, the award presented annually to the Indiana high school basketball player who shows superior "mental attitude" is dedicated in Trester's honor.)

When black schools were allowed to compete, the playing field— to mix sports metaphors—was still far from level. For instance, Indianapolis's Crispus Attucks High School, the largest black secondary school in the state, did not have a suitable gym, so every game was a road game. The Attucks roster was filled with talented players, most notably Oscar Robertson, but often failed to get a fair shake from the local referees. Phantom foul calls and bogus violations were the order of the day. Robertson recalls that the team's coach, the legendary Ray Crowe, would tell the team, "We need to win by at least ten points, because that's how many the refs will give them." When the Attucks team won the state title, they were hardly feted like kings, as the Milan players were the previous year. Though the '55 Attucks team was Indianapolis's first championship team in fifty years, the city was mute in its appreciation. In his outstanding book *Hoosiers: The Fabulous Basketball Life of Indiana*, author Phillip Hoose quotes Robertson's father recollecting his son coming home by 10:30 that night. "[Oscar] didn't say anything for a while," Bailey Roberston, Sr., recalled. "Then he said, 'Dad, they really don't want us,' and he went to bed."

Arguably the best player in Indiana high school history, Robertson led Attucks to the state title again the following year. It marked the first all-black team in the country to win an integrated championship in *any sport*. In the years after, he starred at the University of Cincinnati and became one of the truly elite players in NBA history, a stylish, versatile guard who once averaged a triple double in a single season. Many rank Robertson behind only Michael Jordan and Magic Johnson as the best backcourt player ever. In his life after basketball, he's become a successful businessman in Cincinnati, the principal owner of three industrial companies. He has been happily married to his wife, Yvonne, for nearly thirty-five years and recently donated his left kidney to his daughter. Through it all, he has never forgotten the stinging treatment he received playing high school ball in Indiana a half century ago. "At the time, you're a kid and you don't know differently," he says. "It isn't until later that you realize how bad it was."

When it is suggested that his legacy might have been grander had he not left the state to attend college or had he relocated to Indianapolis after his retirement, he clucks disapprovingly and implies that he would gladly have attended Indiana University had he felt welcome there. "I wanted to be a Hoosier. I grew up in Indiana. I was Mr. Basketball in Indiana. Coach McCracken didn't want anything to do with me. I went to Cincinnati, and I guess the rest is history." He told me that he is particularly embittered by how folks recall the triumph of Milan but ignore the feat of Attucks the next year. "People say, 'Oscar, they like Milan because they were the underdogs.' You know what I say to that? '*Underdog?* What could be more underdog than an all-black school in Indianapolis in the 1950s? The problem is that black people don't write the history books.'"

The situation has improved—steadily if slowly—but some echoes still remain. There are still suggestions that players who don't conform to a certain style are accorded second-class status. To wit: Shawn Kemp, Bonzi Wells, Zach Randolph, Walter McCarty and Calbert Cheaney make for a pretty good starting five. Each starred in college and went on to a fruitful NBA career. Each is an Indiana product, yet none was conferred with the Mr. Basketball honor. Mysteriously, none occupies the same floor of the state hoops pantheon as less accomplished counterparts whose style of play and physical appearance more closely conformed to the time-honored archetype of a Hoosier. "I would hear the N-word at games and, honestly, I didn't even consider it racist. I thought of it as crazy basketball fans doing anything to get on the other team," says Kemp, a star at Elkhart's Concord High who would go on to become an NBA All-Star before sabotaging his career with drugs, alcohol and overeating. "That stuff never bothered me. But I never felt like I got my due. That bothered me much more." Muncie's Bonzi Wells, late of the NBA's Memphis Grizzlies, bristles when he reflects on his treatment by the Indiana basketball institution. "Do you know who beat me out for Mr. Basketball?" he asks. "Bryce Drew. I like Bryce and he's a nice player, but c'mon, man."

Likewise, black teams tended to get short shrift. The 1991 state final pitted Gary Roosevelt against Indianapolis Brebeuf. It was a classic matchup pitching North versus South, an inner-city public school against an esteemed Indianapolis prep school, Purdue-bound Glenn Robinson against Indiana-bound Alan Henderson, both of them currently in the NBA. The contest was well played and fiercely competitive. But the game, won by the all-black team from Gary, is seldom discussed—much less romanticized—by most fans. Except in pockets of the state's black community, where it's considered one of the most significant games in Indiana history.

Writing in the *Journal of Sport History,* Troy Paino, an Indianapolis native and professor of history at Minnesota's Winona State University, goes a step further and makes the case that the proliferation of black players is largely responsible for basketball's diminishing cultural importance. "The growing influence of inner-city African-Americans on the game—arguably more than any other factor—[makes] it increasingly difficult for Hoosiers to use the game as a culturally cohesive force." He is also among the many critics who cite the rise of black players as the catalyst in the switch to class basketball. "No one writes about it, but there is a huge racial angle to the story," says Gary Donna, publisher of *Hoosier Basketball* magazine. "Basically, these small white schools wanted a way to be winners again. They figured the black schools are all the big 4A schools so they wouldn't have to face them."

*I*n Martinsville, ripples from "the Bloomington North thing" quickly became waves. The conflation of hot-button topics—race, class, kids, sports, competing values—turned an incident at a high school basketball game into a full-fledged *cause célèbre.* A reporter for the *Indianapolis Star,* who had been at the game and not reported anything unusual, a week later wrote a withering critique of Martinsville. *The New York Times* sent a writer to town, as did ESPN's fledgling magazine. (I wrote a small, but fairly scathing, account for *Sports Illustrated.*) Soon Martinsville's students were inured to the sight of satellite trucks parked near school grounds. The media flogging, coupled with the Conference Indiana penalty, engendered a siege mentality among the locals. Understandably perhaps, the town closed ranks, their distrust for outsiders deepening by the day.

Then, after the media had turned its attention elsewhere and the news cycle had passed, something remarkable happened. Slowly, but unmistakably, leaders emerged from silence. There was no sackcloth and ashes, no torrent of mea culpas. But the message was clear: We need to confront this. "It was a sense of 'Enough is enough.' We needed to get out of reactive mode and take some responsibility for our reputation," recalls J. Christy Wareham, a local minister. "It wasn't, 'Hey, let's apologize.' But it was, 'Hey, this has gone on long enough and we're not going to shut up this time. We want a relationship with the outside world. Let's figure this thing out and do it in a way so we don't cast ourselves as victims.'"

Wareham was an instrumental figure in the sea change. Amiable and outgoing, he had recently made the unlikely relocation from Los Angeles to Martinsville. While he was, by his own admission, something of an outsider, his status as a popular minister gave him clout. He and some of his congregants at Martinsville's First Presbyterian Church founded PRIDE, an acronym for People Respecting Individuality and Diversity in Everyone. Its ranks swelling, the group invited African-American speakers to address civic groups, coordinated fishing trips to a local lake with a group of kids from inner-city Indianapolis and set up hospitality tents at Martinsville High School football and basketball games.

Meanwhile, there were civic initiatives aimed at luring more African-Americans to relocate to Martinsville. (According to the most recent figures, only eleven of the town's 11,698 residents and none of the high school's 1,507 students were black.) Other Martinsville churches followed suit, holding joint services with African-American churches in Indianapolis. There were personal instances of soul-searching as well. Mary Ann Land, a member of one of Martinsville's seminal families, wrote a heartfelt letter to the Martinsville *Reporter-Times*, conceding that her grandfather was a bigot and asking the community to examine itself and its values.

Better still, there was reciprocation. John H. Stanfield, then the chairman of the African-American Studies Department at Indiana University, made what Wareham calls "extremely generous overtures" to Martinsville. Leaders from black churches in Indianapolis spoke favorably of Martinsville after visiting the town. "One day, I hope us coming to Martinsville, or you coming to Indianapolis, will not be newsworthy—I hope one day we can just be Americans," Delbert Watts, Sr., a black pastor from Indianapolis, told a Martinsville reporter. "This great nation has learned to die together. Now we need to learn to live together."

When Martinsville fans sat in the stands at road games, they heard the whispers and the wisecracks about cross-burnings and "forgetting your white sheets." It stung and it hurt, and at times it took every fiber of their being not to react. But, of course, it also provided some a sense of how it felt to be judged in advance. Says Wareham, "People came back from games and said, 'Just because I was born here doesn't mean I'm like that. How could they think that without even getting to know me?' And you're thinking, 'Exactly.'"

There was also healing at Martinsville High School. Tim Wolf, Martinsville's well-regarded coach, started his tenure at the school the same year McKinney took over at Bloomington North and the two have always had a certain kinship. In the wake of L'Affaire Martinsville, Wolf and McKinney spoke to each other almost daily about how they could improve the relationships between the schools and their teams. Away from the glare of the media, they quietly brought their players together for a meal at one of the Subway franchises Wolf owns. "It wasn't a big thing," says Wolf. "It was just about getting the kids to feel more comfortable around each other." Meanwhile, the Martinsville athletic department took steps to be more hospitable to all visiting teams, dialing back an obnoxious sound system and forbidding students from "greeting" visiting buses.

The shift was also made easier by several coincidences. While not overtly racist, the Martinsville newspaper spoke in a stridently conservative editorial voice, perceived by some as mean-spirited and less than tolerant of outsiders. Several years ago, the paper came under new ownership and a new editor/publisher, Jim Kroemer, was installed. Under Kroemer, the newspaper is decidedly more mainstream and takes pains to include more viewpoints. Moreover, the longtime coach of the football team accused of hyperaggressive play retired. His replacement was an affable, even-tempered former player who just happens to be his son.

Most significant, the murder of Carol Jenkins was solved. In 1968, Jenkins, a black, twenty-one-year-old encyclopedia saleswoman from Rushville, Indiana, was murdered in Martinsville. The crime had gone unsolved; conventional wisdom was that it was a Klan-related murder and Martinsville's civic leaders had swept the investigation under the rug. Jenkins's murder was Exhibit A when critics of Martinsville attempted to paint the town as racist. In 2000, the state police, acting on an anonymous tip, reopened the investigation. Eventually, the daughter of the killer told investigators that as an eight-year-old girl, she was in the backseat of a car when her father, Kenneth Richmond, fatally stabbed Jenkins with a screwdriver. It was a harrowing account and the killing indeed appeared to have been racially motivated. But there were also exhales in Martinsville. Richmond was not a local, but rather an Indianapolis native driving through town. There was no evidence of Klan involvement. As the town's mayor, Shannon Buskirk, put it at a news conference: "It's a great day for Martinsville. [Maybe now] people will say, 'Maybe they're not as bad as they've been

192 o *L. JON WERTHEIM*

labeled.'" (Richmond, who had a long history of mental illness, died shortly after his arrest, before the case could come to trial.)

Change, of course, seldom occurs at thunderclap speed. Just as some still cling stubbornly to the belief that Martinsville is an intolerant backwater, some of the town's residents do little to extinguish that impression. Following the September 11 attacks, the city's assistant police chief, Dennis Nail, acting as a private citizen, wrote an irate letter to the *Martinsville Reporter-Times* that read in part:

> I get offended when I can't show my patriotism because it might offend someone from around the world that landed here to go to school. It offends me when I have to give up prayer in school. Once again because it might upset Hadji Hindu or Buddy Buddha. I don't believe the founding fathers were either of these. Truth is, they were Christian and believed in the one true God of the universe. Our culture is uniquely American unlike any other on the face of the earth. Our country was founded on Christian principles.
>
> Talk about majority. When I look around I see no Mosque, or fat, bald guys with bowls in their laps. I see churches. I'm offended when I turn on a television show and without fail a queer is in the plot just like it's a natural thing. America put God in the closet and let the queers out. When the planes struck the twin towers I never heard anyone utter, "Oh, Ellen." I heard a lot of, "Oh, my God." Now we want to pull God off the shelf, rub His head and expect a miracle.
>
> Offended? Well, get over it, because it's time the dog started wagging the tail. Let's not be led around by a minority of weirdos and feel gooders. I, for one, am tired of it.

At a city council meeting a week after the letter was published, Nail received a standing ovation. At the end of the meeting, one councilman asserted that "99 percent" of his constituents supported Nail. In an age in which information and images fly freely and rapidly, making it increasingly hard to be an insulated community, Nail's remarks and their reception made it onto the pages of the *The New Yorker* and *The New York Times*, among other media.

But this time, there was local backlash. A group of Martinsville citizens circulated a petition condemning Nail. And though, predictably, it went unremarked upon by the national media, several letters to the editors ran the following week rebuking Nail. "I don't know how much of it is attitudes are changing and how much it is a sense that we needed to show that this is not who we are," says Wareham. "But I think it goes both ways. Other people have looked at Martinsville, taken the time to meet people without passing judgment, and they've seen that just because someone might be conservative, just because they might be religious, it doesn't mean they're a racist. To me it's funny to think that a basketball game was the catalyst for all this."

On this polar Friday night, almost six years to the day after the catalytic event, Martinsville bore not the faintest relation to the "hotbed of hate" portrayed by the media. When the Bloomington North bus maneuvered around snowbanks and disgorged the players in front of the school, there was no fomenting mob of students. Instead, the players were greeted by a genial police officer who directed them to the visitors' locker room. As McKinney and the assistant coaches followed the players through the halls, past the wax likeness of Wooden, a man selling tickets rose from his seat. "Good luck, Coach," he said, extending his hand. "Heard you've got some fine kids this season." Caught somewhat off guard, McKinney managed a smile and muttered, "Thanks." Before the players reached their locker room, another well-wisher, this one a middle-aged woman wearing a satin Martinsville

Artesians jacket, cut them off. "Guys, if you're looking for the locker room, it's around the corner and there are pop machines back by the pay phones. Good luck tonight!"

It was clear on this night that Martinsville is another small town in which the importance of high school basketball is diminishing. To be sure, the brutally cold weather didn't help, but the stands were thinly peopled when the jayvee game kicked off at 6:00 P.M. The student section, once so vocal, hardly recalled Duke University's Cameron Crazies. There were a few earmarks of a bygone era. The post-prom committee was selling "delicious homemade cinnamon buns" six for $3.50 and prepubescent "Little Arties" played abbreviated games on the floor during halftime. But overall there was an unmistakable absence of electricity. Recalling what Wooden had told me, I couldn't help think that no local merchant would've wanted to leave his store unlocked on this night.

In the locker room before the game, McKinney didn't mention the Perry Meridian fiasco. Arms akimbo in front of his sweater, he looked down at his shoes and quietly, but sternly, exhorted his aggregation "not to play scared." The possibility of a repeat of the Perry Meridian game was still very much on his mind, but the team had practiced hard during the week, which he regarded as a heartening sign that perhaps his troops weren't apathetic or pride-deprived after all.

In step with the times, the Artesians took the court to AC/DC's ominous "Hell's Bells" (so much for the pep band) while a tape of boxing announcer Michael Buffer intoned, "Welcome to the main event!"—a curious audio selection given the school's recent history. Then it was game time. Faster than one could say déjà vu, Martinsville drained a pair of three-pointers and held a 6–0 lead. Dating back to the second half of the Perry Meridian game, Bloomington North had now been outscored 39–10. His eyes narrowing with concern, but otherwise betraying little emotion, McKinney smacked his hands together. "Come on, now." Predictably, it was Lindsey, the Cougars' most gutsy player, who put an end to the skein. He took a pass from behind the three-point line, barely elevated, and launched a shot laced with backspin that flitted through the net. The crowd quieted, and Bloomington North started to play with ballast. Lindsey was just warming up. Barely a minute later, he hit another three. Then another. And another as the period ended, giving Bloomington North a 17–15 lead.

As the team strutted to the huddle, they projected confidence that they had emerged from whatever trance they were in during the previous game. Lindsey continued his hot shooting, and he had help. Bil Duany played authoritatively and threw down a series of violent dunks. Kyle Thomas played superb defense on the Artesians' best player, Milos Ciric, a 6'7" three-point-shooting center who—another sign of the changing times—came to Martinsville as an exchange student from Serbia. Positioned near the free throw line, Josh Norris picked apart Martinsville's zone defense, either dishing to Duany, kicking a crisp pass out to a shooter on the perimeter or taking the ball to the rack himself. By halftime, Bloomington North held an eight-point lead and pulled away comfortably, 67–56.

It was a sweet win. McKinney agreed with the observation that it was probably the best game his team had played to date. Bloomington North had shot well, passed well, defended well. It was a complete game, free of the lapses that tend to plague even the best teams. And given the circumstances—playing a heated rival following a thoroughly humiliating defeat—it meant even more. "I don't tell them this often, but I was proud of our guys tonight," McKinney said. "It shows something that they got the job done coming up here in a hostile environment."

But in truth, the environment wasn't hostile at all. The competition on the floor was fierce, but it was honest with no traces of bad blood or dirty play. The officiating was unimpeachable. The fans were not merely civil but downright gracious—at one point Duany threw down a dunk so electrifying that two kids in the Martinsville student section exchanged a high five in admiration. Writ small, it was a tableau for everything right and virtuous about high school sports. After the game, McKinney sat contentedly on the empty bleachers as his team showered and dressed in the locker room. A steady stream of Martinsville fans congratulated him. "Well done, Coach," said a fiftyish man in a wool Indianapolis Colts hat. "Your boys play hard," he added, perhaps the highest praise in the Indiana sports lexicon.

Cast as sworn enemies six years ago, the two basketball programs had been bracketed by fate, and now there was even a certain bond between the teams, between the schools, perhaps even between the communities. There was still a chasm. But, trite as it sounds, one left the gym that night feeling that maybe it wasn't unbridgeable after all.

11

AGENT OF CHANGE

ALTHOUGH INDIANA HAS BEEN A STATE SINCE 1816, IT HAS furnished the country with only one president. And he was a quasi-Hoosier at that. Benjamin Harrison was born on the outskirts of Cincinnati but was living in Indianapolis when he was elected to the White House in 1889. On the other hand, Indiana has been home to five vice presidents—Schuyler Colfax (Ulysses S. Grant), Thomas Hendricks (Grover Cleveland), Charles Fairbanks (Teddy Roosevelt), Thomas Marshall (Woodrow Wilson), and Dan Quayle (George Bush)—the most of any state save New York. The veeps are even memorialized at the United States Vice-Presidential Museum, part of the Dan Quayle Center in Huntington, Indiana, outside Fort Wayne, in the state's northeast quadrant.

The abundance of vice presidents is in keeping with the state's ethos. *Don't whisper, but don't roar either. Wield power, but do it with decorum, and do it behind the scenes.* "Hoosiers are a genuinely modest people whose pioneer origins tend toward democracy and equality," says Professor James Madison, chairman of the Indiana University history department. "They distrust strong leaders and leadership, particularly when it drifts toward elitism and arrogance, as it usually does. They like leaders who look and act as they do, with just a bit more smarts and energy, but enough sense not to show it."

The modern-day personification of this ethic is Eugene Parker, who works a few miles from Huntington up State Highway 24. Roanoke, Indiana, is the kind of one-stoplight town that disappears into the folds of your map. And while it is just south of Fort Wayne, Indiana's second-largest city, it bears no characteristics of a suburb. The main drag of Roanoke is prototypical small-town America, something straight out of Mayberry. Walk down Main Street and you'll find the obligatory diner, a small public library, a used-furniture store, an upscale restaurant, a gas station that doubles as a bait barn, and, naturally, the barbershop where patrons come as much for the small talk as for the tonsorial handiwork. Catty-corner from the barbershop is a nondescript office, its windows covered in red, white and blue bunting, that could pass for the local VFW Hall.

The unassuming space is home to Maximum Sports, Parker's sports management and representation agency, which claims as clients some of the biggest stars in the sports cosmos. You'd be hard-pressed to find a less likely locale for a handsome, polished-but-somehow-not-slick African-American in his late forties who ranks among the most powerful agents in professional sports. But then again, Parker has made a living—and a nice one at that—shattering perceptions. Deion Sanders, one of the forty or so pro athletes Parker and Maximum Sports represents, nearly flipped his lid (the Shaft-like fedora with the feather, perhaps) the first time he went to visit Parker in Roanoke. Once an exceptional football player, and unexceptional baseball player, "Prime Time" is as famous for his braggadocio and his abundant jewelry as for his achievements on the field. This is a man who wore a do-rag emblazoned with the word "Jesus" under his helmet. Let's just say that Sanders cut a conspicuous figure as he gamboled down Main Street in Roanoke on the way to meet his agent. "I said, 'Nice town and all, Eugene, but, *man*, what are you *doing* here? Don't you want to move to Atlanta or something?'" recalls Sanders. "Eugene just looked at me and shook his head. Yo, it's something about Indiana, I guess. The man loves it there."

Parker's explanation: Setting up shop in Roanoke is a strategic decision. He can do his job, but is far enough from his players that he doesn't risk becoming a glorified babysitter—a job that befalls other agents who get roped into menial tasks such as making sure their wives and girlfriends don't sit in the same section at games. And if he's in the sticks, he can concentrate on doing deals without tending to the legion of hangers-on and bootlickers that inevitably ride tandem with today's athletes. There are also practical personal reasons he's in Indiana. He is deeply attached to his place of worship, the nondenominational Christian Church. He can leave work and five minutes later—there's never any traffic—be sitting at the dinner table with his wife, June, and five kids ages eleven to twenty-three.

Pressed, Parker concedes there's a much deeper reason he's in Indiana. The state defines him. "In Indiana, there's still the overall work ethic and Midwestern values. People tend to be solid. Character is important. This is not a get-rich-quick state. In other places, things move fast, underlying details get overlooked, people get ignored. Here you still grow up with the notion that good things will happen if you work hard, if you're persistent, if you have an overall sense of morality and fair play."

*P*arker grew up fifteen miles—which is to say: a world away—from pastoral Roanoke. Raised by his mother, Jessie, in the black enclave of Fort Wayne, Eugene had no blood siblings, but the family took in a set of cousins whose mother had died. At any given time, there were eight to ten kids scrambling around the Parkers' modest home. Jessie worked as a beautician and as a clerk for a shipping company and performed various odd jobs, but money was generally sparse. "We didn't have much, we were on the lower end," says Eugene. "But neither did anyone else, so you really didn't think much of it. The memories I have, overwhelmingly, they're good ones."

In the summer of 1967, before Eugene was to enter middle school, the Supreme Court mandated integration of the public schools. The Allen County School System, however, couldn't act quickly enough to accommodate the law and Parker was assigned to attend sixth grade at an annex wing of the local high school. Displeased with the prospect of her twelve-year-old wandering the halls of a high school, Jessie enrolled Eugene in the nearby parochial school, St. Paul's. The tuition was several thousand dollars a year—money the Parkers didn't have—but Eugene's education was too important to leave to chance. Jessie figured somehow she'd make it work.

When the first bill came due, Jessie and Eugene approached the principal and his wife, Gene and Marty Berger, and explained their situation. They reached an agreement. The Bergers granted Eugene a partial scholarship, and to account for the shortfall, Eugene would do odd jobs around school. Still, there was substantial culture shock. He was transitioning from a predominantly black public school to an overwhelmingly white private school. Raised as a Baptist, he was suddenly surrounded by all things Lutheran. And there was an entirely new set of social guidelines to learn. "Where I grew up, we resolved conflict physically; that determined if you were right or not. Now I was somewhere where you resolved conflict verbally. That was completely foreign to me. I was like, 'You don't want to fight?' I think that's when I first started to appreciate the power of persuasion."

One rainy Saturday when he was sixteen, Parker and assorted cousins and aunts decided to take in a movie at the Rialto Theater in Fort Wayne. They chose a gloomy film, *The Spook Who Sat by the Door*, that was so controversial that Richard Nixon, then president, opposed its release. The premise: A young black man joins the CIA as a low-level agent and, keeping a low profile and making keen observations without speaking much, he rises through the ranks of a white bureaucracy. He finally wearies of the CIA and returns to the ghetto, where he draws on the tactics he learned as a spy to start a revolution.

His cousins didn't think much of the movie, but it made a deep impression on Eugene. Even today, not having seen the film for decades, he can still recall scenes and dialogue with remarkable exactitude. To him, the message was clear. "I don't want to cause a revolution from a negative standpoint, but what I've learned is that sometimes the best way to get ahead is to be very quiet and nonthreatening; so people won't shoot you, literally or figuratively. Then, by the time they're ready to shoot you, you've built a fortress so you can withstand their shots."

Parker stayed in the parochial school system, attending Fort Wayne Concordia, a Lutheran high school. Sports, the lingua franca of adolescent boys, helped ease the transition. He was the star of the basketball team, a 6'1" point guard dripping with poise, endowed with a sixth sense for when to delegate power and when to snap the reins. He was named Fort Wayne's best player both his junior and his senior years. Though he'd grown popular with his white classmates and never wanted for friends, he never let it be known that he often arrived to school early and cleaned the football stadium in order to help defray his tuition.

Parker accepted a basketball scholarship to Purdue, which not only afforded him the chance to play for a top program in a top conference but was only two hours southwest of Fort Wayne by car. Fred Schaus, the Boilermakers' coach at the time, recalls his first meeting with Parker. As he did with all his new players, Schaus asked Parker to articulate his goals while at Purdue. "I want to go to law school, Coach," Parker shot back. "Everyone else assumed that I meant basketball goals," recollects Shaus, now retired and living in West Virginia. "He was just so rock solid. He was a natural-born leader, just the kind of guy who breeds success. To this day, Eugene Parker ranks as one of the two or three most special guys I've ever coached." It bears mentioning that prior to coming to Purdue, Schaus was the coach of the Los Angeles Lakers, overseeing players the likes of Wilt Chamberlain, Jerry West and Elgin Baylor.

Unlike college athletes today—who use top-of-the-line equipment and have their own school-sponsored trainers exhorting them—Parker devised his own off-season regimen. He jumped rope for thirty minutes, wearing a thirty-five-pound weighted vest. He ran hundreds of flights of stairs. He kept a basketball on his aunt's porch and honed his jumper late at night on the court of a nearby church. The parking lot lights illuminated his workout. "I remember a line I read in a John Wooden book: 'Fatigue makes cowards of us all,'" says Parker. Parker's work ethic and monastic existence made him something of a cult figure in Fort Wayne basketball circles. "We all wanted to be like him," says Frank Thomas, a childhood friend of Parker's whose son, Chris, is an NBA-bound point guard for Notre Dame. "I remember one time, he wouldn't stop until he hit twenty-five straight free throws. I said, 'This guy is serious.' He does that and then he doesn't want to leave until he hits twenty-five free throws without hitting the rim—swishes. I said, 'This is crazy.' I knew he was *really* crazy when he did that and said he wasn't leaving until he made twenty-five straight without touching the net.'"

Once a hoops star in high school in Fort Wayne and at
Purdue, the understated Eugene Parker is now a top
sports agent. (© *Maximum Sports Management*)

In his unspectacular way, Parker would go on to become one of the
better players in Purdue history, a four-year starter and an All–Big Ten
player as a senior. Shortly after he graduated with a degree in finance,
he was selected in the fifth round of the 1978 NBA draft by the San
Antonio Spurs. Every year following the NBA's draft night, one inevitably hears of marginal and college players so deluded about their
worth that they pronounce themselves "devastated" when their names
are never called. Yet when Parker *was* drafted, he declined to show up
for training camp. Brutally honest with himself, he figured that even

if he made the team he would be a bench player at best. He had better things to do, he reasoned, than to spend a few years as a basketball voyeur. That comparably talented college players—including former Purdue teammates Jerry Sichting and Kyle Macy, who transferred to Kentucky after Parker beat him out for a starting spot—had long and ultimately lucrative careers in the NBA has never been a source of bitterness. "Understand, the NBA was never the goal for me," he says with a casual shrug, "so I never thought of not getting there as failure."

Having turned his back on a pro career, Parker spent a year traveling the world playing for Athletes in Action—the athletic ministry of Campus Crusade for Christ—and then enrolled in Valparaiso University's law school. It was there that he realized just how profoundly basketball had shaped him. "Being aggressive, setting goals, working within the framework of a team, handling success and failure, all those lessons from basketball served me so well," he says. "They took away the ball and the goal, but the formula was the same." Parker did well, soldiering through the notoriously grueling first year, but he never found an area of the law that particularly appealed to him. As a second-year student, he had sufficient spare time to serve as an assistant coach on the basketball team. There was no epiphany, no single moment of reckoning, but at some point he realized his calling. "I always got along with a lot of people from a lot of walks of life. I had the finance background from college. I was getting the legal training. Of course, basketball was something very dear to me. I put it together and said, 'I'm going to be a sports agent.' Whatever that meant."

Sports agents weren't always necessary evils. They weren't always blights on the athletic landscape along the same lines as overpriced concessions, annoying mascots and earsplitting music during breaks in play. Not all that long ago, the industrial relations in sports were little different from those at the local auto plant or steel mill. The owners were management, the athletes were labor and wages were whatever the former was offering the latter. Eventually, collective bargaining and unions and free agency came to sports—but not before lengthy legal wrangling that went as far as the Supreme Court. Even then, there was little need for representation. The salary structure was fairly simple, as contracts spanned a few years at most. An "endorsement deal" for an athlete meant that the local Buick dealer would offer free use of a Skylark during the season if, in exchange, the player agreed to lend his voice to a low-budget radio ad and throw him and the missus some comp tickets from time to time. There were no salary caps to circumvent, no licensing deals to decipher, no player websites to launch.

Most important, the wage scale didn't leave any room for an agent to siphon a cut. Good players earned a little more than mediocre players, who earned a little more than benchwarmers. "Agent, shoot," says Slick Leonard, unleashing his familiar cackle. "My first contract out of IU was for, shoot, I can't even hardly remember. Four thousand dollars, I think. We shook hands and that was that. Agent? Hell, if I gave a cut of my salary to someone else, there wouldn't have been hardly anything left. My best year I made $13,000 playing for Chicago and I scored 16 points a game and led the team in assists. I'd like to have been playing now with those numbers. Times have changed, baby."

And how. As the public's love of sports intensified and both corporate dollars and television revenue have grown at the rate of Jack's beanstalk, the economic picture has changed dramatically. In no small part because of the NBA's $1 billion or so in annual television revenues, the current median salary for an NBA player exceeds $5 million. There are salary caps and option years and base years and exempt roster spots and unrestricted free agencies and offer sheets. Then there are the other revenue streams and tributaries that began to flow for athletes: trading card deals, shoe contracts, video game endorsements, autograph shows. Given the complexities of the modern sports marketplace, the agent is, for better or worse, a dire necessity.

There are currently more than a thousand agents registered with the NBA Players Association. This, of course, means that the majority of registered agents lack that essential asset: a client. Still, it's easy to see why this is a growth field. The standard agent cut is 4 percent on an NBA contract and 15 percent on endorsements, and, well, you do the math. If you can count one run-of-the-mill player as a client, you are assured a six-figure income. Several clients and you're set for life. A stable of clients like Parker? You have to squint to keep the zeroes straight.

Alone, the high stakes and big money would be enough to turn the field of sports representation into a rogues' gallery. But factor in the tsunami of testosterone—virtually all of the agents in the four major sports are males—the ego, the bravado, the poor regulations, the scant barriers to entry, the impressionable clients who seldom bring much in the way of financial sophistication to the table. Put simply, the mix is toxic. "People say, 'Is it really that big a cesspool, all the lying and backbiting and shady behavior?'" says Len Elmore, a former NBA player and Harvard-minted lawyer who briefly represented a handful of NBA players. "It's worse."

A full accounting of the misdeeds, malfeasance and downright criminal acts of ethically bankrupt agents are too numerous to chronicle here. There isn't a marginally talented college athlete who hasn't been approached by an agent or one of his underlings, hoping to seduce him with a siren's song of cash, tricked-up cars and, sometimes, white nasal powder. The prevalence of sports agents and their toadies on Florida campuses was such that the state legislature recently made it a felony for agents and boosters to make illegal payments to athletes. It is the rare college coach who hasn't had to shoo an agent out of prac-

tice. There isn't a pro already under representation who hasn't been approached by a rival agent offering to cut his fees.

A few years ago, I wrote a story for *Sports Illustrated* about Tank
Black, a smooth-talking former football coach who slithered from
nowhere to sign dozens of high-profile NBA and NFL athletes, including Vince Carter, at the time *the* young stud of the NBA. Unleashing
his Southern charm, Black ingratiated himself to the athletes' mothers
and promised that their sons would receive a 40 percent annual return
on their income. Black is now in prison, having bilked his clients out
of millions through an offshore pyramid scheme. More than $15 mil-
lion in clients' assets disappeared, the largest case of agent fraud in
sports history. How could anyone entrust their millions to a man
promising them a 40 percent annual return? "Look, man," Fred Taylor,
a running back for the Jacksonville Jaguars, told *SI*, "when I met Tank
I didn't have a checking account. You think I knew that 40 percent
was bullshit?"

Parker got an early glimpse of his chosen profession's seamy side. In
law school, he served a summer internship with Harvey Lakind, a New
Jersey agent who represented NBA marginalia. His clients—"Basically,
big, white guys," Parker says, laughing—included the likes of Billy
(Whopper) Paultz, Mark Landsberger and Kim Hughes. A few years
after Parker worked for the agent, Lakind was indicted for his role in
a scheme to transfer money from the clients' accounts to a personal account. (He pleaded guilty to accepting kickbacks and tax fraud.)

Parker's first client was Roosevelt Barnes, who grew up with Parker
in Fort Wayne and was a teammate on the Purdue basketball team. At
Purdue, Barnes had a fifth year of eligibility and decided to try out for
the Boilermakers' football team. He not only made the team as a walk-
on, but was a starter and was drafted by the Detroit Lions. He tapped
his buddy to represent him and Parker was on his way. Reciprocating
this loyalty, Parker later made Barnes his partner at Maximum Sports.

On the surface, anyway, Parker would appear to be singularly ill-suited to the profession. A reference to his refusal to "blow smoke up a client's butt" is the closest he comes to swearing. He doesn't drink, doesn't smoke, doesn't even like to drive his car—a hardly ostentatious Chrysler minivan—faster than the posted speed limits. In the course of a three-hour interview, not once does he "go off the record" to trash someone or give life to a rumor. Emmitt Smith, the NFL's all-time leading rusher and another longtime client of Parker, describes his agent as "a lamb among the sharks." But Parker watches calmly as Babylon unfolds around him. Like the title character of *The Spook Who Sat by the Door*, he is hip to the realpolitik and has figured out how to take the ambient ugliness and use it to his advantage.

Though he's adamant that it was by accident and not design, Parker has positioned himself as the anti-agent, guided not by avarice but by Judeo-Christian values. He doesn't proselytize to his clients—"My business card doesn't say 'Eugene Parker: Christian Sports Agent'"—and his office bears no evidence that the proprietor is a devout Christian. But he doesn't exactly suppress his spirituality either. "My motto comes out of a scripture in the Bible," he says. "It's in Matthew. Jesus was talking to His disciples and said He had trained them and now He was going to let them go do things on their own. And He says, 'Behold, I send you a sheep, a sheep in the midst of wolves. Be wise as serpents but harmless as doves.' And my approach has been just that. I want to know every trick of the trade, I want to know all the devices that an agent, a team, whoever might use. But on the other hand, I'm not looking to scheme. I'm looking for the win-win."

This land grab of the moral high ground infuriates rival agents. Both an NBA and an NFL agent independently referred to Parker as a "fraud" who uses his religiosity as a shtick. "Trust me, there are no saints in this business," says a top NBA agent. "Look, it's a lucrative business, it's challenging as hell and sometimes it's even fun. But it's not exactly a higher calling, not even for Eugene Parker." (Asked to respond to these charges, Parker demurred: "When you speak badly of other agents, you're just lowering the profession.")

Nevertheless, neither rival agents nor team executives whom Parker has engaged in knock-down, drag-out negotiations can recite specifics of misconduct. Parker doesn't pay college players. He doesn't aggressively try to poach clients signed to other agents. Unlike most agents, he doesn't have a staff of "runners" or "bagmen," the low-level myrmidons who descend on college campuses so their employers don't have to dirty their hands. The strongest credible charge leveled against Parker is that when it comes to loopholes, he has the nose of a bloodhound. And it's a charge to which he pleads nolo contendere. "I get a rush from doing creative contracts," he admits with a broad smile. "It's the precedent-setting deals, the ones where they have to change the rules afterward, that give me more satisfaction than the ones that might be for more money but are straightforward."

In the mid-'90s, the Dallas Cowboys were so eager for Deion Sanders's services that they flew Parker from Indiana to the negotiation on the private plane of the owner, Jerry Jones. Over a walk in the woods, Jones and Parker agreed in principle that the Cowboys would pay Sanders $35 million over seven years, an astronomical contract at the time. The problem was, the Cowboys had a finite amount of room under the salary cap. Parker structured the deal so that Sanders received a modest "salary" but a whopping up-front signing bonus of $13 million. Sanders (and thus Parker) had his financial demands met while Jones was in the clear for cap purposes. This caused a furor not just in the NFL but in all team sports. If the deal held, owners flush with cash could circumvent the salary cap by paying exorbitant bonuses out of their own pockets. Teams vilified Parker for violating the spirit of the salary cap. But to him, it was born of the twin strains of life: spirituality and sports. He'd reasoned like a Jesuit and had acted like a point guard, simply finding a seam and taking what the defense had given him. The contract stood, but shortly thereafter, the "Deion Rule" stipulated that signing bonuses have to be prorated and count under the salary cap. It's barely perceptible, but Parker still smiles when he recounts the story.

Thanks in no small part to the movie *Jerry Maguire* and the (mercifully canceled) HBO series *Arli$$*, the sports agent is usually depicted as a shame-deprived white male who is heavily bejeweled and dispenses hair gel and half-truths in equal measure—that is to say, liberally. The stereotype held when Parker entered the field more than two decades ago. Though the overwhelming majority of NBA players were black, the overwhelming majority of the men representing them were white. "Sad to say," says Parker, "but it used to be thought that if you signed with a black agent you were going to get inferior representation."

That is changing. Dramatically. An increasing number of agents are black, including some of the highest rollers. Aaron and Eric Goodwin, for example, the Oakland-based brothers who represent Gary Payton, among others, won the derby to serve LeBron James. Within days of retaining the Goodwins, James signed a deal with Nike worth nearly $100 million. Even if the Goodwins charged James vastly less than the standard 15 percent commission, as many of the also-rans contend, they still had a good week.

White agents seldom neglect to bring up Tank Black when they recruit clients, playing, of course, to the shabby stereotype that signing with a black agent is a recipe for trouble. Many black agents incorporate into their pitch a trope of remaining loyal to their race, playing, of course, to the shabby theme that black athletes are "selling out" or neglecting to "keep it real" if they choose a white agent. So perhaps it achieves some sort of karmic balance that evens out in the end.

For his part, Parker claims that he resolutely refuses to deal the race card: "If you're going to choose me," he tells potential clients, "choose me because you think I'm good, not because I'm black." Nonsense, say some of the men against whom he's competing. When he was beginning his career, Parker worked in conjunction with veteran NFL agent Marvin Demoff, who is white. As Demoff once told *Sports Illustrated*: "[Eugene] said it was very important for him to gain credibility by working with someone who is white. Then we reached a point where I no longer served a purpose. It was very much a racial context, which was very disappointing to me. On the one hand, he preached religion and tolerance. On the other hand, [our relationship] was totally racial."

But ask Parker about whether his race has hindered his upward climb and he holds up his hand—a conversational stop sign—and shakes his head. Hindered? If anything, it's imbued him with advantages. He can relate to clients who, more often than not, grew up under similar circumstances. "We can laugh about when friends came over to your house and roaches scatter everywhere and you're hoping they don't see it and they see it." More important, he says that being black in a predominantly white society pays dividends at the bargaining table. "Your whole life, except for your family and your church, chances are the people in authority were white. You had to go through them to get what you wanted. You had to get an understanding of how to relate to them. The most important thing in this business is relating to people and figuring out what's important to them. Being black, honestly I don't even think about that much. I just treat people as people. Some black agents have a hard time because they are challenged relating to white people. Some white agents have a hard time because they are challenged relating to black people. Just like you and I are just talking totally normal, [race] is not an issue with me."

Bearing this out, Parker turned heads in the industry in 2003 when he was retained to represent Rex Grossman, a white quarterback from the University of Florida drafted by the Chicago Bears. Rex is the son of Dan Grossman, a prominent Bloomington eye doctor who captained the Indiana University team in the early '70s and still has close ties to the Indiana program. In the early 1990s, Dan was advising Anthony Thompson, a star Indiana running back who was represented by Demoff and Parker during a brief NFL career. "Back when Rex was nine, Eugene was at our house while representing Anthony," recalls Dan. "Eugene would play basketball with Rex. Obviously, the two got along well then and that just blossomed. . . . Based on our history, as well as some very complimentary discussions we had with two NFL general managers, Eugene was a quick and clear choice. Integrity and contract expertise were the two most important factors in our choice."

Race, the Grossmans claim, didn't even enter their thinking. "We are aware that Eugene is black," Dan says. "But it was in no way an affirmative action move. This was only based on merit." Still, it marked the first time in NFL history that a white quarterback had signed with a black agent. "Other people call it a sad commentary, but I guess I'd rather call it a breakthrough," says Parker. "Kind of funny that it took a kid from southern Indiana and an agent from up north to make racial history in the NFL, isn't it?"

12

THE GUT CHECK

BEFORE THE SEASON, TOM MCKINNEY HAD STUDIED HIS team's schedule of games and tried to divine the Cougars' record. The coach would never have conceded as much to his minions, but there were a few games that were "gimmes." The majority of games were ones Bloomington North *should* win. There were a few toss-up games, the outcome resting on which team made the decisive plays in the waning moments. Then there was one opponent on the schedule that McKinney, ever the realist, could hardly conceive of beating: Pike.

The nine townships of Indianapolis form a tic-tac-toe board not unlike the set of *Hollywood Squares*, and Pike Township occupies the upper left square. For much of Indianapolis's history, Pike was rural terrain filled with small, single-family farms. Today it is studded with office parks and subdivisions bearing quaint, rustic-sounding names.

The three- and four-bedroom homes that sell for between $100,000 and $200,000 come replete with manicured lawns, American flags affixed to the front porches, practical minivans and impulse-purchase Mustangs parked under the basketball goals in the driveways. The streets are clean and quiet. The Pike Township Cultural Center sits at one of the busiest intersections in the area. In short, Pike has all the earmarks of a typical middle-class community in Middle America. Except one: It is predominantly black.

Perhaps because it's smack in the middle of sleepy flyover country, Indianapolis seldom gets its due as a big-time city when, in fact, it is more populous than San Francisco, Boston, Seattle and Washington, D.C. "Naptown" and "India-noplace" are civic nicknames that have outlived their accuracy. Indianapolis has every amenity you'd expect from a large, twenty-first-century city—topflight live theater, a vibrant arts community, fine dining, plenty of Starbucks. And contrary to popular belief, it's not a white-bread town. A quarter of the 800,000 residents in Indianapolis are African-American, comprising a larger black population than that of Newark, New Jersey.

Not unlike the stratification in most American cities, for decades the vast majority of Indianapolis's blacks lived in one enclave, Center Township. While Center Township could hardly be described as a "ghetto," it was—and is—home to the city's worst schools, lowest per capita income and highest crime rate. As the socioeconomics slowly improved—wages in Indianapolis steadily outpaced inflation—many Center Township blacks amassed capital sufficient for homeownership and looked to move out. Where to go? Historically, Indianapolis's south side hadn't been particularly hospitable to blacks. Relocating to the townships due east or due west was seen as a "lateral move." Housing prices in the northeast townships were often prohibitively high. The obvious choice: Pike. In 1970, there were barely four thousand blacks living in Pike Township. By 1990, there were almost nine thousand. By 2000, there were more than twenty-three thousand.

The raw numbers tell only part of the story. As the flavor of the township changed, the trend was self-perpetuating. Families seeking to send their kids to a diverse school—but without sacrificing the quality of education—relocated to Pike. Black professionals new to the area relocated to Pike. Internet chat rooms buzzed with the word that Pike was a hospitable, racially mixed community, liberal in some respects, but traditional and family-oriented in others. Per capita, Pike is home to one of the densest concentrations of biracial couples in the United States.

Take Frank Thomas, a former Indiana All-State basketball player from Fort Wayne, who was Eugene Parker's boyhood friend. Frank, an executive consultant, is black and his high school sweetheart wife, Tammy, a homemaker and former small-business owner, is white. Their brood of four children includes a son, Chris, whose basketball skills were so precocious that Bob Knight stealthily watched his middle school games. It was important to Frank and Tammy that they live in a place where differences were celebrated. Pike was an easy choice. "We're a diverse family and we wanted a diverse community," Frank told the *Indianapolis Star*. "It was important for our children to look around and see African-Americans who are doctors, lawyers, and executives of key businesses. I want them to know successful African-Americans who aren't athletes."

In lockstep with this shift in demographics, Pike High School has become a dominant hoops program, a basketball factory that has started to mint the best teams and best players in the state. For the first sixty years of the school's existence, the Red Devil teams were generally unremarkable. Some teams were better than others, but none came close to winning a state title or even advancing far in the tournament. Since

1998, Pike has won three 4A titles and was runner-up once. Over the past decade, Pike and Bloomington North have had the highest winning percentages in Indiana and the two schools have furnished four Mr. Basketball winners since 2000. *Eleven* former Pike players from the past four teams were playing college ball during the 2003–04 season.

In 2002–03, Pike's freshman, jayvee and varsity teams went a combined 68–1, and the undefeated varsity team won the state title without facing much resistance. The team's best player, Robert Vaden, a dazzling junior swingman some scouts have pegged for the NBA, decided not to return for his senior season. He had already committed to play for Indiana University, so he matriculated at prep school in Maine— where, not coincidentally, he roomed with Mike Davis, Jr.—trying to ensure that he'd be academically eligible to play as an IU freshman. No matter. The Red Devils were still, arguably, the best team in the state.

Asked to explain Pike's transformation from a perennially marginal program to a powerhouse, a rival coach had a simple answer. "They started getting the black athletes." It's a sentiment that gets bandied about the Indiana hoops culture with unfortunate frequency. Later in the year, two hours up the road in South Bend, Notre Dame icon Paul Hornung invoked the identical phrase to explain the Fighting Irish's recent woes in football. Talking on a Detroit radio station, Hornung remarked, "We can't stay as strict as we are as far as the academic structure is concerned, because we've got to get the black athlete. . . . We must get the black athlete if we're going to compete."

The implication that blacks were unable to meet academic standards was as offensive as it was absurd. But was Hornung so far off about the role of blacks on successful teams? The wildly disproportionate success rate of blacks in sports is a radioactive issue, discussed fervently and honestly in private but guardedly in public. The role of race in sports is the 5,000-pound elephant in the room, an obvious topic that's worthy of discussion, but one that goes largely ignored until a dinosaur like Hornung or Al Campanis or Jimmy the Greek makes an indefensible remark. There's a news cycle's worth of righteous indignation, a blizzard of op-ed pieces, and an official apology from the offender explaining, "I meant no offense." Then the topic disappears until the next dunderheaded remark.

Even defining race is an inexact science, which makes an honest discussion all the more difficult. But friends and colleagues whom I consider progressive and reasonable will wonder—in private, anyway—whether blacks aren't endowed with superior ability to run fast and jump high. When I ask to see some hard evidence, they tell me that if the evidence may not be in the science, it's in the statistics. Blacks, they point out, account for barely one in six Americans but make up three-fourths of all the NBA players, virtually every top running back in football, virtually every elite sprinter.

During my winter in Indiana, I was speaking informally with a group of Ball State University students when the topic came up. "Isn't it possible," I suggested, "that the black culture places more emphasis on certain sports because—rightly or wrongly—blacks feel there are fewer opportunities in other pursuits or they are seeking the quickest, easiest way to escape poverty?" Look at Indiana basketball, one of the kids responded. Practically *every* kid in the state—black or white, rural or urban, north or south—is exposed to the sport and learns quickly how deeply the culture reveres it. Yet in Indiana, where blacks make up barely 5 percent of the general population, the overwhelming majority of the top players are black, including the past six Mr. Basketball winners and eight of the ten Indiana natives currently in the NBA. "And," he added, "what about Pike?"

Sticking with Indiana basketball as the focus, I responded that if this were just a matter of genetic superiority, if the "black athlete" was an acceptable generalization, why had it been years since any of the uniformly black teams from Center Township had challenged for a state title? How, earlier in the season, had the racially mixed team from Bloomington North beaten the all-black team from Gary by 40 points? For that matter, how was it that Bloomington North's most athletic player was Josh Norris, the white son of Pentecostal ministers, not Bil Duany, the son of two African parents?

What about Pike's transformation? True, scanning the pictures in the school corridors of Pike's past basketball teams, it is impossible not to realize that the mediocre teams were predominantly white, racially mixed at best, whereas the current dynamo is almost exclusively black. (Of the thirty or so varsity and junior varsity players, I counted a single white face.) But it's just as hard not to marvel at the current amenities. Today's Pike players have access to state-of-the-art training facilities, masses of supportive fans, a strong, dedicated coaching staff. The players' families have the means to send them to summer basketball camps and traveling tournaments. In sum, you could easily make the case that Pike argues as much for "nurture" as for "nature."

Steve Stocker, Pike's amiable athletic director, recounts a story from the team's postseason banquet a few seasons ago. The Red Devils had just won the state title and Purdue coach Gene Keady was the guest speaker. As Keady looked around the room, he was stunned to see so many parents in attendance. He was told that all of the players lived with both of their biological parents. At a time when more than one-third of all kids are born out of wedlock—and roughly 70 percent of African-American kids are—Keady was stunned. "My gosh," he said. "You *all* live with both your parents? You just don't see that these days!"

One of the most shopworn clichés in sports is that a team has "nothing to lose and everything to gain." But buried somewhere in that sentiment is more than a small degree of truth. Sports psychologists will tell you that athletes face the most pressure when they compete against a closely matched opponent. Those are, to lapse into coachspeak, the "gut checks," the games that double as referendums on character, the times when players' hearts pound like jackhammers. Competing against a superior opponent? When defeat is the likely, anticipated outcome, there's little reason to fear failure. You'll simply be meeting expectations. Which is why time and again, underdogs upset overdogs. Liberated from any performance anxiety, they compete with devil-may-care abandon and swing for fences, secure in the knowledge that everyone expects them to strike out anyway.

So it was that the Bloomington North players, facing far and away their toughest opponent of the season—on the road, no less—came to Pike betraying a looser demeanor than they had at any point all season. Earlier in the winter, they would clamber off the bus and walk deferentially through the corridors of other schools. Now the North players oozed a casual confidence as they made their way to the locker room at Pike. Pressure? What pressure?

And there were other reasons for optimism. The team had won its last six games and, after the unqualified fiasco against Perry Meridian, exhibited a newfound sense of toughness. They were rabid in their pursuit of loose balls and rebounds. Defense, already a strong suit, was ratcheted up. The guards were knocking down outside shots, which, in turn, helped carve space in the low post for Duany and Norris. Even McKinney had a discernible spring in his step. "This is a big ballgame," he said. "But if we do a lot of things right, I think we have a real chance." By his standards, it almost qualified as boasting.

The evening got off to an inauspicious start when the locker room doors were inadvertently locked and it took several minutes to find the custodian with the master key. Then, led by a 6'5", 220-pound freshman, Dennis Ziegler, the Pike junior varsity team—which could beat all but a handful of varsity teams in the state—blitzed Bloomington

North's consortium, 61–24. If it augured ill for the varsity game, McKinney wasn't letting on. In the locker room, McKinney addressed the varsity team. His pregame soliloquy was strictly technical. "If you take more than two dribbles," he said, elevating his middle and index finger for emphasis, "you're doing something wrong." . . . "We're going to start out in the 23-offense and use press-breaker number two." . . . "We can't be timid against these guys. If you get your shot blocked, that's okay. We're going to block some of their shots too." Here it was, one of the biggest games of the year, and his voice remained in the same octave the entire time. He closed by asking, "Are there any questions?" Silence. He said calmly, "Well, then, let's get to work."

It was in the hallway leading to the court that the team got pumped. As the coaches remained in the locker room to make a few last-minute adjustments, the players huddled around senior Terrence Warfield in the corridor. Warfield was the closest thing the team had to a free-spirited cutup. As he freestyled, the players moshed and shrieked and slammed balls against the walls and uninhibitedly punched the air. To the uninitiated, they looked intoxicated.

WARFIELD: "What time is it?"
TOGETHER: "Game time!"
WARFIELD: "All my dawgs in da house?"
TOGETHER: "Woof, woof, woof, woof!"
WARFIELD: "What time is it?"
TOGETHER: "It's time to get live. It's time to represent!"
WARFIELD: "What time is it?"
TOGETHER: "Northside soldiers, what time is it?"

With that, they burst through the doorway and streaked onto the court.

For all the do-rags in the stands and the OutKast on the p.a. system, in many ways Pike provided the most traditional—and downright quaint—basketball ambience I encountered all season. Though the game was held on a Thursday night and not a weekend, the crowd was significant, a good many fans wearing Pike sweatshirts and jackets and caps. An army of cheerleaders and a mammoth pep band took turns entertaining during breaks in play. The townspeople—most of them having no direct connection to the players—kibitzed at the concession stands during time-outs. Red Devils basketball had clearly become a rallying point for the community, just as standout teams had served as lightning rods for small towns in decades past.

The player introductions were modest and were followed by a reminder that the players had made a commitment to sportsmanship and Pike expected its fans to do likewise. To reinforce the point, the entire back page of the game program was devoted to checklists enumerating "The Responsibilities of Sportsmanship."

THE PLAYER:
- Treats opponents with respect.
- Plays hard, but plays within the rules.
- Exercises self-control at all times, setting the example for others to follow.
- Respects officials and accepts their decisions without gesture or argument.
- Wins without boasting, loses without excuses, and never quits.
- Always remembers that it is a privilege to represent the school and community.

THE SPECTATOR:
- Attempts to understand and be informed of the playing rules.
- Appreciates a good play no matter who makes it.

- Cooperates with and responds enthusiastically to cheerleaders.
- Shows compassion for an injured player, applauds positive performances; does not heckle, jeer or distract players; and avoids use of profane and obnoxious language and behavior.
- Respects the judgment and strategy of the coach, and does not criticize players or coaches for loss of a game.
- Respects property of others and authority of those who administer the competition.
- Censures those whose behavior is unbecoming.

I asked Stocker, the Pike athletic director, what had brought about this emphasis on sportsmanship. Had there been some unseemly incident—a brawl? a lawsuit? "No, not really," he said. "The conference as well as the IHSAA has made a huge commitment to sportsmanship and we support it." The goal, he added, was to host good, clean, well-played games. And the fans more or less got one on this night.

North started in a 2-3 zone aimed at containing Pike's best player, swingman Courtney Lee. It worked masterfully at first. Looking nothing like the best senior in the state, Lee missed his first four shots and Bloomington North led 10–9 after the first quarter. The ensuing huddle represented the seasonlong push-pull between McKinney and his players. As teammates exchanged whoops and giddy high fives, visions of a colossal upset dancing in their heads like sugarplum fairies, McKinney tried to douse any irrational exuberance, reminding them that 75 percent of the game remained to be played. "You're really doing the job out there," he said. "But, guys, we still got three quarters to go."

Sure enough, Pike gained some traction, hit a few three-pointers and surged to a lead. Still, it was clear the teams were well matched. If Bloomington North had a tough time manufacturing much offense against Pike's man-to-man defense, the Red Devils had trouble penetrating the Cougars' zone. Neither team had a significant rebounding advantage and, as McKinney predicted, both teams blocked their share of shots. They also provided a compelling contrast in styles. Lee was clearly "The Man" for Pike, the fulcrum for every offensive possession. After his dismal start he found the radar on his shot, scoring on a dazzling array of drives, medium-range jumpers and fadeaways. Bloomington North's attack was decidedly more balanced. Both guards, Josh Macy and Anthony Lindsey, took turns stroking cold-blooded three-pointers. As usual, Josh Norris showed a few tantalizing flashes of his potential, slashing to the basket and canning jumpers. Kyle Thomas was a defensive stalwart.

As Duany sat slumped on the bench, North also received a strong contribution from an unlikely source. Even as a freshman, Reed Ludlow was perhaps the tallest kid at Bloomington North. Topped by a mop of blond hair, he stood 6'8" and weighed in excess of 200 pounds, ideal dimensions for a high school center. But for the first three years of his high school career, the only time Ludlow played center was on the power play during hockey games. Though his father, a prominent Bloomington ob/gyn, played for the Indiana University freshman team in the late '60s and his older brother, Clay, was a key contributor on the 2000 Bloomington North team that reached the state final, Reed had little use for basketball. He had taken to hockey as a kid and stuck with it. Routinely, he would get stopped on the street by strangers asking how the basketball season was going. "I don't play basketball," he would say. The response was often a look of shock, if not outright disdain. Somehow, at 6'8", he was shirking an Indiana obligation by not putting his height to use on the basketball court.

Early in his junior year, Ludlow started to suffer headaches that, at first, he didn't think about much. When they persisted, he saw a neurologist. Tests revealed an arachnoid cyst on the right side of his brain. Fortunately, it was benign, but it had grown to the size of a baseball and necessitated surgery. Because his head would be sensitive, the doctors advised against his playing hockey. "I was okay until then," he recalls. "When I heard no more hockey, I kind of lost it." Having learned that Ludlow's hockey career was over, McKinney made his move. He sent Ludlow a note in class, saying, in effect, "No pressure, but if you'd like to give basketball a shot, we'd love to have you." Ludlow demurred at first. But after talking to his brother and father and getting a pep talk from his barber, Hershell Tiemann, a Bloomington icon, Ludlow gave it serious thought. Then Bloomington North was upset in the 2003 sectional by Bloomington South and Ludlow felt a duty to play. "I got home from a hockey banquet, and when I heard North lost I just got so mad," he recalled. "I was like, 'That's it, I'm playing basketball.'"

The learning curve was vertical. He knew that as a center, he would be camped under the basket and wouldn't be tasked with bringing the ball upcourt. But his basketball knowledge more or less ended there. Still, Ludlow worked over the summer to get into shape as his father and his brother inculcated him on the sport's finer points. Clay Ludlow also gave his brother a scouting report on McKinney. "He'll get on you, but don't take it personally. Just listen to the message, because he really does care about making you better."

Ludlow and Thomas formed North's two-headed center. Since Thomas already had his college football scholarship in hand and Ludlow was happy just to be playing sports again, there wasn't much competition between them. Sometimes Ludlow looked discombobulated— very much like a tall kid who had never much taken to basketball but said "What the heck" and decided to play in his senior year. Other times he showed flashes of inspiration sufficient to make him wonder how good he could have been had he played hoops from childhood. In an early-season game against Jeffersonville, he made like a hockey player and filled the lane beautifully on a fast break, awaiting the pass.

When Lindsey delivered a perfect assist, Ludlow caught the ball in stride, took two steps and threw down a dunk. He was fouled in the process and made the ensuing free throw. He played the rest of the game with a smile welded to his face.

Mostly because of his rough edges, Ludlow fell in and out of favor with McKinney. His minutes varied throughout the season. But against Pike he was summoned early and often and made a big impact. Active around the basket, he blocked a shot, grabbed five rebounds and scored a crucial put-back basket. He had saved perhaps the best performance of his abbreviated varsity career for the biggest game of the season.

Unfortunately for Bloomington North, the one player who'd left his A-game on the bus was Bil Duany. With the status of a college scholarship still in abeyance, Bil was a cipher. The effects of his reluctance to lift weights were painfully apparent as Duany was displaced from the blocks and flopped awkwardly as he tried to establish position. On the rare occasions when he caught the ball, he was quickly swarmed by defenders and returned the pass to a guard. Frustrated, he would force a shot that was either blocked or barely nicked the rim. With his older brother Duany Duany looking on from a dozen rows behind the North bench, for most of the game Bil had fewer points than fouls.

With Duany on the bench, Pike streaked to a double-digit lead midway through the third quarter. McKinney called off the zone defense and instructed his players to pick up a man. That left Macy—who's six feet on a good day and sometimes seems to play with cinder blocks tethered to his ankles—tasked with guarding the ultra-athletic Lee. Ironically, the gambit paid off. Macy stayed in front of his man and fought valiantly to extricate himself from picks and screens. Emboldened by his defense against the best backcourt player in the state, Macy hit two big jump shots. Suddenly, deep into the fourth quarter, Bloomington North was very much in the game. The crowd that had been rabid for most of the game had gone quiet.

With fewer than 90 seconds remaining and Bloomington North trailing by three points with the ball, Duany threw a careless pass that was intercepted by Pike senior Mike McCoy. A slashing swingman bound for Murray State, McCoy had been sidelined for a month with knee trouble. He looked no worse for wear in this, his first game back. With only four dribbles he covered sixty or so feet of court. As he neared the basket, he cocked his arm and soared. North's guards were a step slow and McCoy threw down a fierce dunk. Ballgame.

There was palpable ambivalence in Bloomington North's locker room, the vibe a mix of satisfaction and abject disappointment. The team had played the defending state champs—the dominant program in the state—and stayed in the game until the final seconds. A few plays here and there, a few of the jumpers that lipped out, and they could easily have scored the upset. And yet any moral victories felt hollow. The fact remained, they were returning to Bloomington with their mission unfulfilled, their record pocked by another loss. McKinney was similarly torn. Having steeled himself for a blowout, he was pleased that his players had not flinched. They competed with passion, played blind and deaf to the crowd, and, as he said, summoning his typical postgame coachspeak, "We gave ourselves a chance to win."

If McKinney was conflicted, disappointment won out when he pored over the stat sheet. Duany, who had resisted advice to take a scholarship to a smaller school when he had the chance, scored four points and managed just one field goal. It was not exactly the big-game performance that draws interest from top Division I programs. Then there was the team's seasonlong bugbear, free throws, "unguarded fifteen-footers," as McKinney calls them. Inexcusably, Bloomington North shot 9-of-19. That the team missed ten free throws and lost by eight points, 55–47, hardly escaped the coach's notice. "Guys, I can't shoot 'em for you," McKinney said plaintively to no one in particular. It was already past 9:30 and it was a school night, so the coach hustled his team out of the building and onto the bus. There was no savoring the moment, no pausing to reflect that his coaching career was now down to its last few games.

13

PUT DOWN
PLAYING PICKUP

BY MARCH OF 2004, HAVING SPENT INNUMERABLE HOURS ON backless bleachers watching Hoosiers and Hoosierettes of all shapes, sizes and colors play basketball, I finally gave in. On most afternoons, I dragged myself to the Bloomington YMCA for a workout, clambering aboard the treadmill and embarking on the Sisyphean exercise of trying to liberate myself from a few hundred unwanted calories. On this afternoon, I headed to the basketball court. I grabbed an overinflated Spalding off the rack and shot around, hoping that a pickup game would break out.

One of basketball's real shortcomings is that all that time spent watching late-night games, cogitating about the NBA's Eastern Conference or pontificating about the likely outcome of the NCAA Midwest regional, does little to improve your on-court performance.

Deep as my passion runs for the sport, I've never been a particularly skilled practitioner, at least not by Indiana standards. Even at the height of my powers—such as they were—I was a C+/B- player. And as I press up against the ceiling of the 18–34 demographic, the days of being able to slap the backboard or play for hours on end with no physical aftermath are the haziest of memories. Whiling away an afternoon playing pickup—as I did *every* afternoon the summer before college—is unthinkable. *Lives in Manhattan. Father of two young kids. Holds down full-time job.* It's not exactly the scouting report for a recreational player with an improving game.

Still, if there's one thing I can do, it's shoot the jumper. Not unlike riding a bike, it's a skill that never really deserts you, even as everything else enters a state of irretrievable decline. Back home again in Indiana during my father's illness, I kept a ball in my rental car. There are courts across the street from the Bloomington Hospital, and I would head there after the rough days and "shoot buckets," as we say in Indiana, sometimes just for a few minutes, sometimes in dress shoes. There was something therapeutic about the diversion, the physical activity, the sweating. But there was also something instantly familiar. Fingertips against the ball's pebbly grip, I extended my arms, released and followed through, as I first learned to do in elementary school. Every shot brought back a flood of memories. That euphonious *puh-zzzip* as the ball went through the net—and even the harsh clang of rubber on metal when it didn't—was my Proustian madeleine.

It's not just me, of course. Toss anyone from Indiana a ball and, regardless of how long it's been since they last played, odds are good they'll hit an uncontested fifteen-foot shot. During NBA games, fans are often summoned to the court during time-outs to shoot for prizes. I've noticed that in most markets, the lucky stiffs heave the ball awkwardly, barely draw iron, then cup their hands to their mouths in mock embarrassment and walk off, happy with their consolation prize. At

Pacers games, the fans are different. No matter the age or gender, those chosen to shoot, unfailingly, have better technique than half the players on the court. When the fan hits the shot that wins him round-trip airfare to Vegas and four nights at the Mirage, he is ecstatic. But when he misses, he is authentically pissed off, more because of the indignity of missing a shot than because of the squandered prize, I'd bet.

*T*he Bloomington YMCA has all the facilities of a swanky health club, but it maintains a soulful, egalitarian feel. It is utterly affordable and the members represent every demographic. Emeritus professors orbit the jogging track listening to NPR on their headphones while frat boys and workers off their shift at the RCA plant pump iron. Hardly anyone bothers applying a lock to their lockers. Unlike at my Manhattan sweat temple, no one is there simply to be seen. You won't find personal trainers. No juice bar or herbalist on site.

The centerpiece of the complex is a pair of full courts, the stages for reasonably competitive pickup games during lunch and again in the late afternoon and early evening. On this afternoon, there were six of us shooting, scattered among the four goals. Even eyeballing everyone from a distance, it was clear I had ten years on the field. After a few minutes, we engaged in the universal mating ritual that precedes pickup games. Pretending not to notice, you pay heed to the other players' skill level and size, making mental notes of preferred teammates. You hold the ball around your waist, sending the clear message: "Hey, I could be talked into playing a game." Dribbling eventually slows to a trickle and everyone mills around for a few minutes, then gravitates to the center. "Wanna shoot 'em up?" someone inevitably asks.

So it was that we shot for teams. The first three players to hit a free throw formed one team; the three of us who didn't formed the other.

One of my teammates was a stocky, muscle-bound high schooler with a nascent goatee whom I thought I recognized as the son of one of my father's former colleagues. Or maybe not. The other was a lanky kid, early twenties, who looked like a quintessential slacker. In addition to a vacant, self-contained look, he wore a Radiohead T-shirt, black shorts as baggy as sails on a schooner, leather bracelets on his wrists and a psychedelic tattoo on his upper right arm. Without exchanging a word, we matched up with the opposition. I paired with a kid wearing a backward baseball cap and a Pacers jersey. He had a wristband on his left forearm, though I suspected it was a fashion accessory and served no functional purpose.

Even as we divided into teams, I felt like Margaret Mead observing a foreign and exotic tribe. The five other players on the court, all in their late teens and early twenties, shared a language of grunts, looks, single-word sentences and gestures. Different handshakes were freighted with different meaning, a knuckle-knock denoting something entirely dissimilar from a standard "five." What exactly these meanings were, I couldn't decode. I attempted to announce my bona fides by making abundant use of the word "dude." It was clear I would have been better off speaking Old English.

There was also the matter of footwear. I have never quite comprehended the "cult of shoes." I have friends—otherwise rational thirty-something types with children and mortgages—who collect high-tops as if they were matchbooks, amassing dozens of pairs of "kicks," some of them stored in a closet never to be seen again. I own a pair of high-tops but prefer playing ball in cross-trainers and have never given it much thought. On this afternoon, I felt as though I had worn a plaid blazer to a black-tie affair. Looking down, I realized that not only was I the only person not wearing high-tops but I was the only one wearing white shoes. Even Joe Slacker in the Radiohead shirt had a pair of the $200 black Nikes to which Tracy McGrady had lent his imprimatur. My mid-'90s models were too outmoded to be acceptable, but too new to pass for retro hip.

In keeping with house rules, we played winners out. And the winning team would be the first team to eleven by ones. Standard baskets were worth a point, three-pointers counted as two. The game started fairly typically, lots of firm passing and conservative shot selection, no one wanting to appear exceedingly intense or exceedingly nonchalant. On an early possession, I passed to Muscle Man, whose defender raked him across the arm. The slap was audible. But no apology was forthcoming and no one seemed troubled by it. This set a precedent.

There was enough violent banging and jostling underneath the basket to resemble a mosh pit. Defenders challenged shots by trying to block the ball with one hand and simultaneously poke the shooter's arm with the other. Slaps and prods that would have merited a comment ten years ago—"Dude, take it easy, huh?"—went unremarked. There was perhaps something symbolic: Our culture has become increasingly less civil, more violent, and less respectful of personal space, and these values have bled over into the way we play. But there was nothing malicious about the physical contact and no one else seemed bothered by it in the least. Maybe kids are just becoming tougher, the human body better armored.

It was astonishing to me how athletic everyone else was. Riveted to the floor, I watched hopelessly as they soared for layups and rebounds and executed effortless behind-the-back dribbles. At one point I unfurled a ten-footer from the baseline that bounced high off the rim. A pillow of air under his feet, Joe Slacker snatched the offensive rebound and, in a single motion before he touched the ground, guided a touch pass to Muscle Man, unguarded on the other side of the basket. At least by my standards, it was a sensational play. But it didn't seem to elicit much awe from anyone else. "We're up by two, right?" Muscle Man mumbled.

And while there was a conspicuous absence of grit, there was a great deal of rococo flash. Lots of improvisational moves—plays completely at odds with basketball conventions and the fundamentals drilled into me at a young age—that were nonetheless successful. At one point the tallest player on the opposing team grabbed an offensive rebound. It's an article of faith that tall players refrain from dribbling, lest pygmies like me slap at the ball. This guy, however, dribbled twice, spun away from the basketball (another taboo) and then wafted a fadeaway. It swished cleanly.

It occurred to me that during my basketball-besotted summer fifteen years ago, Trevor Brown, Pat Hallagan, Azad Raiesdana, Adrian Martin and I were at a similar rung to this quintet of kids—avid and capable players, though not nearly good enough to have made our high school team. We were of comparable size and were in comparable physical condition. On our best day, we wouldn't have stood a chance against these kids.

It took two, maybe three possessions before my defender got hip to my inability to dribble with my left hand. Naturally, he cut off my right every time. And my lone asset, the ability to knock down an open jumper more times than not, was really no asset at all. Even recreationally, the sport's geometry has changed. Double-teams are almost nonexistent, so it's rare that a big man would kick the ball out to an open teammate stationed on the perimeter. Only the old fogies set picks and screens—if anything, it's come to be regarded as an affront, an implication that your teammate is not self-sufficient—so it's imperative you can create your shot. And it wasn't just specific to this game. It's no different in the games at the famed West Fourth Street court near my apartment in Manhattan. No different at the Sportsplex, Bloomington's other recreational basketball venue.

There's been plenty of hand-wringing about basketball's plummeting values, imparted by the NBA and the highlight-show culture that glorifies style over substance. But this "bastardization" is trickling up as much as it is trickling down. As basketball evolves, even recreational players are able to make moves that their antecedents could only imagine, fending for themselves instead of relying on the collective. The NBA is just the highest representation of this shift.

As the game progressed, a natural order set in. It became clear that Slacker was the best player on the court. Shoes squeaking loudly against the floor, he assumed the role of our go-to guy. At 9–9, he scored on a clever inside move. On the next possession, I threw him the ball on the baseline. He spun and missed a short jumper but then rose over everyone else to collect the rebound. Without dribbling, he faked twice and then muscled in a bank shot. "Ballgame," he said, clapping before the six of us exchanged ritual hand slaps.

We had won 11–9, no thanks to me. Guarding the weakest player on the opposing team, I held my own defensively, grabbing a few rebounds and loose balls that had fortuitously come my way. But I was a nonentity on offense. I missed an early three-pointer, prompting Slacker to say—felicitously, I should add—"Let's work for better shots." After that I attempted just two jumpers from shorter range. Both missed. My line score would have read: 0-3 0-0 0.

As I slogged over to the drinking fountain, I felt old, I felt obsolete and I couldn't wait for the next game to start.

14

A CRIME AGAINST CULTURE

TIME HAS FROZEN IN TINY MILAN, INDIANA. DRIVE THROUGH town and there's little indication that it's a day past 1954. The barber on the main drag is the same genial man, Chester Nichols, who's been cutting patrons' hair and applying copious fistfuls of pomade since the '50s. ("Closed: I'll be back when the doctor releases me," read the sign on the door when I last visited town.) A general store struggles to transition to an era of specialization. One of the few thriving businesses is a down-home restaurant where the locals come less for the biscuits and gravy than to discuss the topic of the day, usually basketball. As if on cue, cell phone reception cuts off the instant you cross into town.

You can hardly blame folks for trying to resist the onslaught of change. Times were never better than that magical spring more than fifty years ago when the Milan High Indians won the state basketball tournament and, at least in Indiana, Milan had every bit as much status as its Italian namesake. The story, of course, has a biblical ring to it. A rural school in the southeast corner of the state with a student body of 161, seventy-three of them boys, fields a basketball team that's pretty darn good. After snaking through the tournament—the sectional, the regional and the semistate rounds—they reach the state final and meet a Big City school with ten times the student body. The score knotted at 30 in the waning seconds, Bobby Plump, the team's best player, uses the buffer known fittingly as the picket fence to free himself from the defense. Plump elevates, albeit modestly, and unfurls an impeccable jump shot. By the time the ball passes through the hoop and Milan has won the title, the team's story is embedded in history. One of the many books devoted to the team's unlikely run is titled *The Greatest Basketball Story Ever Told.*

Rose McKittrick does her share of retelling. An irrepressible, thoroughly disarming grandmother on the far side of sixty, Rose is the de facto curator of a museum devoted to the team. A Milan resident since the 1950s, she had been running an antiques shop in town, a menagerie of wooden tennis rackets, out-of-production board games, plates adorned with the likeness of a smiling Mamie Eisenhower and ashtrays from "Scenic Atlantic City." The official name of the shop is "Milan Station Antiques and Collectibles," but she has nicknamed it "The Store of Three Wonders." Quoting from Rose's business card:

1) You wonder if I have it
2) You wonder where it's at
3) Everyone wonders how I find it

A few years ago, she and her husband split up after more than forty years of marriage and Rose decided she'd be the one to stay in town. When visitors passing through Milan stopped into her shop, they all wanted to talk about the team. So she converted the front of her store into a shrine. The display isn't just the typical assemblage of game jerseys and snippets of net. Artifacts include the popcorn bags used at the concession stands and old ticket stubs and photos of the lucky local policeman tasked with chaperoning the team. "What those guys did is such an inspiration," says McKittrick. "We have to keep making sure people know the history."

Rose's goal is to raise enough money to establish a permanent museum in the adjacent bank building. Members of the 1954 team—now in their mid-sixties, sporting thatches of white hair and well-upholstered bellies—have helped out with fund-raisers, autographing balls and showing up to shoot the J at charity games. Her slightly quixotic dream: Rose will build the museum and then have money left over to re-create the old soda shop across the street where the team would repair for malteds and egg creams after games. "It'll be like a wax museum, just the way it used to be," she says, pausing to lose herself in reverie. "Oh, this was such a great place. A great place to raise your kids. Everyone knew everyone. Your social life was your school and your church. Now . . ." She pauses for a good five seconds. "Well, everyone is just so *busy.*"

For decades, kids in Indiana have heard about the "Milan Miracle" as if it were another Bible story. But the story "went national" when it was memorialized in celluloid in the 1986 movie *Hoosiers.* Though the film—written and directed by a pair of Hoosiers, Angelo Pizzo and David Anspaugh—captures the state's passion for basketball, it took a certain amount of artistic license. For one, there was no Hickory High.

The team's coach, Marvin Wood, was not, like Gene Hackman's

character in the movie, a middle-aged vagabond trying to reclaim his good name. A receding hairline and measured demeanor belied his age, but Wood was only in his mid-twenties during the magical year, less than a decade older than most of his players. Neither was he a hot-head who begged referees for technical fouls and had the stentorian presence that recalled Bobby Knight in his saner days. Rather, Wood, who died of bone cancer in 1999, was cut from the mold of John Wooden, a student of the game who spoke in parables and rarely raised his voice. "He came in and there was respect right away," Bobby Plump recalls. "There was this real dignity, this real speak-softly-and-carry-a-big-stick quality to him."

But the most glaring difference between fact and fiction may have been the movie's *underselling* of just how deeply Milan's title resonated in the state. The best estimates are that upward of 90 percent of the state was tuned in to the radio broadcast for the final game. (Compare this to Indiana University's last NCAA title in 1987, when barely half the television sets in the state—still, a phenomenal proportion—were tuned in.) Just as Americans still recall where they were on November 22, 1963, most Hoosiers of a certain age can remember their whereabouts the night of March 20, 1954.

The morning after the championship game, Milan High's victory was the top story in the *Indianapolis Star*. Yellowing, crisping copies everyone in Milan has kept to this day reveal a banner headline—in point size usually reserved for presidential assassinations, declarations of war and other events of national significance. The players were conferred instant celebrity status. Chris Volz, a General Motors dealer in Milan, promised the team that if they won the sectional, the first of the four rounds of the state tournament, he would have them driven around town in a Pontiac. As the team won the regional and semistate titles, they would trade up the GM food chain, and were chauffeured in Buicks and then Oldsmobiles. After the title, the automotive ne plus ultra awaited: a ride in a new Cadillac. (Pause here to consider that midway through his senior year of high school in 2003, LeBron James received a $60,000 Hummer as a birthday gift from his mother.) "Bobby hit that shot and we knew our lives were going to change," says Glen Butte, a player on the team. "We had no way of knowing that fifty years later we would still be asked for autographs."

It wasn't just the exploits of this underdog that fueled a love affair in Indiana, transforming teenagers into icons. It was what Milan represented. Put five guys on the basketball court and anything is possible. Teamwork and faith form an insuperable combination. David really can stand up with his slingshot and, under the right circumstance, do some damage. But Plump has a theory about why the story still has so much currency, why the Milan Miracle is still shrouded in so much gauzy hagiography: "I think what really keeps nostalgia in the Milan Miracle is that people know it can never happen again."

For all the factors that helped basketball accumulate its tradition in Indiana, none did more than the annual high school tournament. An institution since 1911, it was the ultimate Big Dance, open to every team in the state, spawning rivalries and civic pride in equal measure. Invariably, each year a team of plucky, winsome underdogs from a small town captured the state's affection as it moved on to play the Goliaths. The tournament was one of Indiana's real touchstones. As John Wooden eloquently put it to me, "A state treasure that went deep in the soil."

Then the treasure disappeared, never, it seems, to be unearthed.

Though the change from the "all-comers" format to so-called class basketball has been in effect since 1998, the outrage it wrought persists. The Indiana High School Athletic Association's decision to scrap the all-comers state high school basketball tournament and replace it with a new format that divides schools into four classes (1A, 2A, 3A and 4A) based on student body size, has been an experiment that's failed as abjectly as New Coke. The difference: While Coke executives had the good sense to recognize the error of their ways and reissue the original formula, the IHSAA executives, accountable to neither market forces nor constituents, continue with a format that has sucked both soul and revenue from the tournament.

Roe versus Wade. Gay marriage. Free trade. All are polarizing topics that inspire spirited debate. While class basketball is every bit as much a hot-button issue in Indiana, it doesn't cleave public opinion. In the course of my return to Indiana it became painfully clear that, all but uniformly, Hoosiers despise it. Wooden, who played in the tournament in the '20s, calls the switch to class basketball "a crime against the culture." Oscar Robertson, who played in the '50s, asserts, "It's a terrible thing that was too drastic and did a lot of damage." Brad Miller, the NBA All-Star center who played for East Noble High School near Fort Wayne in the '90s, calls it "a joke." Stephanie White, who went to teeny 2A Seeger Memorial High School, hates it. So does Bonzi Wells, who went to 4A Muncie Central. And unless you have an afternoon to kill, don't even get Larry Bird started on the topic. Says Gary Donna, publisher of *Hoosier Basketball* magazine: "The fans hate it, the coaches hate it, the players hate it, the media hates it. I go to two hundred games a year, and not a single person has ever come up to me and said, 'You know, I like class basketball.' And you know what? It doesn't matter. The IHSAA is like Communist Russia. They're not elected and so they do what they want."

Momentum for the change had been building for years. The principals of small schools, tired of seeing their teams walloped by bigger teams from bigger schools, slowly began to occupy some of the seventeen seats on the IHSAA's executive board. When they had reached a critical mass, they put class basketball up for a vote, a move supported by the then-commissioner, Bob Gardner, who had, ironically enough, served as principal of Milan High but had a football, not a basketball, background. The executive board approved the change to class format by a vote of 12–5 and the measure was approved by a majority of the state's 382 high school principals. There was something underhanded about the entire process. A state full of straight shooters, Indiana doesn't do backroom politics. The issue was never put to a popular vote. The coaches and athletic directors had little input. The decision was made by principals—many of them raised in other states, products of to-day's transient workforce—unable or unwilling to grasp the sociocul-tural importance of the all-comers tournament.

The decision was stunningly tone-deaf to a statewide code of val-ues. As Phillip Hoose deftly put it in *Hoosiers: The Fabulous Basketball Life of Indiana*, the single-class tournament was a representation of the Hoosier mentality: "It gave everyone a chance, but no one a handout." Adds Plump with slightly less nuance, "Why not have eight classes? Ten classes? Twenty classes? These are the same namby-pamby princi-pals that don't want to give kids grades because they might get their feelings hurt. Give me a break."

In going against the political grain, the IHSAA autocrats also made the mistake of focusing on the final rounds and not the opening ones. The tournament was made at the sectional level. The sectionals—the opening brackets—pitted a half-dozen schools from the same county or cluster of towns. The school that won would then receive the sup-port from the entire county as it moved forward to the next round, the regional. "I would rather have beaten one bigger school in the sectional than won a state title for small schools," says Bird. "You'd win that sec-tional and you'd have bragging rights all summer." As it stands now, teams travel hours to play like-sized—but otherwise unknown—opponents. Even on the occasions when local rivals meet, the games are often held too far out of town to elicit much interest. For instance, in 2004, Terre Haute North faced its rival Terre Haute South in the Plainfield, Indiana, sectional, more than an hour from both schools.

The consequences have been dramatic. The distances teams now have to traverse for games are so vast that fans don't bother making the trip. The absence of David-versus-Goliath games has bleached so many compelling story lines from the tournament. It has also eroded the symbiotic relationship between towns and teams. With four times as many titles to go around, coaches at even the dinkiest schools are under heightened pressure to win. As diluted and generally meaningless as the 1A titles are, there is also a nagging asterisk adorning the 4A title. How would a powerhouse such as Lawrence North have fared against the 1A champs, Waldron, a tiny school from Shelby County that went through the season undefeated? We'll never know. "You might have four times as many champions," observes Plump. "But no one is really satisfied."

Not least, class basketball has been a financial disaster. The tournament isn't losing money; it's hemorrhaging it. When Bloomington North beat Delta to win the last all-comers state title in 1997, roughly 780,000 attended the tournament. In 2003, total attendance was 440,000—a drop of more than 40 percent. Though it featured no team from the capital city region, the 1997 final drew a 14.1 viewership, more than 140,000 viewers in the metro Indianapolis area. The 2003 final showcasing Pike—an undefeated Indianapolis team—did a 1.6 rating, representing roughly 16,000 homes. Revenue has fallen accordingly. The situation is so dire that many athletic directors predict that sectional revenues once divvied up among schools will now go directly to the IHSAA to account for the shortfall. There are also murmurs that the IHSAA will charge high schools dues to join.

With millions in its war chest before class basketball was inaugurated, the IHSAA is unmoved. The company line is that it's not about the money, it's about serving the kids. But this response is more than a little disingenuous. When the dried-up revenue streams from basketball mean that services—possibly entire sports—will have to be cut, it's hard to see how kids are being served. When small schools win titles that few care about, how are kids being served? "Everyone still knows that, say, Marion won the 1986 title," says Gary Donna. "No one knows who won the 3A title last year."

The proprietor of an Indianapolis restaurant—Plump's Last Shot—and a partner with Oscar Robertson in senior living developments, Milan's hero led the charge against class basketball. Shortly after the measure passed, Plump founded a preservationist group called Friends of Hoosier Hysteria to Fight Class Basketball and even solicited a $10,000 donation from Nike to fight for a return to the all-comers format. Like so many, Plump holds out hope that common sense will take hold—or perhaps the legislature will intervene—and euthanize class basketball. A logical compromise proffered calls for sectionals to pit smaller school against smaller school and larger school against larger school. Then the sixty-four sectional winners would be pooled together à la the NCAA tournament. It's a compromise that restores a single winner but guards against the first-round massacres that so inflamed the principals from small schools. (The IHSAA did not respond to more than a dozen calls and e-mails seeking comment.)

So it's been seven years and the IHSAA bureaucrats continue to fiddle while high school hoops burns. Plump tells a story of attending a game at Conseco Fieldhouse and being recognized by a teenager. "Check it out, Mr. Plump, I got a championship ring, too," the kid said, holding up his hand.

"That's great," Plump responded.

"Not really," the kid replied. "It was 2A. I would rather have won a sectional [title] than won a 2A title. They won't be making any movies about the 2A champs."

Plump could only sigh.

In one of the goosebump-inducing scenes from the movie *Hoosiers*, Hickory High player Merle Webb (played by the late Kent Poole) stares wide-eyed at the big-city arena, like a tourist peering at the pyramids of Egypt for the first time. He exhorts his team: "Let's win this one for all the small schools that never had a chance to get here." Today, all the small schools do have a chance to get there. The shame of it is, Indiana high school basketball is immeasurably worse for it.

15

"THIS IS AWFULLY SWEET"

THE GODS OF THE BRACKET PAIRINGS SHOWED A KEEN SENSE of irony when, in 2004, they divined that Bloomington North and Bloomington South meet in the first round of the 4A sectional in Columbus, Indiana. Since the heated intra-city, regular-season game in January, Bloomington South had gone undefeated, winning the Conference Indiana title. The team entered the tournament ranked No. 5 in the state, picked by many to win the whole 4A shebang. Bloomington North, on the other hand, finished the 2003–04 campaign with a 16–4 record and a No. 12 ranking. It was, by any measure, a respectable season. But the team had finished sluggishly. Coach McKinney wondered whether his players had, perhaps subconsciously, reckoned that a state title was beyond the realm of possibility, and figured that the sooner they lost, the sooner they could depart for spring break or hang out with their girlfriends or start baseball season.

After the team's last regular-season game, McKinney walked up to the locker room chalkboard and drew an abstract sketch. The players looked puzzled trying to decipher the drawing, as if they were on a losing Pictionary team. When McKinney explained that his drawing depicted a pair of scissors clipping a basketball net, the players cracked up, fixated more on McKinney's lousy rendering than on the message. The mood was less giddy at practice the next day. When McKinney heard nothing but silence—no players communicating with each other, no shoes squeaking on the maplewood—he called his team together. When they encircled him, he told them to go home for the day. "And don't bother coming tomorrow," he barked, "unless you want to work a little."

By the end of the week, he had lightened. On the day before the tournament, he massed his players. "Guys, I've computed the statistics," he told them. "We're 16–4, Bloomington South is 17–3. We were both undefeated at home. The bus leaves here at four-thirty tomorrow. The trip takes fifty-five minutes to get to the gym. I'm fifty-six years old. I've done all the math, and we're going to win by seven points. Write it down: seven points." There was an awkward curtain of silence as the assistant coaches and players shot each other *Has he completely lost it?* looks. The coach couldn't keep his poker face and busted up laughing.

But McKinney was a wreck on the inside, flooded by huge amounts of stress, much of it self-applied. The end of his estimable coaching career was drawing near, but he had told no one, except for his wife, Judy, his assistants and a few close friends. He cringed at the thought of a grand send-off. Not his way. He also figured that the longer he held off announcing his departure, the less time it would give others to angle for his job, and the administration would be more inclined to replace him with his top assistant, Andy Hodson, a young, hardworking, faithful lieutenant.

McKinney desperately wanted to see Hodson's loyalty repaid but realized that hundreds of established coaches from all over the Midwest would give their eyeteeth to take over such a successful program. (In fact, McKinney later learned that some coaches had already submitted their résumés, playing a hunch that he would be gone after the season ended.) Plus, much as he tried to shoo away thoughts of losing his final game to rival Bloomington South, albeit in the sectional for the second straight year, he was realistic enough to know the odds were against him. So much so that after the team's final practice before the game, he approached Brian Reitz, the team's beat writer, and thanked him for all his good work during the season. McKinney was taking nothing for granted, and Reitz interpreted this as a good-bye.

The site of the sectional bracket wrung out even more pressure and emotion. Every year since the move to class basketball, the Bloomington North team had ventured forty miles east to Columbus for the sectionals. A gem of a town, Columbus was once described by Ladybird Johnson as "The Athens of the Prairie." It's probably best known for its architecture, but it's also the birthplace of Chuck Taylor, an unremarkable basketball player but one whose eponymous canvas shoes have sold more than 500 million pairs. Columbus is also the hometown of McKinney.

As the Bloomington North team walked into the Columbus North gym for its first pre-sectional practice, the players passed a series of large portraits of the glaringly Caucasian Columbus teams from decades past. The 1964–66 vintages feature a gangly forward with closely cropped hair nicknamed "Goose," identified as T. McKinney. "Man, Coach was skinnier than I am," Bil Duany marveled. McKinney's coach was Bill Stearman, a Mount Rushmore–like figure in the Indiana basketball annals who coached at Columbus for forty-four seasons. He won 714 games, third most in state history, and his retirement in 1996 was covered by CNN. Stearman was McKinney's first mentor, a kindred spirit who shared a distaste for cutting corners, a reverence for defense, and a fondness for old-school basketball virtues. Whenever North ventured to Columbus, Stearman sat in on McKinney's practices and the two men sometimes talked basketball late into the afternoon. When Stearman returned for the game, McKinney always made a point of knowing where his old coach was sitting.

In the fall of 2003, Stearman passed away at the age of seventy-nine. This time, when McKinney brought his team to the Columbus gym—now christened the William Stearman Athletic Complex—for a practice, it felt oddly hollow. Time and again, McKinney reflexively looked over for Stearman, only to catch himself. He sighed audibly as he looked up at the rafters and saw his coach's retired jersey above the court. For McKinney to lose his final game in his old high school a few months after his mentor had gone to the great slab of hardwood in the sky . . . It came with more emotional knots than he cared to contemplate.

At 7:30, the Columbus gym's 7,000-seat capacity was close to being filled. Caravans from Bloomington had arrived and the atmosphere was electric. In *Hoosiers*, the crowd scenes depict buzz-cut boys in letter jackets and modest girls in their camellias and plaid skirts and knee-high socks, earnestly cheering on their classmates throughout the state tournament. Today, the pageantry is still in evidence, but it's taken on a decidedly different dimension. The "Big Game" has morphed into a kind of house party that almost renders the action on the court secondary. The student sections were seas of retro jerseys and campy baseball hats and togas and bowling shoes and Hawaiian shirts and straw wigs. There were dozens of kids in army fatigues, oblivious to the irony that thousands of their peers were fighting a real war half a world away. The stands were deafeningly loud, so much so that one girl in a cowboy hat whined, "How are we ever going to hear our cell phones ring?"

Underneath the bleachers, McKinney walked into the same locker room he had inhabited as a player in the '60s. He addressed his players as if this were just another game. No facile homilies. No "do or die" pep talk aimed at the eight seniors. No sentences ending in exclamation points. Not the slightest indication that this could well be his final game as a basketball coach. "That wouldn't have done anyone any good," he would say later. "We just had to concentrate on the game plan. There was enough emotion as it was."

The game began as a virtual repeat of the earlier clash. Bloomington South's viperously quick guards slithered through North's defense and kicked the ball out to deadeye shooters. North countered with superior inside play and toughness. South stormed to an early lead, but North went on an 18–3 run in the second quarter and led by eight at halftime. "We still got sixteen minutes to play, guys!" McKinney snapped, as his players sashayed into the locker room. "You know they're going to make a run, so let's be ready and really try to win the third quarter."

It would have been good advice had they heeded it, but Bloomington South outscored North in the third period. Owing in no small part to the team's ritually lousy foul shooting, North trailed for much of the fourth quarter. Through it all, McKinney was the picture of poise. Across the court, a different career of sorts was drawing to an end. Julia Duany reckoned that she had been to a hundred or so Bloomington North Cougars games for each of her five kids. Now Bil—"My baby. My 6'7" baby"—was a senior playing in a single-elimination tournament. Even in the ambient bedlam, it wasn't hard to hear Julia's distinct accent as she shouted at the North players, at the refs, at no one in particular.

With barely a minute to play and North trailing by three points, Bloomington South botched a defensive switch and Josh Macy found himself wide open underneath the basket. As he caught the pass, the defense arrived. Macy went up and was slapped on the left arm. Justifying every early-morning weight-lifting session, Macy still had the strength to guide a shot that trickled into the hoop. He made the ensuing free throw, and suddenly the game was tied. It was somehow poetic that in the era of the three-point shot, a conventional, old-fashioned three-point play made for the single biggest interlude of Bloomington North's season. As McKinney looked on dispassionately, South held for the final possession but missed a series of shots. The game, fittingly, went to overtime.

During the break, a collective delirium had washed over the crowd. The fans, raucous throughout a thoroughly entertaining game, were in a frenzy. Proud parents of players exchanged group hugs. Radio announcers strained to be heard over the din. Two well-regarded coaches tried their best to exude grace under pressure and not let their kids stop to ponder just how momentous the occasion was, both men knowing that regardless of the outcome, the game was going to be seared into their memories for the rest of their lives. It all made for a tableau you wished you could freeze and present to folks who try to grasp Indiana basketball distilled to its essence.

Bloomington North bounded out of the huddle like a prizefighter who can't wait to leave his corner for the decisive round. The Cougars won the opening tap. On their first possession, Terrence Warfield, a burly senior reserve who was a seasonlong regular in McKinney's doghouse, muscled in a basket and was fouled. He made the free throw and North would never trail again. With his wheelchair-bound grandfather looking on from courtside, Josh Norris played spectacular defense on Bloomington South's hot shooter, Cole Holmstrom. Duany grabbed every available rebound to garnish his 22-point game. Reed Ludlow scored six points, including a ferocious dunk off an outlet pass. It was hard not to smile, thinking that the kid who a year earlier had a brain tumor and played hoops largely to help avenge the 2003 loss to South had acquitted himself remarkably well. Dominic Parker, who started the season on the jayvee team, iced the game with four late free throws, complementing a pair of vital three-pointers he had drained earlier in the game.

When the final horn honked like a sick duck, and Bloomington North had won, fans swarmed the court. South players draped their jerseys over their heads to stanch the onslaught of tears. McKinney looked quickly at Stearman's jersey above and held up a finger. It was his three hundredth victory as the coach of Bloomington North and, unquestionably, it ranked among the sweetest. As for the seven-point win he had predicted the previous day after "computing all the statistics"? Final score: Bloomington North 73, Bloomington South 66.

In the locker room, McKinney—not a bead of sweat on his face, not a hair out of place—served up liberal helpings of praise. Then he quickly warned the team that the sectional final was less than a day away. "No one is cutting down any nets yet," he said. "Let's win tomorrow and then we can celebrate a little." But in truth, McKinney was already celebrating, suffused with a kind of joy he hadn't felt in a long time. There was joy that his team had reached that blissful, symphonic state and had finally played better than the sum of its parts. Joy that he could exorcise the memory of the 2003 sectional. Joy that he had won his final North–South game. Joy that he had paid homage to his mentor. And joy that he wasn't retiring just yet.

*T*he evening after Bloomington North upset their archrivals in a fever-pitched game, there was an inevitable letdown for the sectional final. Reed Ludlow declared that the North–South game "was like our state championship game," and his classmates seemed to agree. Few of the thousands of vocal fans on hand for the Bloomington South game bothered returning to Columbus. Bloomington North had won the war, beating South. And besides, what the heck was East Central High?

In a back-and-forth game, East Central resembled those arcade moles that get whacked with a mallet and, undaunted, continue popping up. The superior interior team, Bloomington North continually fed the ball to Duany in the low post and built a series of modest leads. Each time, a member of East Central's buzz-cut brigade would counter with a three-pointer. With Bloomington North nursing a three-point lead late in the game, East Central—clearly in possession of an accurate scouting report—began to foul. Departing from tradition, the Cougars drained a succession of free throws. Duany was particularly poised, uncharacteristically swishing his foul shots. Bloomington North graduated to the regional round with a 52–49 victory and proceeded to cut down the nets, just as McKinney had inartistically depicted the previous week.

In a rejoinder to the cynics who lament the death of sportsmanship, the East Central players and their young coach, Dave Disbro, showered and then returned to the court, where they stood and congratulated the Bloomington players as they received the sectional trophy—as classy a display as any Bloomington North follower could recall witnessing all season. One by one, the players descended the ladder and pumped a fistful of nylon at their parents and girlfriends and class-

Bonding experience: Josh Norris (*left*) and Anthony Lindsey (*right*) helped the 2003–04 Bloomington North Cougars advance to the "Final Four" of the Indiana high school basketball tournament. (*Jeremy Hogan/Bloomington* Herald-Times)

254 ○ L. JON WERTHEIM

mates. Their celebration was leavened by a sobering thought: They were suddenly serious contenders to win the state title.

The regional games provided another graphic illustration of the failures of class basketball. Bloomington North was one of four 4A teams that sojourned to John Mellencamp's hometown of Seymour. Meanwhile, the 1A, 2A and 3A schools were playing their regional rounds in nearby towns. The net effect: Fan support and media coverage was diluted everywhere. When the Cougars tipped off against Evansville Central in the first game, Seymour's cavernous gym was less than half full. Complicating matters, the round was scheduled for 10:00 A.M. on the first Saturday of spring break, so many Bloomington North students and fans had skipped town—even the school's athletic director decided his time was better spent elsewhere—and the team felt as though they were playing on the road.

The game matched McKinney against his former assistant, Brent Chitty, now the Evansville Central coach. During the week of buildup, both men took pains to downplay any Plato-Aristotle dynamic. Which was a good thing, because on this day, the teacher remained the teacher. Time and again, Chitty tried to confound his mentor with creative offensive sets. Time and again, McKinney was equal to the task. When Evansville took an early lead, its players making hash of North's man-to-man defense, McKinney switched to a match-up zone. Chitty called a time-out to readjust to the zone. When play resumed, he smiled resignedly and shook his head: Everything he had just told his team had been rendered useless as McKinney had tinkered with the defense. Late in the fourth quarter, Evansville solved the riddle of North's defense and sent the game to overtime. McKinney switched to a gimmicky "no help responsibility defense" (essentially face-guarding the two best players), which he later credited Chitty for conceiving years before.

In overtime, Bil Duany asserted himself. For the first time anyone could remember, he bellowed to his teammates to feed him the ball. When they obliged he delivered, scoring five quick points. Again, North hit critical free throws to close out another win, 64–57. McKinney was quick to heap praise on his players for their ability to adjust, for their aplomb, for their skill at overcoming the lukewarm fan support. But it was his superior chess playing that had ultimately won the game. Gracious in defeat, Chitty repeated the same mantra for every reporter: "We got beat by a very well-coached team."

When Bloomington North returned to the gym at eight that night for the regional final game, the crowds had thinned and the atmosphere was oddly anticlimactic. Against a feisty, undersized team from Northview, Bloomington North raced to an early lead it never surrendered. Flicking jumpers as if he were playing Pop-a-Shot at the arcade, Lindsey scored 20 points. Though he scarcely scored, the hero was Norris, who played flypaper defense on his man, Northview's star Zack Keyes, who scored just seven points, 14 below his average. North hit a sloppy patch in the fourth quarter and saw their lead diminish to two points, but Ludlow—who suffered the indignity of air-balling a free throw in the morning game—knocked down a pair of critical foul shots and Bloomington North pulled away to win, 55–48.

The team that had been blown out by 39 points a few weeks before, the consortium of players whose coach constantly doubted their mettle, had reached the semistate, Indiana's answer to the Final Four. It was the fourth time since 1997 that McKinney would take a team to this rarefied round. As he watched his players snip the nets yet again, ecstatic that their season would extend still another week, McKinney smiled and conceded, "This is awfully sweet." For the moment, he was unambiguously happy and could not have cared less that his team was facing the state's best player in the next round.

A seven-foot, 245-pound leviathan with size 19 shoes, Greg Oden
was regarded not merely as the best player in Indiana but the
best sophomore in the country. Though the center for Indianapolis's
Lawrence North High School was still a work in progress and had the
touch of a lumberjack, his mere presence could change the entire tex-
ture of a game. Defensively, he was swift and agile, batting away shots
with his long arms. He betrayed his Hoosier bona fides, comprehend-
ing the game with court smarts that belied his age. Bill Benner, the
former ace columnist for the *Indianapolis Star*, once described Oden
to me as a "Bill Russell type," not exactly a comparison one commonly
hears made about a fifteen-year-old prodigy.

As the season progressed, so did Oden. By the time Lawrence North
beat top-ranked Pike in the last week of the regular season, Oden was
simply an unstoppable force. In that game he had 31 points and 14 rebounds. Time was, Oden was the type of player who would have college coaches salivating and recruiting him with fervor. By the spring,
it was NBA scouts that frequented his games. Here he was, yet to
reach the age required to drive a car and already it was a foregone conclusion that he would go directly from high school to the NBA. Some
scouts have already predicted him as the top pick in the 2006 draft.
"The only way Greg Oden spends a day on a college campus," says Gary
Donna, the basketball journalist, "is if he visits a friend." Oden was also
what stood between Bloomington North and another trip to the state
finals.

The Bloomington North–Lawrence North semistate game was
held in Bedford, where the Cougars had begun their tumultuous season four months earlier. The team spent the week before the game deep
in preparation, much of it centered around how to contain Oden.
"Remember, he's only a sophomore and he doesn't like to get pushed

around," McKinney reminded his charges. "Let's body him up, play him physical and see what happens."

What happened was that Oden withered from both the contact and the weight of the occasion of playing in such a high-stakes game in front of a standing-room-only crowd. He scored six points, his lowest total of the season, didn't even consider shooting from beyond eight feet and missed all four of his free throws. He still dominated the game, blocking shots and changing countless others. Mostly on account of Lindsey's torrid outside shooting, Bloomington North led by a point at halftime, 31–30. But the Cougars' inside game was nonexistent and the team's lone two-point field goal was a seventeen-footer. In a sweltering locker room, McKinney and staff feared that as soon as the outside shots stopped falling, as soon as Lindsey felt fatigue from bringing the ball upcourt against a merciless press, the bottom could fall out.

In the third quarter, Lawrence North's superior athleticism and depth manifested itself. With Oden out of sorts offensively, another sophomore, point guard Mike Conley, Jr.—son of the 1992 Olympic gold medalist in the triple jump—took the baton. Cunning and quick, he hounded Bloomington's guards and scored on nifty drives to the basket. Irretrievably, Bloomington North lost both its lead and its momentum.

The game was more closely contested than the final score, 63–54, indicated. Far from playing poorly, Bloomington North gave a fine accounting of itself against the team that would go on to win the title the following week, routing Columbia City 50–29. The least athletic player on the floor, Lindsey scored 16 points. Exhibiting the toughness McKinney had tried for years to cull from him, Duany scored 12 of his game-high 17 points in the final period, as an assistant coach from Bradley looked on. Thomas and Ludlow played unrelenting physical defense against a player bound for the NBA. At one point late in the game, when Thomas missed a block-out, McKinney summoned him over and pantomimed the proper technique for riding. "Ride him on your hip, Kyle," he said. Not only was the game out of reach, but Thomas, the IU football recruit, was unlikely to play another organized basketball game again. Still, McKinney was teaching.

In the locker room after the game, the players were sullen and stunned, but not inconsolably dejected. There were small and scattered tributaries of tears, but no undertows of emotion. There is no such thing as a painless defeat, particularly when it marks the final game for eight seniors. But when you compete honorably and play well against a superior team, it's hard to stake a legitimate claim to profound disappointment. The loss would stick in McKinney's brainpan for weeks, months, years, his slumber sure to be interrupted by thoughts of *What could we have done differently?* But teenagers? The start of baseball season was a few days away, the senior prom was coming up, then graduation. Soon enough, the pain would fade, and the game would become another page in a mental scrapbook of adolescence they might revisit from time to time.

His voice raspy as if he had caught a cold during the game, McKinney pierced the silence of the locker room, addressing the team for the last time. "I'm proud of you guys. There's only been one time when I haven't lost the last game of the season. But we had a great run. You played together. You worked hard. We were one of the final four teams in the state. I have no regrets, and you shouldn't either."

He emerged from the locker room to favor the assembled reporters with a few vanilla quotes. He locked eyes with his wife and gave her a subtle wave. He read over the postgame statistics and made sure the team left the locker room in respectable condition. It struck me as intensely sad that he would never go through these small rites again.

Unsentimental till the end, the coach still had told only a handful of confidants that this marked his final game after thirty-four years as a high school basketball coach. It would be weeks before he would break the news to his players and then to the press. But as valedictories went it wasn't bad. For all the winds of change buffeting the sport of basketball, McKinney had adjusted gracefully to the times. He was pliable but unbreakable. Now he was going out on top. His head high, McKinney strode confidently and with purpose through the halls and walked out the doors into an Indiana spring afternoon. He had done the job they had paid him to do.

EPILOGUE

TIME WAS, BASKETBALL IN INDIANA WENT INTO HIBERNATION during the summer. Kids shelved their high-tops for either baseball cleats or work boots, the lucky ones spending their vacation from school playing Little League, the others laboring on the family farm, detasseling corn or dispensing swirl cones down at the Dairy Queen. It was too damn hot to play hoops outdoors, and most schools disabled their air conditioners during summer. If you could get a pickup game at all, it was in the early evening when the sun was descending and the temperatures were sliding back into double digits.

No more. It's not just that basketball has become a year-round sport. Summer might be *the* pivotal season, the time when college recruiters do their most intense scouting and make their most impassioned pitches. Summer is now synonymous with AAU ball, the controversial

'70s. Stotts was quick to land a job as an assistant with the Golden State Warriors.

In sleepy Roanoke outside Fort Wayne, business was still booming for Eugene Parker. He represented more players in the first round of the 2004 NFL draft than any other agent, including global leviathans such as SFX and IMG. And he still has no plans to leave Indiana.

Across the state in West Lafayette, the Purdue women's team was upset in the 2004 NCAA tournament, losing an early-round game. Katie Gearlds, named an All–Big Ten freshman, hit a crucial three-pointer, but the Boilermakers missed a point-blank layup at the buzzer. Coach Kristy Curry tearfully described the loss as "gut-wrenching." There was, however, this consolation: The Boilermakers won intense recruiting wars and signed 6'5" Amber Harris and 6'6" Tashia Phillips. At the time of their signing in the spring of 2004, Harris was a sophomore, Phillips a freshman. Meanwhile, Stephanie White, the former Purdue star, turned in a respectable season for the WNBA's Indiana Fever, scrapping and clawing to keep up with more athletic opponents. In the off-season, she agreed to a job as an assistant coach for Kansas State's women's basketball team.

In Bloomington, Mike Davis spent the summer bracing for a make-or-break season. The Hoosiers finished the 2003–04 campaign with a 14–15 record—the program's first losing season in thirty-four years—amplifying calls for Davis's head on sports talk radio, on editorial pages, at barbershops and water coolers, and especially on Internet message boards. Davis's saving grace, a highly touted class of incoming recruits, was dealt a blow when Josh Smith rescinded his commitment and opted to head directly from high school to the NBA. (Who could blame him: He was drafted by his hometown team, the Atlanta Hawks, midway through the first round.) Then another recruit, 7'1" center Robert Rothbart, renounced his scholarship in order to play professionally

league that, depending on your view, either supplements or supplants the high school game. AAU ball gives kids a chance to travel the country and play organized games against top-notch competition. It is also a crucible of everything wrong with youth basketball. The ragtag games often cultivate flash while placing no importance on defense. Conniving, profiteering coaches use their AAU teams to line their pockets and insinuate themselves with colleges. Highly unregulated, AAU ball has become an opening for shoe companies to turn teenagers into potential pitchmen. Ask coaches at any level what poses the biggest threat to the soul of basketball and, uniformly, they will cite summer ball.

In late May, more than fifty teams from around the country converged on Bloomington for an annual AAU tournament. The tournament was previously sponsored by Nike, but Adidas has recently colonized Bloomington—winning a bid to outfit the Indiana University teams—and won the right to promote the tournament. As the summer cicadas chirped outside, teams played high-scoring games that doubled as swap meets. College coaches sat surreptitiously in the bleachers, taking notes and evaluating talent. Adidas reps made the rounds, slapping the backs of kids they hoped would one day make the NBA and then pledge their fealty to the brand. The players competed knowing that future scholarships might hang in the balance.

For Bil Duany, the Adidas Spring Classic was another opportunity to show a big-time school that he was worthy of a full ride. After Bloomington North's season had ended, he continued to spurn schools such as Bradley, clinging steadfastly to his belief that he could land a scholarship offer from a major Division I program. "He's keeping his options open," his mom, Julia, said cheerfully early in the summer. As the humanitarian crisis in Sudan raged on, Julia had a certain amount of perspective about her youngest son's basketball future, uncertain as it was.

While some people close to him rolled their eyes, perhaps Bil's optimism wasn't delusional after all. Playing against a welter of future NBA guys, he held his own in the AAU tournament. He was named to the Indiana All-Star team and played well in the annual home-and-home series against their Kentucky counterparts. As the summer came to an end, Bil accepted a full-ride to play basketball for Eastern Illinois. It wasn't North Carolina or Syracuse or Wisconsin. But it was a respectable Division I program and a fine academic school, barely two hours by car from Bloomington. It marked a terrific achievement and set an unofficial record: the Duanys were going to send their *fifth* child to college on a basketball scholarship.

Shortly after the AAU tournament, Bil Duany and his senior teammates graduated from Bloomington North, most of them with academic honors. Anthony Lindsey, the star quarterback and preternaturally poised point guard, had cooled on West Point when a new football coach who favored a running game was brought in. Instead, Lindsey accepted a scholarship to play football at St. Joseph's College in Rensselaer, Indiana, a three-hour drive from Bloomington. He started summer workouts first on the team's depth charts. Reed Ludlow, the hockey refugee who hadn't played an organized basketball game until his senior season, acquitted himself well enough to earn a basketball scholarship to the University of Indianapolis. Kyle Thomas, the obelisk of a power forward, went to Indiana University on a football scholarship. Josh Norris, the mercurial swingman, accepted a football scholarship to Franklin College, an hour from Bloomington, close enough to return to his father's church on Sundays.

In early June, a few of the players gathered at the Duany household to watch the Pacers play in the Eastern Conference Finals. The Pacers had finished the 2003–04 season with the best record in the NBA. In the Eastern Conference finals, they matched skills with the Detroit Pistons in what—depending on your hoops aesthetics—was either a

masterful defensive struggle or some of the most unsightly basketball ever played. With the game tied in the waning minutes of Game Six, Ron Artest, whose behavior had been generally exemplary all season, reverted to his old form. After receiving a cheap elbow to the groin from Detroit's Rip Hamilton, Artest responded with an elbow to Hamilton's head. As always happens, the referees missed the provocation but caught the retaliation, and cited Artest for a technical foul. Detroit scored four straight points, never trailed again, and went on to win the NBA title two weeks later. Within days, Larry Bird was speaking to other teams about trading Artest. Bird no doubt wished he had acted on his instincts to trade Artest. On November 19, 2004, Artest committed the cardinal sin of entering the stands to fight Detroit fans who had doused him with beer, igniting a riot and earning him the largest suspension in NBA history.

For Larry Bird, there were extra-basketball concerns as well. His hometown of French Lick was the site of a heavy-duty bidding war for a casino. Bird and a group of business partners submitted a bid that was burnished by Bird's vow to donate any profits back to the town. In another era, it would have been a no-brainer. Once the local-boy-makes-good had entered the derby everyone else would have dropped out. But in 2004, money talks. Even in French Lick, Indiana. Donald Trump's Hotels & Casino Resorts outbid Bird's group. So did a French gaming concern, Groupe Tranchant. ("Whoever offers the county the most money, that's who I want in here," one resident told *Fortune* magazine. Another asserted that she just wanted Groupe Tranchant to lose. "The French knife America in the back every chance they get," she notes.) In the end, Bird was "trumped" and the bid went to The Donald.

It was also a busy summer for Terry Stotts, the Bloomington North grad who coached the Atlanta Hawks during the 2003–04 season. Stotts was fired and replaced, ironically enough, by Mike Woodson, an Indianapolis native and star for the Indiana Hoosiers in the late in Europe. Davis did, however, get some welcome news over the summer. First, Bracey Wright decided to ignore the sirens and did not turn pro. The following week, two players from Auburn, Marco Killingsworth and point guard Lewis Monroe, announced they were transferring to IU after the school had abruptly fired coach Cliff Ellis. Such is life in college basketball.

At Bloomington North, the post-McKinney era was afoot. Every weekday morning, by the time the summer sun had crept above the horizon, a dozen kids were already on the floor being run through a battery of drills by the new coach. Despite dozens of applications, the North administration and school corporation tapped McKinney's loyal lieutenant, Andy Hodson. A twenty-six-year-old natural-born coach, Hodson was known to go to sleep early and rouse himself at midnight to watch telecasts of West Coast teams that featured innovative offensive formations. Having just graduated eight seniors, including all five starters, Bloomington North was facing a harsh winter, a heavy-duty rebuilding season. But the consensus was that Hodson would be an able caretaker.

As for McKinney, he retired not just from coaching but from teaching as well. For weeks after his retirement announcement, he declined any sort of grand send-off—"Nobody wanted to hear 'Boy, what a great guy' all night long," he reasoned—but shortly after the school year ended, he grudgingly agreed to be feted. Hundreds of former players and assistant coaches, Bloomington North boosters, faculty colleagues, friends and family members packed into a sweltering gym for a roast. It was somehow fitting that for all the heartfelt toasts, the unquestionable highlight came when former assistant coach Tom Bowers rapped to Eminem's "Real Slim Shady." McKinney, of course, didn't have the vaguest idea who Eminem is. Still, he couldn't help suppress a smile as a roomful of Hoosiers joined in the hip-hop chorus in his honor.

'Cause he's [Coach] McKinney, he's the real McKinney
All the other ball coaches haven't won so many
Won't the real [Coach] McKinney please stand up,
Please stand up, please stand up?

His guide is what is best for these growing men.
Even though he's tough when he's in the gym
And not just on the court but also in his class
He prepares them for a life that will come to pass
He teaches them to work and also how to grow
So I'm here to tell you all what you already know
That a million could be coaches like he
They may dress like he, have a pen over their ears like he
But few of them, you see, care for their players like he
And sure as can be, they don't win like he!

'Cause he's [Coach] McKinney, he's the real McKinney
All the other ball coaches haven't won so many
Won't the real [Coach] McKinney please stand up,
Please stand up, please stand up?

ACKNOWLEDGMENTS

In the past, when I watched the Academy Awards, I've snickered when the Oscar winner for "Best Beekeeper" or "Best Icelandic Dancer" gave an interminable thank-you speech. Now I understand. This project would not have been possible without the contributions of many.

My most obvious debt of gratitude is to the coaches and members of the 2003–04 Bloomington High School North basketball team. Coach Tom McKinney, in particular, could not have been more gracious—welcoming me into his enclave, answering all manner of questions and staying in contact long after the season had ended. I envy the parents whose sons had the chance to play for him. As for the players, "great bunch of guys" gets bandied around locker rooms too often, but I'm hard-pressed to think of a more fitting description. For all their surface differences, collectively and individually, they are intelligent, warm, self-possessed and authentic young men. They were unfailingly cooperative, answering the questions of a graying alum and taking his calls at all hours. And at a time when the conduct of athletes is at a low ebb, it's worth noting that not once did any violate their coach's cardinal rule and embarrass the program.

Dozens of others were exceptionally generous dispensing time, advice, information and contacts. Among them: David Khan, Donnie Walsh, Ron Artest, Dave Benner, Jeff McCoy and Slick Leonard with the Pacers; Katie Gearlds and Kathleen Offer (MC '96) at Purdue; Eugene Parker; Jeff Sagarin; Wayne Winston; Wal and Julia Duany, Mike Davis, Bill Wiggins, Jim Madison, Murray Sperber, Mark Miles, Tom Bowers, David Pillar, Mike Pegram, Chris Griffin, Angelo Pizzo, Sheryl Spain, Chris Hunt, Hank Hersch, Jack McCallum and Alex Wolff. Pat McKee at the *Indianapolis Star* was a font of valuable information, as was Andy Graham at the Bloomington *Herald-Times*.

I had the good fortune of working with a pair of cub reporters who have a bright future in sports journalism. Brian Reitz, Bloomington North's ace beat writer last season, was willing and able to provide updates and observations when I couldn't make it to games. Jo'el Rouse was a thoughtful and industrious assistant whose contributions added a great deal.

This book would never have gotten off the ground without the diligence of my agent, Scott Waxman, and the conviction of Rob McMahon. A second-half sub, David Highfill, was absolutely first-rate as an editor and a pleasure to work alongside. Thanks, too, to his assistant, Sarah Landis.

J. J. Carter, Angelo Pizzo, Jeff Pearlman, Gabe Miller, Pat Hallagan, Albert Lin, Jeff Spielberger and Sam Silverstein all read various drafts of the manuscript and provided immensely helpful feedback. Special thanks to Grant Wahl, my journalistic partner in crime, who is a terrific writer and terrific friend. As ever, Terry McDonell, Rob Fleder and my other editors at *Sports Illustrated* could not have been more accommodating and encouraging.

Finally, the proverbial shout to the family: Gerald Wertheim, Raluca and Alexander Verona, Velma Colquhoun, Ann Seregi, Larry Kallenberg, Gail

Drillings, Lily Seregi, my grandmothers, Gerta Wertheim and Lilly Barr, and my mother, Judith Wertheim, whose courage and fortitude after a losing season have been genuinely inspiring.

My deepest gratitude goes to my front line: Ben, Allegra and Ellie.

L. JON WERTHEIM is an award-winning senior writer for *Sports Illustrated* and the author of *Venus Envy*. He lives in New York City with his wife and children.